101 UK CULTURE TIPS

A Field Guide to British Culture

Other Books by Anglotopia

101 Budget Britain Travel Tips
101 London Travel Tips
Anglotopia's Guide to British Slang
Great Britons: Top 50 Great Brits Who Ever Lived

Other Books by Jonathan Thomas

Adventures in Anglotopia
Anglophile Vignettes: 50 Little Stories About Britain

101 UK CULTURE TIPS

A Field Guide to British Culture

By
Anglotopia

Anglotopia Press - An Imprint of Anglotopia LLC
www.anglotopia.press

Printed in the United States of America

1st US Edition: September 2021

Published by Anglotopia Press, an imprint of Anglotopia LLC. The Anglotopia Press Name and Logo is a trademark of Anglotopia LLC.

Print Book interior design by Jonathan Thomas, all fonts used with license.

ISBN: 978-1-955273-13-8

TABLE OF CONTENTS

GEOGRAPHY

BRITISH BASICS

ASPECTS OF CULTURE

HISTORY

BRITAIN'S HERITAGE

BRITISH FOOD

TEA

PUBS

LONDON

BRITISH ENTERTAINMENT

INTRODUCTION

This is a book that changed substantially in the writing. When I came up with the idea a few years ago, I had a clear vision of what it would look like – 101 quick bites about British culture. Then I went to write the thing, and this ended up being a book that was completely different. The end goal was the same; I wanted to create a basic guide to British culture for the curious that covered questions we commonly get running Anglotopia.net.

As I began to plan the content for the book, I found that about half the things that would fit in the book we'd already written about. So I've done the sensible thing and gone through our archive to find these articles and then adapted them for the book. But once I'd done that, I realized there was so much that we hadn't written about yet that needed to be in the book. Half the chapters in this book have not appeared anywhere else and were written for this book.

Inevitably something will have been left out. The format of the book was 101 UK Culture Tips – we could easily write 1001 tips about British Culture! So, we tried to keep it focused on the most important aspects of British culture that outsiders have questions about, wonder about, and like to experience when they travel there. So, there's a big focus on heritage, history, language, places, tourism, etc.

The result has ended up being twice as long as I planned, and we ended up having to change the format of the book to make it larger. So, while the book is not a comprehensive encyclopedia of British culture, hopefully, it feels comprehensive.

It's been rather fun being immersed in British culture for the last few months writing this book; I do find it endlessly fascinating. I do hope you enjoy this eclectic exploration of all things British.

Jonathan & Jackie Thomas
Publishers
Anglotopia

GEOGRAPHY

1. WHAT IS THE UK?

The United Kingdom is a country in Northern Europe made up of four constituent countries spread out over the two British isles of Great Britain and Ireland. Those countries being:

- England
- Scotland
- Wales
- Northern Ireland

This does not include the Republic of Ireland, which is its own separate country. This also does not include places like the Isle of Man or the Channel Islands, which are not part of the United Kingdom but are rather Crown Dependencies that the UK has sovereignty over, but the people are not part of the United Kingdom. Places like Gibraltar or the Falkland Islands are British overseas territories.

The Kingdom of Great Britain was officially formed in 1707 when the Kingdoms of England and Scotland, whose crowns had already been joined, politically integrated by creating one Parliament based in London. Wales, by this point, was already considered part of England (this is no longer the case).

The Kingdom of Great Britain transformed into the United Kingdom of Great Britain and Ireland in 1801 when the Parliaments of Great Britain and Ireland were officially joined. Ireland was part of the union until the 20th century, when it became independent.

The official name of the country is now the United Kingdom of Great Britain and Northern Ireland (Northern Ireland being the six counties of Ulster that did not wish to become part of the Republic of Ireland – it's complicated!).

2. THE COUNTRIES OF THE UK

ENGLAND

Taking up the lower two-thirds of the Island of Great Britain, England has long been the most powerful and most populous part of the island. Its Kings have either ruled most of the island or tried to rule it (and the island next door). When we think of 'British' culture, we usually mean 'English' Culture since England's culture is the dominant force on Great Britain. British Imperialism was essentially English Imperialism (backed up by the Scots and Welsh and occasionally Irish). Separating 'Britishness' from 'Englishness' is very difficult and beyond the scope of this book (and we will irritate pedants by using the terms interchangeably). While England is its own 'country' within the UK – it does not have its own devolved government like the other countries do. Its government is the United Kingdom Government, where it dominates the rest of the UK politically and culturally.

SCOTLAND

Taking up the northern third of the island of Great Britain, Scotland has long been a powerful challenger to the English. It resisted English rule for most of its history, developing its own distinct political traditions and legal system. But it could not resist English dominance forever. First, the crowns were joined when James VI of Scotland, became James I of England, and united the crowns. The countries joined together into the United Kingdom around a hundred years later and are still together, despite talk of independence. When the UK was formed, Scotland dissolved its parliament, but in 1997, it was given the power to legislate back and now has a strong government already independent of the British parliament. Scottish culture is very distinct from English (and wider 'British' culture). They have their own traditions, many based on the Highland clan system. They have their own patriotic songs, their own accents, and a tradition for doing things that is very different from the English (buying a house and marriage are completely different in Scotland, for example). They even have their own language, which now has legal recognition.

WALES

Wales is a 'rump' of a country on the western coast of the Island of Great Britain. Very mountainous, it played a major role in Britain's industrial development due to the quantities of coal in its hills. It has been a declining region since coal mining went away all over Britain. It's struggled in recent years. Culturally, it is very distinct from Scotland and England. Like Scotland, they have their own traditions; many rooted in the hills and valleys that make up Wales. They have their own Celtic language (separate from Scottish Gaelic), and it's an official language (with its own radio and TV stations). The Welsh consider themselves to be the original 'Britons' as they're the closest in relation to the original inhabitants of the British Isles before the Romans arrived. Wales now also has its own devolved government, but independence isn't really at the forefront of political thought like in Scotland. Until very recently, Wales wasn't even considered a 'separate' country; legally, it was just part of England. That has changed, and Wales is developing and proudly showing off its separate identity to the rest of the world.

NORTHERN IRELAND

This one is complicated. The Republic of Ireland used to be part of the United Kingdom but has had independence for over 100 years. But the six counties in the North never joined the Republic and wanted to remain part of the United Kingdom. This has led to a century of conflict known as 'The Troubles' that is too complicated for this short entry. But basically, there's a constituency that wants to remain part of the UK, but there's also a constituency just as big that would like to join the Republic in a new United Ireland, which seems feasible in the new post-Brexit order. The Northern Irish are a distinct culture from Ireland and from the rest of the UK. There are those that see themselves as just Irish, those that see themselves as British, and those that see themselves as both. They have their own devolved government, but it's very unstable, and the British government occasionally has to intervene through 'Direct Rule.' Even as I type, this Northern Irish politics are in turmoil and will remain so for the foreseeable future. As I said, it's complicated. For a good explainer on it – I recommend the TV comedy Derry Girls.

3. GEOGRAPHY OF THE UK

For what might seem like a tiny island to those in the great big United States, the United Kingdom is a very diverse country when it comes to Geography. In fact, much of its diverse natural features are known throughout the world, from the White Cliffs of Dover to the Lake District to the Scottish Highlands. The natural beauty found in England, Scotland, Wales, and Northern Ireland has been praised in poetry, literature, art, and music. The regions in the United Kingdom are almost defined by their geography as much as their cultures, so we will look at each one to give you a basic overview of what Britain has to offer.

LONDON AND SOUTHEAST ENGLAND

London is the most central place in the United Kingdom in terms of its importance more than its physical location, but it is the River Thames that both defines Greater London and has made it important since the Romans first established a settlement there. Once you get out of the city and the home counties, the rest of Southeast England is filled with luscious green hills. It's also in the Southeast that you'll find the famous White Cliffs of Dover, which reach 350 feet high and owe their color to being made of chalk and flint.

EAST ENGLAND

East England, sometimes referred to as East Anglia, is defined by both agricultural land as well as its waterways. This includes the Norfolk broads, a network of navigable rivers and marshlands that offers some of the most ecologically diverse animal and plant life. These marshes also encompass the Fens or Fenlands, a number of which were drained over time to produce arable land. The Fens also help to buffer storms that come in from the east.

SOUTHWEST ENGLAND

Much like the East and South East, Southwest England is full of rolling green hills, farmland, and quaint villages. These hills are made primarily of limestone and chalk, though some are artificially made barrows that provide the final resting places of importance of the pre-Roman chiefs of yore. Its shores see perhaps the greatest number of ports in the United Kingdom. The Southwest peninsula has the longest coastline of anywhere in the UK at 700 miles, and the amount of igneous and metamorphic rock that makes up parts of East Devon and Dorset has labeled it "Jurassic Coast."

EAST AND WEST MIDLANDS

The most geographically central part of England, the Midlands, is an idyllically green place from whence rose the Industrial Revolution. It's also here that you can find the Peak District, which is home to both grassland moors and upland elevations that mark the very southern end of the Pennines mountain range. It should be no surprise that this region contains a number of Areas of Outstanding Natural Beauty, such as the Shropshire Hills and the Cotswolds.

YORKSHIRE AND THE HUMBER

The Pennines practically divide our next two entries. Yorkshire and the Humber sit between the East Midlands and Northeast England, and its beauty has caused the locals to dub it "God's Own Country." It's here that you'll find some of the largest moors in the North York Moors. It's also home to Yorkshire Dales National Park as well as the most northern part of the Peak District. The Yorkshire Peaks are three relatively close mountains that comprise Ingleborough, Whernside, and Pen-y-Ghent.

NORTHEAST AND NORTHWEST ENGLAND

Also collectively known as "The North," Northwest and Northeast England can also lay claim to the Pennines mountains and is full of numerous other hills and mountains. It's a hard land that, over the centuries, has produced an arguably hardy people. It is also home to the Lake District, a series of waters and meres that proved popular with artists and writers of the Romantic Period.

NORTHERN IRELAND

Northern Ireland comprises just 17% of the island of Ireland and is mostly uplands and low mountains. It does, however, also possess the United Kingdom's largest freshwater lake in Lough Neagh. Another striking feature are the basalt columns that make up the Giant's Causeway. It also has its share of mountains, including the Mourne Mountains, Slieve Croob, Slieve Donard, and the Antrim Mountains that rise up to the Antrim Plateau.

WALES

Occupying much of western Great Britain, Wales can be divided into a mountainous region to the north and lowlands to the south. Most of the northern mountains can be found in Snowdonia, including, of course, Mount Snowdon as the country's highest peak. There are also the Cambrian Mountains, the Black Mountains, and the Brecon Beacons. The lower regions are covered by a coastal plain filled with valleys. Approximately a quarter of wales is covered in national parks and Areas of Outstanding Natural Beauty, and at least 80% of the land is dedicated to agriculture, whether crops or livestock.

SCOTTISH LOWLANDS

While Scotland is a pretty diverse country in its own right, it's primarily divided into the Lowlands and the Highlands. The Lowlands comprise the Central Lowlands and the Southern Uplands, which border England. The Lowlands are full of sedimentary rocks and valleys that have produced most of Scotland's agriculture over the centuries. Most of Scotland's largest cities are found in the Lowlands, and the thinnest point of the lowlands is only 30 miles across. The hills down near the border in the Southern Uplands are rounded, and their peaks are covered in peat, a composition of plant matter that looks like soil and was once burned as fuel.

SCOTTISH HIGHLANDS

The Scottish Highlands are considered one of the most romantic and beautiful parts of the country. Thousands of years ago, glaciers carved out the mountains that created high mountain ranges and deep valleys. It should be no surprise that the Highlands are the highest elevations in the United Kingdom and also feature the nation's highest peak, Ben Nevis, which rises to a height of 4,413 feet. The Caledonian Canal is a major waterway that bisects the Highlands and runs from Inverness to Fort William. It's the untamed beauty of this land that has inspired TV programs such as Outlander.

4. WHAT IS A BRIT?

This is a complicated question to answer. You'll see why shortly. On the surface, a Brit is someone from the Island of Great Britain. But quite a few Scottish and Welsh people might not appreciate being called 'British.'

That's the paradox of being a citizen of a country made of our four different countries. Each has its own identity.

On the most basic level, it is fine to say someone from the United Kingdom is British. When they're outside the UK, calling them British, or a Brit for short, is perfectly fine, and that's how the UK government would refer to them or itself – the UK government is the 'British' government. The Queen is the British Queen. The Royal Family is the British Royal Family. The BBC is the British Broadcasting Corporation.

Someone from Scotland is Scottish, and they call themselves Scots. While they're technically British, a separate Scottish identity is very strong these days, so you will find they will identify more with being Scottish than British. Some nationalist Scots will be insulted if you call them British. Some Scots view themselves as Scottish first, British second if at all.

Someone from England is English, and they call themselves English. While they're technically British, Englishness and Britishness are practically the same things. They will use 'English' and 'British' interchangeably. Some English people hate the term 'Brit,' but most don't really care. It's all very confusing!

Someone from Wales is Welsh, and they call themselves Welsh. While they're technically British (and until only recently were part legally of England anyway), they identify with being Welsh first and British second. Welshman or Welshwoman are common terms. But they might keep it simple by saying they're British. Welsh Nationalism is not nearly as strong as Scottish Nationalism, but they're still proud of their separate Welsh heritage.

Northern Ireland is a whole other matter entirely.

So, Northern Ireland is made up of the six counties on the island of Ireland that did not join the Republic of Ireland when it gained independence. Mostly because there's a huge population of Anglo-Irish and Scots who moved there over the centuries, most of these people are Protestants (so joining majority Catholic Ireland was not appealing). Many of these people call themselves Unionists and consider themselves to be British and would probably call themselves Brits.

However, there's a large population of Irish Catholics who consider themselves to be solely 'Irish' even though they live in Northern Ireland. Then there's a group of people who just consider themselves to be Northern Irish. According to the Good Friday Accords, which brought peace to Ireland in the late 90s, people in Northern Ireland can choose to be either 'Irish' or 'British,' and it comes down to personal choice (they can apply for both Irish and British passports). As I said, it's complicated!

So, if you're interacting with someone who appears to be English ... Scottish ... Welsh ... or British – it's best to let them lead in the conversation. Which accent they speak and how they speak about themselves will indicate how they like to call themselves. And there is absolutely nothing wrong with just asking how they prefer to be referred to. That way, no Scottish people or Welsh people are harmed in the course of your conversations!

5. DEMOGRAPHICS OF THE UK

We've covered what the British call themselves and the constituent countries. But that doesn't cover exactly WHO the British people are. This data is based on the 2011 census (data from the 2021 census was not available at the time of writing).

Historically the people of Great Britain were white Northern Europeans. But with a history of empire and immigration, that picture is much different today.

The United Kingdom has 66 million people.

The countries break down as follows:

- England – 56.2 million
- Scotland – 5.5 million
- Wales – 3.2 million
- Northern Ireland – 1.9 million

The following numbers are broken down for the entire country of The United Kingdom. Race breaks down into the following groups:

- White: 92.12%
- Asian: 4.39%

- Black: 1.95%
- Mixed: 1.15%
- Other: .39%

The White population of Britain is a mixture of native Brits and also other Europeans who have immigrated over the centuries. This also includes a large number of Irish people and people of Irish descent.

The Asian population of Britain is rather diverse as it's a broad term. The biggest proportion is people from the Indian subcontinent who came from former British colonies. Chinese and other Asians are lumped into this, but percentage-wise, they're rather small.

The Black population of Britain mostly comes from its former colonies in the Caribbean. Most came in the 1950s and 1960s to fill labor shortages in Britain after World War II and stayed – starting families and becoming part of the British fabric.

6. UK CLIMATE 101

What most people outside of the United Kingdom think of when it comes to British weather is rain. Rain, rain, rain, rain, and more rain. Maybe some gray clouds or fog as well, but it's mostly rain. This is most definitely an exaggeration, even if it isn't too far off the mark. Britain's climate from Cornwall to the Shetland Islands of Scotland is actually rather nice most of the time. Perhaps surprisingly to non-Brits, you might even find it sunny more often than not.

The United Kingdom is actually in a temperate zone. This is the climate zone that actually exists between the tropical zone to the south and the arctic zone to the north. A good chunk of the world exists in temperate zones in the northern and southern hemispheres, including the United States. Compared to the tropical zone that runs around the middle of the planet, a temperate zone has less biodiversity when it comes to plants but a greater number of environments. This is mostly due to the fact that temperate zones enjoy colder winters, which limits the growing time for plant life.

Britain falls neatly into a temperate climate with cool winters and warm summers, though it can be a bit wet in any season. Being a moderately large island, Great Britain doesn't get as much biodiversity in its environments as larger countries like the United States, Canada, and Russia do. Additionally, being surrounded by larger bodies of water means that cold or warm fronts can move in and affect most of the country easily, and weather can change daily (and sometimes hourly) from rain to shine and back again. Indeed, British weather is almost entirely at the mercy of whatever is happening in the Atlantic Ocean and the North Sea.

However, that doesn't mean there is no diversity from one end of the United Kingdom to the other. Dover in southeast England can quite often be warm and dry, while Cumbria in the northwest can be cooler and tends to experience more rain. Southern England stays warm even though the southwest, in Cornwall, for example, can be wetter than Dover. In fact, while rain is a constant throughout the UK, it tends to get steadier the further north you go. The rainfall in Western Scotland can reach 60 inches per year and experience approximately 200 days of rain. On the opposite side of Great Britain, in London, there was only about 23.5 inches spread out over 109 days. Manchester, which sits roughly in the middle of the island, gets about 31.5 inches over 149 days.

Part of the reason that the more mountainous regions further north are more snowy is that the warm air brought in by the Atlantic tends to rise, and by the time it reaches the higher elevations, it cools and turns into precipitation. Needless to say, if you're heading to Scotland, it's best to make sure you have a rainproof windbreaker or umbrella handy. However, despite all the rain that most of the country gets throughout the year, snow is exceedingly rare as the temperatures rarely get cold enough for the precipitation to freeze. The last time there was widespread snowfall in the United Kingdom was actually 2010, and before that, it was 1991, so it appears the country can expect winter weather about every twenty years. On average per year, the percentage of weather stations reporting snow hardly even gets into double digits.

Much like here in the States, July and August can be the country's warmest months, but whereas the highs in the US can reach the 90s or even 100s, in Britain, the highest you might see is a balmy 75-degree Fahrenheit. Additionally, the further north you go, the cooler it gets. And interestingly, while in the States, we're used to winter temperatures that can get down to the 30s or even the 20s on the most extreme wintery days, the average winter low in the United Kingdom hovers in the low-40s. As such, temperatures tend to be fairly mild by comparison to those of us across the pond.

Summer is perhaps the best time for visiting the United Kingdom, and you'll find it to be a lot cooler than the average American summer. You may find yourself needing a sweater or jacket and some Chapstick in parts of Scotland. Also, be aware that July and August can be some of Scotland's wettest months, so that raincoat or umbrella will definitely be useful. January and February tend to be the coldest months, but with lows in the 40s, it can be quite pleasantly cold depending on what part of the United States you call home. And do keep in mind that the weather can change pretty quickly, so always be sure to dress in layers for cool-to-warm temperatures so you can shed what you don't need. If you plan to visit Scotland in the colder months, a jacket is a must, along with a warm hat, some gloves, and maybe even a scarf.

To conclude, the United Kingdom isn't all about rain, even if there is quite a lot of it depending on when and where you go. Holiday destinations along the south will be a fair bit dryer in contrast to the stereotypical image of a drizzly and gray London. In truth, all parts of the country are generally pleasant for most of the year, and you can find yourself starting out with a coat in the morning only to ditch it by midday, then whip out the umbrella in the evening when the rain starts (if it starts). The best time to visit will be in the summer months, but due to Britain's moderate temperatures, you really could visit any time of year and be quite comfortable. So long as you're well-prepared for all the potential weather and temperatures you might encounter, you can expect to have a lovely visit to any corner of Great Britain.

7. BRITAIN'S LARGEST CITIES OTHER THAN LONDON

When most foreigners think of Britain, they think of London. But contrary to what most Londoners think – there are several very large cities throughout Britain, all with their own unique cultures and history (and who have quite a chip on their shoulder about the focus on London). Here's a list of the ten most populous and what they're known for. All are easily reachable by train or motorway – so there's no reason not to explore them!

Birmingham – Also known as Britain's 'second city,' Birmingham is located in the heart of the Midlands. Birmingham was an economic powerhouse during the Industrial Revolution as its location helped fuel its growth. This declined after World War II, and much of the city center was destroyed, giving Birmingham a checkered reputation, but it's had a bit of a renaissance in recent years. Those from Birmingham are known as Brummies, and they have a distinctive accent.

Leeds – This is the largest city in the county of West Yorkshire. It grew to prominence during the Industrial Revolution and a center for processing Wool – it was a major mill town. The beautiful city has impressive civic buildings and a strong Yorkshire culture. Now it's an important center of culture and tourism for the greater Yorkshire area.

Glasgow – Despite the reputation of Edinburgh, Glasgow is actually the biggest city in Scotland, and it was an industrial engine of the British Empire at its height. It was called the 'Second City' of the British Empire at its industrial height. The city is now a strong center of Scottish culture and tourism, and also it's become famous as a film shooting location – its long, straight streets in some places give it an American-like grid feeling – it even stood in for New York City in the Captain America film. Locals in Glasgow are known as Glaswegians and have their own unique lilting Scottish accent.

Sheffield – This large city in South Yorkshire is known for one thing: steel. Its foundries made steel that built the world. Stainless steel and crucible steel were developed locally and led to a tenfold increase in the local population. It's still known as the Steel City, even as steel production has declined (as it had in most post-industrial nations in the West).

Bradford – Known in history as the 'Wool City,' it was a center of the textiles boom during the Industrial Revolution; its proximity to supplies of coal meant that industrial capacity grew quickly. Though the city declined in the 20th century, its proud history and heritage has meant that, like the other post-industrial towns in Northeast England, it's had a 'second life as a center of culture and tourism.

Manchester – Pretty much everyone knows the name of Manchester these days, thanks to the fame of one of its football teams – Manchester United. Manchester really developed during the Industrial Revolution, and when the canal was built linking it to the Irish Sea, it became a textile powerhouse – some say the engine of the British Empire as goods from all over the Empire were brought here and finished into products that were then exported. It declined in the 20th century as textile production moved to the former Empire. But the devastation of the IRA bombings in 1996 led to massive investment and redevelopment in the city, turning it into a Northern economic engine again. Locals in Manchester are known as Mancunians.

Edinburgh – The stately capital of Scotland, and it has been so for over a thousand years. It was a center of knowledge and culture for hundreds of years. It's where the Scottish Parliament is based, and the Queen has her own residence there. Many Scots feel about Edinburgh how most Englishman feel about London – it's a distant, rich place that may not understand all that is happening outside its boundaries.

Liverpool – This city is most famous for one of the most popular bands in history – The Beatles, who came from this former industrial powerhouse. Its location on the coast made it an important port in

Britain – one of the most important in the entire Empire. Liverpool had a dark role in the operation of the Atlantic slave trade. Important cargoes also went through here – as products made all over Britain were funneled into the port and exported around the world. Many Irish and English immigrants to the new world departed from here – leading to major shipping conglomerates like Cunard and the White Star Line (who later merged). It's now one of the most popular tourist destinations in Britain (thanks to the Beatles connections) and was at one time designated a European Capital of Culture. Locals are known as Liverpudlians and have a lilting accent distinctive from Manchester, which is only 37 miles away.

Bristol – Another important port city for Britain, which like Liverpool, grew thanks to the Atlantic Slave Trade. When it was abolished, it continued to be an important port city for Britain. It was heavily damaged in World War II bombing. Despite this, it was a great center of aerospace engineering – all of the Concordes were constructed in nearby Filton.

Cardiff – The capital of Wales and its largest city, Cardiff grew as an important port in Wales due to the ease of getting coal from the Welsh valleys to the water. Welsh coal helped fuel the British Empire. As coal declined in the 20th century, Cardiff declined as well. But thanks to massive investment and planning, it's had a bit of a renaissance. It also became an important center for television production as the BBC built studios on the former docks – hit British shows like Doctor Who are filmed there.

8. THE NAMES OF BRITAIN

There are so many names for the United Kingdom that it can be hard to keep them straight. Some were used interchangeably as if they mean the same thing. Some are used incorrectly. Oftentimes people are mistaken when they refer to something in Scotland as being in England or that the word 'English' means the same thing as 'British.' Here is a list of words and explanations for some of the places and peoples in the United Kingdom.

UK – The official name is the United Kingdom of Great Britain and Northern Ireland, which consists of England, Wales, Scotland, and Northern Ireland.

(Great) Britain – The island of Great Britain itself but often used when talking about the United Kingdom. Does not include Northern Ireland.

British – A term usually used to mean anyone from the United Kingdom though this may annoy some of the Northern Irish. It is also not advisable to call a Scotsman British. While they are technically British, they are Scottish first. Someone like Andy Murray is Scottish until he's winning at Wimbledon, at which point he becomes British (this is a well-worn joke).

Britannia – An outdated Latin term for the island of Great Britain that was coined by the Romans. They also founded Londinium, the city that became London. Britannia is also the female symbol of the UK – the shield maiden used on older currency. Britannia was also a symbol of British Imperialism.

Briton – Essentially citizens of the United Kingdom, the Isle of Man, the Channel Islands, or of one of the British Overseas Territories. The shortened version is 'Brit,' which is commonly used by Americans to refer to the British. There are some who don't like the usage of that term.

The British Isles – The Geographic name for the islands that make up Great Britain and Ireland, though it's falling out of use because the Irish don't like being called British for good reason.

Hibernia – Classical Latin name for Ireland.

Éire – Irish Gaelic for Ireland

Albion – Another outdated term for the island of Great Britain. This is the oldest known name of the island and comes from Ancient Greek.

Caledonia – The Latin name given to the northern part of Britannia, which is now called Scotland.

Cymru – The Welsh language name for Wales.

Ulster – The northern UK part of the island of Ireland (the independent Republic of Ireland is the bottom part). Though not all of the original 'Ulster' was incorporated into Northern Ireland.

England – The largest country in the United Kingdom, where most people live in the UK. South of Scotland and East of Wales.

English – 1. The language spoken by the British (but as in Scotland and Wales, not the only language). 2. The people who live in England. Someone from Scotland is not English. Someone from Wales is not English. Only someone from England is English.

Blighty – An older term for 'Britain' that evokes misty-eyed golden images of Britain. 'Dear Old Blighty.' Originated in India.

Rosbif – A derogatory French term used by the French to describe the British. Because the British love Roast Beef (or at least that's what the French think).

Sassenach – Term used by the Scottish and other Celts to describe the English.

Team GB – The official Olympics team for Scotland, England, Wales, and Northern Ireland. Some people believe the name discriminates against the Northern Irish.

Grande Bretagne – French for Great Britain.

Angleterre – French for England.

Grossbritannien – German for Great Britain.

Gran Bretagna – Italian for Great Britain.

Limey – Limey is a derogatory predominantly American slang nickname for a British person.

Pom or Pommy – An Australian term for British people that is derogatory in nature. Brits will often be called 'whingeing poms' if they come to Australia and complain about anything.

Toff – In British English slang, a toff is a derogatory stereotype for someone with an aristocratic background or belonging to the landed gentry, particularly someone who exudes an air of superiority.

Jock – A derogatory nickname for Scottish people used by the English.

Tan – A derogatory nickname for the British used by the Irish, a reference to the 'Black & Tans' sent to Ireland in an attempt to quell the Irish Uprising (who were quite harsh and unforgiving to the Irish rebels).

9. PRONOUNCING BRITISH PLACE NAMES

One of the most perplexing things travelers in Britain can come across is how to properly pronounce the place names in Britain. Places that have the same name in somewhere like the USA or Australia, will be pronounced completely different in the UK.

This is by no means an exhaustive list – there are plenty of those out there. We've kept the list focused on popular places that Americans would be likely to visit and also places that are particularly indecipherable to an American tongue. There are also local pronunciations that will differ – we've tried to focus on how anyone in Britain would say it based on convention.

- Alciston, East Sussex – Aston
- Alfriston, East Sussex – All-Friston
- Allerton, Bradford, West Yorkshire – Ollerton
- Aldwych, London – Old witch
- Alnmouth – Allenmouth
- Alnwick (Northumberland) – Anic
- Althorp (where Princess Diana is buried) The village is pronounced Olthorpe, but the House is pronounced Orltrop (notice the reversal of the O and the R!)
- Ansty, West Sussex An-Sty
- Ardingly (Sussex) – Ardingl-eye

- Bamburgh (Northumberland) – Bambruff or Bambro?
- Beaconsfield – Bekonsfield
- Beaulieu – Bewley
- Bedworth – Bedduth
- Belvoir – Beever
- Berwick on Tweed – Berik on Tweed
- Bicester – Bister
- Boughton, Lincolnshire – Bootun
- Borough, London – Burra
- Brough, East Yorkshire – Bruff
- Burpham, Surrey or West Sussex – Ber-Fam
- Cadogan Square, London – Ca-duggan
- Castle Combe, Cotswolds – Castle Coombe
- Chippenham – Chipnam (locally)
- Chiswick, London – Chizzik
- Cholmondeston, Cheshire – Chumston
- Cholmondley – Chumly
- Clapham, London – Clap-em
- Deptford, London – Det-ford
- Dulwich, London – Dull-tich
- Edinburgh – Edinboro or Edinburah (just NOT Edinburg)
- Eltham, SE London – El-tum
- Etchilhampton (near Devizes Wilts) – Eyeshalton
- Fowey (Cornwall) – Foy
- Frome – Froom
- Gillingham, Kent – Jillingham
- Gillingham, Norfolk & Dorset – Gillingham (hard sounding "g" as in girl)
- Gotham, Nottinghamshire – Goat'am
- Glasgow – Glazga
- Gloucester – Gloster
- Greenwich – Grenich
- Grosmont, North Yorkshire – Grow-mont
- Grosvenor – Grovenor
- Harrogate – Harrowget
- Hainault, London – Ay-nolt
- Hastings, Sussex – Haystings
- Holborn, Central London – Ho-burn or O-bun
- Homerton, London – Ommer-tun
- Hunstanton (Norfolk) – Hunston
- Isleworth, London – Eye-zul-worth
- Keswick, Cumbria, England – Kezik
- Kettering (Northamptonshire) – Ke'-rin (apostrophe indicated glottal stop)
- Launceston (UK) – Lawnston

- Leadenham, Lincolnshire – Led'nam
- Leicester – Lester
- Leominster – Lemster
- Lewes, East Sussex – Loowis
- Marylebone, London – Marly-bone
- The Mall, London – The Mal not Maul
- Mildenhall (Wilthsire) – Minal (to rhyme with spinal)
- Milton Keynes – Milton Keens
- Mousehole, Cornwall – Mowzel
- Norwich – NORRich
- Pall Mall, London – Pal Mal not Paul Maul
- Penge, London – Rhymes with Henge as in Stonehenge
- Penistone – Penny –stun
- Plaistow, London – Plaaah-stow not Play-stow
- Plymouth – Plimuth
- Rotherhithe, London – Rother-hive
- Ruislip, London – Ryeslip
- Salisbury, England – Sawlsbry
- Scone, Perth, Scotland – Skoon
- Shrewsbury – Shrowsberry
- Slough – Slow (to rhyme with how/now)
- Southwark – Suth-uk
- Streatham, London – Stret-em
- Theydon Bois, London – Theydon Boyce
- Tottenham, London – Tott-num
- Truro, Cornwall – Tru-row
- Warwick – Warrick
- Wapping, London – Kind of rhymes with shopping
- Welwyn – Wellin
- Weymouth, Dorset – Waymuth
- Woolwich, London – Wool-idge
- Worcester – Wooster (as in Bertie Wooster)

10. FAMOUS STREETS/PLACES

There are many streets in places in Britain that have become metonyms for something else. You'll hear them often in the British news or in British TV or film. Here is a list of the most common ones to help you translate.

Savile Row – The street with a high concentration of tailors. Getting a proper Savile Row suit is considered a very nice thing to have, indeed.

Harley Street – While Britain has a nationalized health service that everyone has free access to, there is still a parallel private health system (and private health insurance). Many of the 'top' private doctors will practice on Harley Street. It's popular for wealthy foreigners to come to get their procedures done here.

Shaftesbury Ave – The central avenue in London where there's a heavy concentration of theaters (for plays and musicals). It's now a metonym for referring to the musical and theatre world in general.

Bond Street – A shopping street in London with a high concentration of high dollar designer stores. It also extends to' New' Bond Street as well.

The Mall – The red road leading from Trafalgar Square to Buckingham Palace and usually the center point of many national ceremonies and celebrations.

Charing Cross Road – This used to be a Mecca for bookstores, but there are not as many today – though there are still a few. Cecil Court, just off Charing Cross Road, has more bookstores these days and retains some of that charm.

Downing Street – The location of the Prime Minister's home and office. It's one of those things that wasn't planned and just kind of happened and stayed that way. The Chancellor of the Exchequer (the money man) lives next door. Downing Street has come to symbolize the seat of the British government, even though actual governing takes place down the street in the Palace of Westminster.

Whitehall – The Main Street through London's 'government quarter' and has come to be the stand-in phrase for the actual functions of government in Britain.

Scotland Yard – The original public entrance (via "Great Scotland Yard") to the headquarters of the London Metropolitan Police Service. It is no longer located there, but the name persists when referring to the Metropolitan police in London.

The Old Bailey – This street in central London is synonymous with the most important building on the street – the Central Criminal Court – which is now usually called The Old Bailey.

Fleet Street – Many of Britain's newspapers were based on this street in the late-Victorian and early-Twentieth century. It became a metonym for referring to the press 'what Fleet Street thinks.' It's a name that's stuck when talking about the British press, even though there are no longer any newspapers actually based on Fleet Street.

Gold Hill – Probably the most famous street scene in Britain due to its appearance in an iconic Hovis Bread Commercial, this picturesque row of cottages in northern Dorset is one of the most perfect English scenes. It has ancient cottages rolling down a cobbled hill with beautiful green hills and valleys in the distance. It is sublimely perfect (in this author's opinion).

Castle Combe – This small English village in the Cotswolds has come to epitomize the perfect English idyl. Nestled in an enclosed valley, this small village built of local Cotswold Stone is one of the most beautiful places in Britain (and absolutely swamped with tourists in the peak season).

Arlington Row – Bibury – Another famous location in the Cotswolds – Arlington Row is a street of weaver's cottages along a small stream that has become famous as one of the perfect English places. Again, popular with tourists, you will struggle to see it as a calm and beautiful place in peak tourist season.

Steep Hill – Dorset doesn't have a monopoly on steep street scenes; this street in Lincoln is very famous, lined with Georgian villages and providing views of the surrounding city and countryside; it's a very beautiful place.

Stormont – An estate in Northern Ireland where the Northern Irish assembly meets, and the NI government operates from. So, when the media refers to issues in Northern Ireland, you'll often hear the name when referring to the government there.

Holyrood – A street in Edinburgh where Holyrood Palace is located, as well as the new Scottish Parliament. It's now a metonym for the Scottish government, and you'll often hear 'Holyrood' invoked when speaking of the Scottish government or First Minister.

11. AMUSING PLACE NAMES IN BRITAIN

It's not just streets and roads in London that have unique names; many of Britain's villages have them as well. As this chapter shows, there are plenty of unique names in the whole of England, Scotland, Wales, and Northern Ireland. Of course, what you think their names might mean and where they originate can be very, very different.

BEER

Located in Devon, the Village of Beer is not named after the alcoholic beverage. Instead, its name comes from the Anglo-Saxon word "bearu," which meant grove, like the one that surrounded the village long ago. Located along the southern coast, it had a pretty good fishing industry once upon a time but also was a point for smugglers to bring their goods into the country.

CRACKPOT

This village in North Yorkshire derives its name from the Old English word "kraka" (or crow) and the Viking word "pot" (meaning a deep hole, in this case, a rift in limestone). Crackpot Cave has a pretty impressive geological feature, a column made from an intersecting stalactite and stalagmite.

LOST

More a hamlet than a village, only about two dozen people live in Lost. The name comes from the Scots Gaelic word for inn, taigh ósda, with the village's name being Lósda in Gaelic. The Aberdeenshire Council wanted to change the name to "Lost Farm" after a number of understandable thefts of the village sign, but the some two-dozen people who lived there resisted, and eventually, the Council let them keep the name.

THREE COCKS

Get your mind out of the gutter, lad, or you'll be doing lines for the rest of term! The Welsh name for this village located in Powys is Aberllynfi. The English name is a relatively recent addition, taken from the former Three Cocks railway junction (now a garden center), which itself was named for the Three Cocks Inn (which is still there), which itself was named for the heraldry of the Williams family who were local landowners.

MUFF

That's it, lad, to the headmaster's office with you! Found in County Donegal of Northern Ireland, it sits right on the border with the Republic of Ireland. Its Irish name is Magh, and plays host to the Muff Festival every year, including competitions, street parties, and music performances. It is also home to the "swear-to-God-I'm-not-making-this-up" Muff Diving Club. The club offers discounts for its members at Malin Head Wrecks in County Donegal, a place for divers to check out shipwrecks from WWI and WWII.

UGLEY

This hamlet in Essex has no alibi (think about that joke for a second). The first documentation of its name is in 1041 as "Uggele" and later in the Domesday Book as "Ugghelea." Its name may mean "woodland clearing of a man named Ugga." Ugley has at least two Grade II listed buildings that are anything but ugly.

PRATTS BOTTOM

Found in Kent, Pratt comes from the Latin word "partum" meaning "meadow," though another source suggests that it means "valley of a family called Pratt." The village is part of Greater London and the Borough of Bromley.

SHITTERTON

I do apologize for all this bottom humor (not really). Another hamlet, this one located in Dorset, has a name that literally meant "town on the stream of a sewer." A survey back in 2012 named this the most unfortunate place name in Britain. As with Lost, town residents have had to suffer numerous thefts of their sign, and they eventually replaced it with a stone one that's much harder to lift.

BROKENWIND

Don't breathe in too deeply in this Scottish hamlet. The name was spelled "Broken Wynd" in the 19th Century and actually referenced a narrow path that winds up between two larger roads.

BITCHFIELD

Not a place where you can make complaints, this village in Lincolnshire first appeared in the Domesday Book as Billesfelt. Apparently, the best thing to see there is the local parish church, which provides practically unaltered Norman and Perpendicular Gothic architecture.

BRITISH BASICS

12. DATES AND MEASURES

Britain is a hybrid country. It invented the system of Imperial measurements, but they now mostly use the metric system. The keyword there is mostly. As with all things British, it's more complicated, but no worries, we're going to try and break it down for you.

TEMPERATURE

Britain uses the metric system for temperature measurement in all situations. For those not familiar, it's really simple, but 0 degrees is freezing, and 100 degrees is boiling. But where it gets confusing is when you're trying to read the weather forecast. Having to convert is a bunch of math that most people don't want to do. So, here's a quick breakdown of what those temperatures mean (with a little humor thrown in).

- -10 Siberia
- -5 Freezing your Bollocks Off
- 0 Cold
- 5 Do I Need a Coat?
- 10 Basically a Spring Day
- 15 Heatwave
- 20 Pleasant

- 25 A Real Heatwave (And you start to realize that AirCon isn't common in Britain)
- 30 Basically Dubai
- 35 Typical Southern USA Summer
- 40 The Face of the Sun

DISTANCE AND WEIGHT

Now weights and measures are another matter. Officially Britain uses the metric system; in practice, there are still a few holdouts.

The metric system is based on 10. For length:

- 10 millimeters (mm) = 1 centimeter (cm)
- 10 centimeters = 1 decimeter (dm) = 100 millimeters
- 100 centimeter = 1 meter (m) = 1,000 millimeters
- 1000 meters = 1 kilometer (km)

While this is the official system, in practice, speed is still measured in Imperial Miles, speedometers are in miles, but you buy gas by the liter. It's so odd, really. Roads signs will all be written in miles as well.

Here is a breakdown for weight:

- 10 milligrams (mg) = 1 centigram (cg)
- 10 centigrams = 1 decigram (dg) = 100 milligrams
- 10 decigrams = 1 gram (g) = 1,000 milligrams
- 10 grams = 1 dekagram (dag)
- 10 dekagrams = 1 hectogram (hg) = 100 grams
- 10 hectograms = 1 kilogram (kg) = 1,000 grams
- 1,000 kilograms = 1 metric ton (t)

In practice, you will mostly see weights broken down by grams or kilograms. However, there is a completely different weight the British used called 'Stone.' This is usually used when measuring the weight of a person. A stone is equal to 14 lbs or 6.3503 kilograms. A person would say they weigh 6 stone, and that would translate to 84 lbs. It's an odd system.

VOLUME

Here is a breakdown for volume:

- 10 milliliters (ml) = 1 centiliter (cl)

- 10 centiliters = 1 deciliter (dl) = 100 milliliters
- 10 deciliters = 1 liter (l) = 1,000 milliliters
- 10 liters = 1 dekaliter (dal)
- 10 dekaliters = 1 hectoliter (hl) = 100 liters
- 10 hectoliters = 1 kiloliter (kl) = 1,000 liters

In practice, you'll generally see liquids in milliliters, liters, or kiloliters. Beer and Milk are the only things sold by the pint nowadays. FYI, a British pint is 20 fluid ounces compared to an American pint which is 16 fluid ounces.

13. BRITISH ETIQUETTE

Good etiquette is always something that travels well, no matter whether you're in the United States or the United Kingdom. Table manners are especially important when dining, and Britain is a place where they are an absolute necessity, from fancy dinner parties to dining at someone's house for the first time. We'll cover the basics of what you need to know before you dine in Britain, from basic table settings to what to do during the meal and some other helpful tidbits.

At this point, you have responded to a casual invitation or a formal RSVP to dinner at someone's house. If you have any dietary restrictions, please let the host know prior to the event. It can be customary to bring something with you if dining in someone's home, like flowers, candy, or a bottle of wine for your host. The host may not open the bottle for the meal, but that doesn't mean the gift isn't appreciated. They may simply save it for another dinner party or add it to their wine cellar to enjoy another time. Also, be sure that you arrive on time, if not a bit early (just not too early). Also, be sure to dress for the occasion based upon the type of dinner party it is. It's hard to go wrong with business casual, but if you know it's going to be a fancier party than that, dress appropriately with a coat and tie or a nice dress.

Once seated at the table, you may notice the setting is a bit fancier than you're used to back home. The fanciest you might see will have three plates, three knives, three spoons, three forks, and at least two glasses: one for water and one for wine or another beverage. Your salad plate should be placed over your dinner plate, while your bread plate sits above and to the left of the others. On the right side, you'll have a dinner knife, then your salad knife, followed by your dinner spoon, and lastly, your soup spoon. On the left side will be your dinner fork closest to the plates with your salad fork on the other side of it. The idea is that you use the utensils in the order of the courses, with soup and salad going first, followed by the main course. Your butter knife should be positioned with your bread, but its sole use is for butter, and it's actually permissible to pull the bread apart before spreading butter. The dessert fork and/or dessert spoon will sit above the plates. Your napkins should be folded and off to the left side or placed on the plate until it is time to eat and then placed in your lap when the meal begins.

Furthermore, you should not eat until your host signals that it is time. The placement of the utensils partially indicates which hand you should use. The forks should always remain in your left hand, while the knives should always be used with your right. Hands should be kept in your lap when you're not using your utensils, and you should not place your hands or elbows on the table. If dishes are passed around the table, it is customary to pass to your left, not to your right, or across the table. When you're finished with your part of the meal, the appropriate utensils for that course should be placed on the side of the plate to indicate that you're finished.

These are just some basic table manners to follow. Dining etiquette can be ever more intricate depending on the type of meal you're having, or it can be even less formal. For example, it is perfectly acceptable to eat with your hands at a barbecue in someone's backyard. If all else fails, carefully observe your host and fellow guests for clues about how they behave. And of course, no matter how formal the event, be sure to thank your hosts for the meal and a wonderful time.

14. BANK HOLIDAYS

The simplest answer is that a bank holiday is a day on which the banks are officially closed. They're now a day that most people have off. However, just because a day is a holiday doesn't mean it's a bank holiday. And just because the bank is closed, that doesn't make it necessarily a bank holiday either. Bank holidays have a lot of history and a set of rules that make them a bit different from a holiday in the United States. What's more, depending on the country in the UK, certain holidays are celebrated while others are not.

Going back to the Medieval Period, there were approximately 45 feast days associated with various saints and figures in the Catholic Church. The observance of the feast days didn't necessarily include a day off from work and was subject to the whims of those in power, such as when Christmas feasts were banned during the Protectorate period. Despite this, however, until 1834, the Bank of England recognized 33 feast days. In that year, it reduced the number of holidays for which it closed to four: May Day (May 1), All Saints Day (November 1), Good Friday, and Easter.

The first legislation recognizing official bank holidays would not occur until Sir John Lubbock, a member of the Liberal Party and a banker, introduced the Bank Holidays Act of 1871. This officially designated four official holidays in England, Ireland, and Wales and five in Scotland. For England, Scotland, and Wales, these holidays became: Easter Monday, the first Monday in August (later changed to the last), Boxing Day, and Whit

Monday, which follows Whit Sunday, the celebration of Pentecost, and can vary between May and June. In Scotland, the holidays were: New Year's Day, Good Friday, first Monday in May, first Monday in August, and Christmas.

These remained the same until 1971 when Whit Monday was replaced by the Late Spring Bank Holiday on the last Monday of May, and the August bank holiday was changed from the first to the last Monday as well. Additionally, Parliament made it so that bank holidays were recognized each year by royal proclamation. Rather than falling on a particular date that moves with the day of the week, this permitted the bank holiday dates to be determined on a yearly basis. The ability of the monarchy to announce bank holidays by royal proclamation has been used for royal weddings, to celebrate the Queen's Silver Jubilee, and to recognize the new millennium.

1974 saw the recognition of New Year's Day in England, Wales, and Northern Ireland, while 1978 included May Day (May 1) with the bank holidays. St. Andrew's Day received royal assent in 2007, bringing the number of bank holidays in Scotland to nine. In Northern Ireland, St. Patrick's Day has been a recognized bank holiday since 1903, and the Governor of Northern Ireland first recognized the Battle of Boyne as a bank holiday on July 12, 1926. The latter is still proclaimed by the Secretary of State for Northern Ireland each year.

Another term often used interchangeably with bank holidays is public holidays. However, while public holidays can also be determined by statute or royal proclamation, the banks don't necessarily close for them. Additionally, while banks may not close for public holidays, shops, attractions, and public buildings may be closed. Further, there is no statutory right to paid leave on bank or public holidays, though leave is often provided for by employers, especially if the business is affected by either or if the employer decides to close the business.

If you're planning a trip to Britain, it is often a good idea to avoid the bank holidays as that's when tourist attractions and country roads will be flooded with British people on holiday themselves. Anyone who has sat in a tailback on the A303 to the southwest can sympathize with this.

Holidays, whether bank or public, are a great time for many to go on a weekend holiday or just enjoy the time off from work. After all, even your banker needs a holiday once in a while.

15. FLAGS OF THE UK

Flags have long been used to identify groups of persons and nations. They often contain symbolism that is relevant to the country's national identity. Since 1484, the College of Arms has possessed the authority under the Crown to officially designate flags for the United Kingdom, including England, Wales, and Northern Ireland. Meanwhile, the Lord Lyon, King of Arms, who is the chief officer of the Lyon Court, regulates the coats of arms for Scotland. Between the two bodies, they have established flags with their own unique symbols and histories.

ENGLAND – ST. GEORGE'S CROSS

Conventional belief states that King Richard I was the first person to adopt St. George as the patron saint of England and carry standards with St. George's Cross (a red cross on a white field) into the Crusades, though there isn't much evidence to support this idea. It was much later during the reign of King Edward I during the 1200s that England adopted George as its saint and Edward's men began to wear a red cross on their uniforms to distinguish themselves from the rebel troops who wore white crosses. Later, King Edward III would credit George's intervention with his victory at the Battle of Crecy, and George's Cross saw more and more use. Over time, while the Union flag became the de facto flag of the United Kingdom, St. George's Cross came to represent England.

WALES – THE RED DRAGON (Y DDRAIG GOCH)

The red dragon has long had an association with Wales. It is believed that the dragon originated with the Roman forces coming to the area in 48 A.D. bearing dragons on their banners. With the withdrawal of Romans, the earliest Welsh kings (supposedly including the fabled Arthur) began to use the dragon as a symbol of their authority. Legend has it that the wizard Merlin foretold of a battle between a white dragon (representing the Saxons) would do battle with a red dragon (the Welsh) and that the red dragon would triumph. Later, Owain Glyndwr used the Red Dragon as his standard in his rebellion against the Crown, and with King Henry VII's conquest of Wales, his son, King Henry VIII, adopted the Laws in Wales Acts to make Wales a full partner of the United Kingdom and he also adopted the Red Dragon as well. It wouldn't be until the 20th Century that a sense of Welsh nationalism led to the flag being adopted as an official symbol (with the Red Dragon on a green field) in 1901 and is recognized as the national flag of Wales by Queen Elizabeth II in 1959.

NORTHERN IRELAND – ST. PATRICK'S SALTIRE AND THE ULSTER BANNER

With St. Patrick as Ireland's patron saint, his cross was adopted as a symbol of the Kingdom of Ireland in the 1780s. With the Acts of Union in 1800, the red saltire (x-shaped cross) was adopted as the Irish national flag and incorporated into the Union flag. With the end of the Anglo-Irish War and the subsequent treaty that split Ireland into the Republic of Ireland and province of Northern Ireland, the Government of Northern Ireland was granted a royal warrant for its own coat of arms which included the dexter hand of Ulster, itself associated with the Irish legend of Labraid Lamh Dhearg (Red Hand Labraid), under the symbol of the Crown. This aspect of Northern Ireland's coat of arms was adopted as the Ulster Banner and the national flag of Northern Ireland until the government was abolished in 1972. Technically the official flag of N.I. is the Union Flag, but this is a very controversial and emotional subject. Irish Nationalists prefer the flag of the Republic of Ireland, some Unionists continue to use the Ulster Banner, and yet others will use St. Patrick's Cross as a less politically divisive symbol, such as the Church of Ireland.

SCOTLAND – ST. ANDREW'S CROSS

Similar to Northern Ireland, Scotland's official national flag is the saltire of its patron saint, St Andrew. Legend states that the Scottish King Oengus II prayed on the eve of battle that he would make Saint

Andrew the patron saint of Scotland if he won. The morning of his battle against Anglo King Æthelstan, the clouds formed a white cross against the sky, similar to the cross on which Andrew was martyred, and Oengus succeeded against much superior numbers. It is this legend that may have motivated the Guardians of Scotland to adopt it as their official seal in 1286. A 1388 statute made it the official symbol of Scotland. It was adopted as a flag around the 16th Century, first hoisted in 1512, and is believed to be the oldest flag still in use today.

UNITED KINGDOM – UNION FLAG

The Union flag, or Union Jack as it's also known, was born in 1603 when the ascension of King James I to the throne resulted in a combination of St. George's Cross with the St. Andrew's Saltire. The Laws of Wales Acts effectively made the English flag the flag of Wales as well, which is why Welsh symbols were not incorporated into the new flag. King James introduced the new flag by proclamation in 1606 by which it was simply known as the "British flag" or "flag of Britain." The flag's use on a jackstaff for ships is thought to be the origin of the term "Union Jack." This simpler combination of the two crosses would be used until King George III gave consent to the Acts of Union in 1800, which officially united the Kingdom of Great Britain and the Kingdom of Ireland into the United Kingdom of Great Britain and Ireland. It was through the act and George's proclamation that St. Patrick's Saltire was incorporated into the Union flag, giving it the familiar appearance it bears today.

THE THREE LIONS

England is foremost represented by three lions. These came about from the coat of arms for King Richard I, also known as the Lionheart. His successors continued to use this symbol, combining it with the fleur-de-lis to represent lands in northern France claimed by England until King George III finally gave up the claim, and so dropped those symbols. Meanwhile, King William I of Scotland adopted the rampant red lion as his heraldic symbol. It eventually came to not just represent him, but as his successors adopted it, all of Scotland. Both of these lions are regularly seen on alternate flags for England and Scotland.

ROYAL COAT OF ARMS

The Royal Arms includes the coat of arms of the United Kingdom while adding many elements, including a crowned lion on the left side and a unicorn on the right to represent Scotland. It was said that a free unicorn was a very dangerous beast, so it is chained in both the England

and Scottish versions of the Royal Arms. The Scottish Royal Arms flip the positions of the two animals while also giving the unicorn a crown. The field in the English, Irish, and Welsh Royal Arms includes the Tudor rose, a shamrock, and a thistle to represent all three nations, while the Scottish Royal Arms uses only the thistle.

16. MEETING THE QUEEN

So you have a chance to meet Her Majesty, Queen Elizabeth II, but you're not sure what to do, eh? Okay, maybe you're not that lucky, but just curious anyway. Well, have no fear because we at Anglotopia have thought long and hard about this on the off chance it should ever happen to us. Protocol is very important in any dealings with the Royal Family and while the Monarchy's website states that "there are no obligatory codes of behavior when meeting the Queen or a member of the Royal Family," you can certainly expect to make the news if you don't follow "traditional forms."

It doesn't matter whether you're an ordinary citizen or the President of the United States; there is quite a list of protocol rules to follow when meeting Queen Elizabeth. One of the first things one must do is to be early. It's normally rude to keep someone waiting, but it's especially rude to keep the Queen waiting, considering she is the single most important person in the kingdom. The next is the formation of everyone who will meet her. Sometimes visitors will be lined up for greetings, but in more intimate gatherings, semi-circles might be more prevalent.

Once the big moment arrives, the rules diverge a little for men and women. Men are expected to give a neck bow (just the head bowing at the Queen), while women are expected to curtsey. If you're not a British citizen or Commonwealth citizen, this isn't expected but is still considered polite. Typically one should wait until spoken to, and then the first address to the Queen should use "Your Majesty," while any subsequent address can use this or "Ma'am," pronounced as in "jam" as we would say in the United States.

Conversation is also strictly observed. It should be limited to "small talk," and no personal subjects should ever be addressed. If you're sitting next to her at dinner, she will always speak to the guest of honor on her right during the first course before turning to the guest on her left in the next course. Formula I driver Lewis Hamilton found this out the hard way when he tried to engage her in conversation, only to be told he had to wait his turn.

Touching a member of the Royal Family is a big no-no. Normally, a formal handshake is permitted, and one must wait until she extends her hand first, but anything beyond that is seen as a breach of protocol. A hug, a kiss on the cheek, or even a light touch on the shoulder is not permitted unless she initiates it, as she did with former First Lady Michelle Obama during a formal state visit, though the First Lady's hug went too far according to the British press. In 1992, former Australian PM Paul Keating got quite the media drubbing when he put his arm around Her Majesty uninvited. Giving gifts is permitted, though mostly reserved for heads of state and visiting dignitaries.

Lastly, one should never do anything before the Queen. It's customary to wait to sit until she does, and one should not begin eating until she begins the meal. Conversely, when she finishes the meal, you should be finished too. However, the dinner portion of a formal state visit can take quite a while, especially when table conversations are involved, so it's not been an issue in years. Most importantly, unless you have a special permission to do so by the private secretary, you should not leave before the Queen does. When you do leave, you should avoid turning your back to her.

And now you have a basic guide to meeting Queen Elizabeth II. With some differences, roughly the same rules apply to meeting any other member of the Royal Family, so you'll be fairly prepared for the Duke and Duchess of Cambridge, the Duke and Duchess of Sussex, Prince Andrew, Prince Charles, and more. More can be found on the Monarch's website and other sites online, so if you have more specific questions, there are plenty of sources available to help you.

17. THE UK LEGAL SYSTEM EXPAINED

Disclaimer: This chapter does not constitute legal advice and should not be taken as such.

Whether you're planning a trip to the United Kingdom, just happened to watch British crime dramas, or you nicked an arseload of McClelland's mini-bottles from your hotel in London, you may find yourself a bit intrigued with the British legal system. What follows is an overview of some of the differences between the two systems, focusing mostly on the criminal side and a bit on the civil side in England and Wales.

BASICS OF UK LEGAL SYSTEM

British and American legal systems have a lot in common, and this is no mistake. Having been an English colony, our own legal system is directly descended from English courts, especially what we know as the "Common Law." Also known as case law, common law doesn't come from the government but from case decisions. If a court decides what a law means, then the court's definition becomes the standard other courts use to decide cases.

After the United States gained its independence, it formed its own common law based upon the Constitution. While Common Law remains the primary legal system in England, Wales, and Northern Ireland, Scotland has a hybrid system of common law and civil law, from which the majority of laws come solely from statutes and legislation. Common law defers heavily to past cases, while civil law is not bound by such precedent.

One noticeable difference if you've seen shows such as "Law & Order UK" or the Stephen Fry series "Kingdom" is that lawyers aren't necessarily called such in Britain. While in the U.S., a lawyer can do just about any civil or criminal matter, in the U.K., most attorneys are either "Solicitors" or "Barristers."

Solicitors can deal with most legal matters, drafting documents, providing advice, and even representing clients in minor criminal matters. They have the power to act directly for their clients.

A Barrister, on the other hand, specializes in trial advocacy and acts for the litigant or defendant in High Court, building the case and arguing before the judge and jury; he cannot act for the client without the solicitor's consent. Often they will work together during important cases where the solicitor manages legal documents, prepares evidence, and even conducts negotiations outside the courtroom while the trial continues.

UK COURT SYSTEM

In Britain, as in America, a criminal case begins with an arrest. In America, the next step is a grand jury hearing, in which a jury decides whether there is enough evidence for the court to issue an indictment (a formal accusation of a crime) which allows the criminal case to proceed to a full trial. Except in certain cases, the right to a grand jury is guaranteed by the Fifth Amendment to the U.S. Constitution. In Britain, following an arrest, the Crown Prosecution Service (the British equivalent of the District Attorney's office) brings its evidence before the Magistrates' Court, where a panel of three judges or district judge issues the indictment.

In England and Wales, the right to an attorney for a criminal defendant came from the Prisoners' Counsel Act of 1836 and guarantees the right to counsel for felony cases, over 100 years before the Gideon v. Wainwright decision guaranteed the right for Americans. Before this, an attorney was only permitted when a defendant was accused of treason. Legal aid is available for free courtesy of the Legal Services Commission, with the Community Legal Service providing legal aid for civil matters and Criminal Defence Service doing so in criminal cases. Most of these attorneys come from private firms of solicitors and barristers assigned to represent the defendant.

Once the judge or magistrates hand down the indictment, the case goes to the Crown Court for a trial by jury, though in some cases, the

Magistrates Court may retain jurisdiction over a summary offense. Trial by jury in Britain goes all the way back to the Magna Carta, and the jury in the Crown Court can range from 9-12 people. Eligible jurors are individuals who are registered voters age 18-70, resided in the U.K. for five years from the age of 13, mentally competent, and are not disqualified for any other reason.

Unlike the U.S., where the Prosecution and Defense attorneys agree on the jury members and strike (or dismiss) jurors they find unfavorable (called voir dire), in England and Wales, the Clerk of Court will select twelve names at random or draw cards with the jurors' names on them until the jury box is full. The trial then proceeds similar to trials in the United States, and the jury renders one of several verdict options: Guilty, Not Guilty, Guilty of a Lesser Offense, or a Special Verdict. In case of a special verdict, the jury determines the facts of the case but leaves it to the judge to convict or acquit based on the law.

The High Court handles most civil cases, including Family Law cases in the Family Division (divorce, child custody, alimony, etc.) and money matters in the Chancery Division (contested wills, corporate wrapping up, trusts, bankruptcy, etc.). The jury for a civil case has the same amount of jurors as a criminal case, and the right to a jury trial for civil cases exists for actions in Fraud, Libel, Slander, False Imprisonment, Malicious Prosecution, Breach of Promise to Marriage, and Seduction (being induced to have sex under false pretenses – only available to women).

In conclusion, this is really just the tip of the iceberg. While the legal systems in England and Wales are very similar, Scotland and Northern Ireland have some differences that I won't get into because this chapter is long enough already. If you find yourself in trouble in the U.K., do ask about your right to counsel, and in a criminal or civil case, please consult with a solicitor and/or barrister.

18. THE POUND AND CURRENCY

Pink Floyd once said that money is a gas, the Beatles said that it can't buy love, and others have said that it's what makes the world go 'round. British money pre-decimal gets a bit confusing, with many different types of coins representing fractions of pennies and larger currency. The official name for British money is the Pound Sterling, often referred to as simply the pound. While bills have tended to be fairly simple over the years, the coins that comprised a pound pre-decimalization can get pretty complicated. Join us as we look at the history and breakdown of English money both before and after 1971.

After the Romans, Anglo-Saxon King Offa reintroduced an institutionalized monetary system in the 7th Century, producing coins that became the earliest silver pennies. These early pennies were made from pure silver, but by the reign of King Henry II, they were about 92.5% silver, and the remainder included copper and other metals. These were dubbed the pound sterling. It wasn't necessarily a shortage of silver or cheapness that motivated the change, but the sterling silver coins proved to be much more durable and lasted longer in circulation.

The original Royal Mint, responsible for the manufacture of coins, dates back to Alfred the Great in 866 AD. In 1279, the mint moved to the Tower of London and remained there for another 500 years before branching out beyond the Tower to more modern buildings. During this time, the first pound coin was produced in 1489 under King Henry VII.

Banknotes, or what we think of as paper money, began to appear in 1694, and the earliest ones were hand-written. Sir Isaac Newton unofficially moved to the gold standard in 1717 when he was Master of the Royal Mint, and the gold standard would be adopted officially in the 19th Century after the value of silver decreased such that most coins contained only trace amounts of the metal. The Bank of England ultimately abandoned the gold standard in 1931.

The earliest breakdown of the pound divided it into shillings and pennies. One pound equaled 240 pennies, and twelve pennies equaled one shilling. Pennies were further broken down when the halfpenny (also known as a ha'penny) and the farthing were introduced in the 13th Century, representing one-half and one-quarter of a penny, respectively. Another coin, the three farthings, had the value of 3/4 of a penny. Multiple penny (or "pence") coins were introduced later on, including the twopence, threepence, groat (worth four pence), and the sixpence.

From 1502 until decimalization, the shilling (also known as a "bob") was worth twelve pence. After decimalization, it became worth five pence until it was eventually phased out. A coin worth two shillings was known as a florin, while a half-crown was worth two shillings and sixpence. A crown was five shillings or 1/4 of a pound. Pound coins were often referred to as a sovereign, while a half-pound was known as a half-sovereign, both so named due to their tendency to have a portrait of the monarch on them. A larger coin was known as a guinea, often made out of gold from the Guinea coast of Africa and was worth one pound and one shilling. The largest coin in circulation for the most time was the five pounds, which remained in circulation until 1990.

In 1960, the British government set up the Committee of the Inquiry on Decimal Currency, and on their recommendation, the British government set up the Decimal Currency Board to change over to a new system in which one pound would equal one-hundred pence. As part of the transition, certain coins were phased out of use, including halfpennies, half-crowns, and farthings. Everything switched over officially on 15 February 1971, known as "Decimal Day," though some shops and institutions used both for a limited time as people adjusted.

Under the decimal system, new coins were introduced that broke down into 1 pence, 2 pence, 5 pence, 10 pence, 20 pence (introduced in 1982), 50 pence, £1 (introduced in 1983), and £2 (introduced in 1997). While pre-decimal coins are not considered legal tender, the public outcry permitted the sixpence to continue use until 1980 and was worth 2.5p under the new system. One pound notes were also in circulation under the decimal system but eventually ceased in England in 1988, though they are still issued by the Bank of Scotland and the Bank of Ireland. Other typical banknotes include £5, £10, £20, £50, and £100 (as well as larger amounts, though they are unlikely to be found in a billfold).

And that's the end of this primer on pre-and-post-decimal currency.

While this only scratches the surface, there is plenty more information that goes into even greater detail concerning the history of English money and the many types of coins that have been available over the centuries. And of course, there's also the Euro to consider, but that's a topic for another time.

19. EXPLORING YOUR BRITISH HERITAGE

As genealogy grows more popular, paid and free resources for amateur researchers tracing family trees continue to proliferate. The good news for descendants of British ancestors is that Great Britain, and England in particular, has maintained an organized official records system, including parish registers and census documents, dating to the 1600s and, in some cases, earlier.

There is even a British TV show called Who Do You Think You Are where famous people search public records for information about their ancestors. It's one of the most popular shows on British TV!

Given the increasing interest in genealogy, it is no surprise that websites such as Ancestry.com are gaining customers. Such sites charge for their services, and they are extensive. Ancestry has most of the recent UK census records, so you can find out a lot about your British ancestors. However, it is possible to track your ancestry largely free of charge if you are willing to devote your time to it.

The free website British-Genealogy.com offers the following advice for those new to researching their family trees:

- Make a note of everything you know, or think you know, about your ancestors, working backward from your parents, to your grandparents, and so on.
- Check this information with other family members as well as

with family photo albums and diaries and revise any incorrect information.

- Visit FreeBMD.org.uk, an ongoing volunteer-based project, the goal of which is to transcribe the Civil Registration index of births, marriages, and deaths in England and Wales beginning in 1837.
- If you are researching Scottish ancestry, begin by visiting ScotlandsPeople.gov.uk, the official website of the General Register Office of Scotland.
- For those with British and Irish ancestry, Genuki.org.uk provides a virtual reference library of genealogical information of particular relevance to the UK and Ireland. It is a non-commercial service, maintained by a charitable trust and a group of volunteers.
- Post queries on as many genealogy forums as you can. Sometimes these queries lead to information on your family provided by other researchers.
- Most importantly, keep going. You never know when you will discover a key piece of information.

If you live in the United States and know you have British ancestry, but don't know the names of your British ancestors, you can start with the following websites that offer genealogy help free of charge:

- FamilySearch.org, which is maintained by the LDS Church, is easy to use; the site only requires you to know a given ancestor's last name to begin searching.
- Established in 1996 by a group of genealogists, the USGenWeb Project is comprised of volunteers who provide thousands of free genealogy websites in every county in the United States. These sites include query boards, listings of local sources for records, county and state histories, online genealogy books, research tips, maps, and links to helpful Internet resources.
- Rootsweb.Ancestry.com is the largest free online community for genealogists. It contains interactive guides and a number of research tools for tracing family histories.
- Another way to research your family history involves creating a family tree. MyHeritage.com offers a family tree builder. This free software supports 35 languages and allows the user to create maps, charts, and photos, among other features.

Many online genealogy databases are updated on a regular basis. In March 2012, the British Forces War Records added 250,000 searchable military records from the Boer War, which occurred in the late 1800s and early 1900s in South Africa, to its database. Forces War Records provides British military records going back to the 1300s.

Hoping to find a British ancestor who can pass you British citizenship so you can move to Britain? Unfortunately, these days the furthest you can go back is through a grandparent (and one of your parents would have to have British citizenship).

20. BRITISH CHRISTMAS TRADITIONS

Being the Anglophile that I am, I have often sought out classic British traditions and tried to incorporate them into my own holiday celebrations here in America. I've picked them up from British TV shows, books, and magazines (and a few when we spent Christmas in England in 2013). Some are quintessentially British; others might be a little fringe and honestly not very British at all. Still, having had the joy of experiencing a British Christmas, we now count many of these traditions as part of our usual American Christmas traditions.

MINCE PIES

Mince pies aren't really a thing here in America. I couldn't even tell you where to buy them locally. Most Americans probably think they're actually still made with meat. They're not part of Christmas traditions here. Instead, we eat cookies, cakes, and other types of pies. It's actually rather odd to us to call a Mince Pie and pie – our pies are usually the size of a frisbee. Until you've tasted a Mince Pie, really one from any grocery store will do (but homemade are better); you don't know what you're missing. They're simply delicious. It feels like you're taking a bite of Christmas when you're eating one. Children also usually leave out a few mince pies, a carrot for the reindeer, and a class of Sherry instead of milk (to warm his cold bones!).

CHRISTMAS CRACKERS

Christmas crackers have also not been a tradition here in the States, they're popular in Canada, and the tradition has started to leak down south of the border. This is partly because there's a small bit of gunpowder in them, so in many states, they were classed as fireworks and banned. Now, you can usually find them in finer stores or in import stores (Costco even had them one year). For those that don't know, a cracker is a cardboard tube invented by the eponymous Tom Smith. The tube is usually filled with a gift, a paper crown, and a poorly written joke. To access the treats inside, you must pull apart the two ends of the tube, and a small crack happens (most of the time, when it doesn't, it's a disappointment!). Crackers are good fun, and much laughter is usually shared when family members share their jokes or trade their horribly cheap gifts that were inside. No Christmas picture is complete without your paper crowns!

CHRISTMAS DINNER

The traditional Christmas dinner feature is a Turkey or Goose (in America, usually it's ham or turkey). Christmas dinner is usually eaten in the afternoon on 25 December after presents have been exchanged and the Queen's Speech has been watched. The dinner usually consists of roast turkey, although other poultry such as goose, chicken, duck, capon, or pheasant, served with stuffing and gravy. Sides include pigs in blankets; devils on horseback, cranberry sauce or redcurrant jelly, bread sauce, Yorkshire pudding, roast potatoes (sometimes also boiled or mashed); vegetables (usually boiled or steamed), particularly brussels sprouts and parsnips; with a dessert of Christmas pudding (or plum pudding), sometimes mince pies or trifle, with brandy butter and/or cream. There are definitely elements that an American would recognize in a Thanksgiving dinner. If you're traveling in the UK during Christmas, it's like having two Thanksgivings. Word of advice: always order your Turkey in advance and make sure you have everything you'll need – almost all stores will be closed on Christmas day.

TELLY SPECIALS

In America, most TV shows go on hiatus for the weeks around Christmas and New Year's. Consequently, we get re-runs of movies aired in their places. The logic is that people would rather spend time with their families than watch their favorite shows (perhaps they haven't met some families ...). In Britain, TV plays a big role in Christmas celebrations. Instead of going off the air, many networks and shows create Christmas specials just to air on Christmas – it's a chance to see your favorite shows with a Christmassy theme. Doctor Who is by far the most famous Christmas special, but lesser shows also have one (and Downton Abbey had one every year when it was still on). The Christmas TV schedule revolves around them. The major networks also save one-off shows or mini-series to run during the Christmas period – sometimes they have nothing to do with Christmas at all.

SCHOOL NATIVITY PLAY

While it's true that Britain is a much less religious nation than it used to be, a centerpiece of the holiday season is still the yearly school Nativity play where the story of the birth of Christ is told to an audience of friends and family. Many people don't know that the Church of England is the official State Church in England, so consequently, most state-run schools have no problems running a Nativity play. Some schools get very creative and seek to tell the stories in new ways (parodies in Love Actually) or tell the traditional story. They even made TWO movies about the drama and comedy that goes into producing one of these plays (starring Martin Freeman and David Tennant – not to be missed!).

GERMAN CHRISTMAS MARKETS

What better way to celebrate a British Christmas than to visit a German-themed Christmas market. Most major cities and bigger towns will have a German-themed Christmas market that features German-style chalets and vendors selling handmade goods or food. Many are local producers. Not all of them have anything to do with Germany; it's just a theme for the market. But it's usually a good spot to get Haribo treats and German Chocolates. Many Brits will bundle the family up, enjoy the various treats on offer, do a spot of Christmas shopping, and enjoy warm mulled wine and chestnuts (often roasting on an open fire!). It's a fascinating reminder of how many British and American Christmas traditions actually have their roots in Germany.

CHRISTMAS BELLS

Throughout the English countryside, many Brits still live in small towns and villages where a church is still a centerpiece of the community – even if very few people still attend services. But one thing happens every Christmas: the bells ring out in celebration. This Christmas bell 'peal' is often a roaring celebration as all the bells are rung at the same time, filling the village or town with a beautiful sound that is a joy to hear. The bells were silenced during World War II – if the bells rang – that meant invasion by the Germans. How wonderful it must have been to hear them ring for the first time in years at Christmas in 1945.

CHRISTMAS NUMBER ONE

Christmas number ones are singles that are at the top of the UK Singles Chart in the week in which Christmas Day falls. Novelty songs, charity songs, or songs with a Christmas theme have regularly been at the top of Christmas charts. Sometimes the songs don't have anything to do with Christmas. Often, 'song fever' will hit Britain as people rush to buy the song they love so that it can be number one. Traditionally the volume of record sales in the UK peaks at Christmas, with the Christmas number one being considered especially prestigious, more so than any other time of year. Many of the Christmas number ones were also the best-selling song of the year. The most recent Christmas number one single is "A Bridge over You" by the Lewisham and Greenwich NHS Choir. In past years the Christmas Number One has ranged from Robbie Williams to Rage Against the Machine. The Beatles are the only band to have ever had 4 Christmas Number Ones. The process has been lovingly parodied in Love Actually when washed-up former music star Billy Mack seeks to turn a cover song into the Christmas Number One, ensuring a return to fame and wealth (for the week of Christmas at least).

MULLED WINE

Mulled wine is very popular and traditional in the UK at Christmas and less commonly throughout winter. Mulled cider (and sometimes mulled ale) is also served, with a mulled apple juice as a non-alcoholic alternative. What exactly is mulled wine? It's wine that has been warmed and infused with various spices (you can usually buy a pre-made packet of spices). It is commonly a combination of orange, lemon, cinnamon, nutmeg, fennel seed (or star anise), cloves, cardamom, and ginger. The spices may be combined and boiled in a sugar syrup before the red wine is added, heated, and then served. It's a hard drink to describe if you've never had it before, other than to say it tastes like Christmas. You will find it easily at any outdoor Christmas celebration or German Christmas Market – it certainly warms you up when you're cold.

THE QUEEN'S SPEECH

The traditional Christmas message from the reigning British Monarch started with the advent of radio and has since become a fixture of British Christmas celebrations. The message is always non-political and usually focuses on the positive qualities of Christmas – families, and people coming together to celebrate something positive. The Queen has given one every year of her reign, usually at 3 pm on Christmas day. Most people, except for Republicans and those that don't care, will stop to hear her speech which will be broadcast on every major British network (they take turns producing it every year). Often, this is the only time of the year that so many people can hear personally from the Queen, especially with her advancing age. Many older Brits will stand out of respect for the Queen (and even remove their hat if they're wearing one); younger generations care less for decorum such as this. The speech has adapted well to the internet age and is released on YouTube and Facebook at the same time. Sometimes it's even broadcast in the US. It's certainly a British anachronism, but it's a lovely one, and the British would miss it if it were gone.

21. ENGLISH EDUCATION SYSTEM

The English education system operates completely differently than the US education system. This can lead to great confusion when having conversations with Brits or when watching British TV. British students aren't in 'grades.' It's natural for Americans to say, "a promising ninth-grader" or "a third-grade class." For Brits, that's as confusing as if they told you that their children are in the second-year juniors, key stage 3, and the Upper Sixth. We'll explain what all this means! This chapter is focused on education in England. It can be slightly different in Scotland, but a lot of the terminology is the same; it just varies in the details.

First, the entire education system in Britain is overseen by Ofsted (the Office for Standards in Education, Children's Services and Skills), part of the British Government.

British children can start pre-school from the age of 2½ (it's free once they turn 3), and then start in the reception (kindergarten) class at Infant School in September following their fourth birthday. The following year they enter "year 1", and their education counts up in years, much as with the US grade system. This system is relatively new here, however. Previously the numbering began again each time the children moved up to the next school.

The school year is divided into three terms, each punctuated by a week's holiday (known as half-term) somewhere around the middle. After the Autumn term, there is a two-week break that coincides with

Christmas and New Year, and after the Spring term, the two-week break usually falls over Easter. The Summer term runs through to the end of July. No "104 days of summer vacation" for British children – they usually get just six weeks.

Almost all schools have a uniform. At the Primary level (years R-6), it's usually relatively simple. Black, gray, or blue trousers, shorts or skirts, and a polo shirt and cardigan or jumper (sweater) with the school logo. In the summer, girls can often wear pretty gingham dresses in the school colors. Supermarkets sell school uniforms relatively cheaply and stock the appropriate colors for the schools in their community.

Unlike the US, religion is standard in (some) schools, especially Primary schools. There is a regular assembly during which hymns are sung and which may sometimes be led by leaders of local churches. In many schools, children say or sing a rote prayer (often a short poem) to open and close each school day. Many schools, these days, are now more secular and inclusive, but the Church of England still runs a great many of England's 'good' schools. Strangely 'public schools are not, in fact, public – rather, these are what the private schools and boarding schools are called (Hogwarts would have been a 'public school' if it actually existed).

There are no yellow school buses in the UK. Parents are responsible for getting their children to and from school, although since the UK public transport system is relatively good (compared to the USA at least), it's not unusual for older children to take the bus.

In year 7, children move up to secondary or senior school. Here, the uniform is more formal and usually means a shirt, tie, and blazer, even for the girls. In year 9, children take their "options." Each child chooses which subjects to specialize in and which to drop. All students have to do Maths, English and a science subject, and to that, they add three or four subjects they enjoy and excel at.

Years 10 and11 are the serious study years, as the students work towards their GCSE (General Certificate of Secondary Education) exams. The importance of these cannot be overstated. Employers judge candidates on how many GCSEs they have and at what grades. Anyone with fewer than four GCSEs probably faces life in a service industry job.

Students don't "graduate" from school; there is no ceremony or event to mark the end of their time there. Prom is a relatively new import (there are no other school dances), but most schools now have them for their leaving year, 11 students, once exams are over, albeit with no corsages, no theme, no official photograph, or Prom Queen. Yearbooks are also a new idea imported from the US, but as yet, very few schools are doing them.

The next stage – years 12 and 13 – is still generally known as Sixth Form (from the old numbering system) and is only now being made compulsory. Some senior schools have their own sixth-forms, but there are also sixth-form colleges. Here students study either A (advanced) levels or vocational courses for two years. Again, the grades they achieve help employers to judge them when it comes to applying for jobs. For those going to University, places are offered based on A-level grades.

University is always called University, never "school" and rarely "college," so it sounds strange to British ears when Americans talk about Harvard being "a good school" because school is for children. Most University courses are three years, and maximum tuition fees are set by the Government. The system of student loans is very good, with loans effectively interest-free, and they don't have to be paid back until the student is earning a good salary in their chosen profession.

There is no "choosing a major." Students study a single course during those three years. They finally get to graduate when they get their degrees at the end of University, where they have a graduation ceremony that resembles American university/college graduations. Graduate school is now more common, and its length varies on the subject studied (PhDs take a very long time to get, just like they do in the USA).

22. WHAT IS 'THE SEASON?'

For watchers of British culture (and fans of British TV), 'The Season' is the most interesting time of the year in Britain. Also known as the social season, it was a time during the year that aristocrats left the countryside for the bigger cities and engaged in various activities like balls, dinner parties, charity events, coming out ceremonies, weddings, etc.

In modern times in the United Kingdom, 'The Season' is known to encompass various prestigious events that take place during the spring and summer. According to The Sloaney magazine's online guide "Sloaney Season," it starts with Cheltenham Festival (March) and includes the Grand National (April), The Boat Race (April), Badminton Horse Trials (May), Chelsea Flower Show (May), Epsom Derby (June), Royal Ascot (June), Test matches at Lord's (July), Wimbledon (July), Henley Royal Regatta (July), Edinburgh Festival Fringe (August) and others, ending with Goodwood Revival (September).

As with most things in Britain, this 'event' evolved over the centuries – starting in the 17th and 18th centuries. It's a key plot point in most of Jane Austen's novels, as many of the stories revolve around 'The Season' in some fashion. After World War I, 'The Season' went into decline as most aristocratic families lost their heirs or sold their London houses to stay afloat. However, the events that evolved from the historical 'Season' are still very popular today and enjoyed by everyone, not just aristocrats.

According to the peerage guide Debrett's, the traditional social season runs from April to August and comprises of the following events:

Arts

- Glyndebourne Opera Festival
- The Proms
- Royal Academy Summer Exhibition
- West End theatre

Horticulture

- Chelsea Flower Show

Equestrianism

- Royal Ascot
- Cheltenham Gold Cup
- Badminton Horse Trials
- Grand National
- Royal Windsor Horse Show
- Epsom Derby
- Glorious Goodwood
- Cartier Queen's Cup

The Crown

- Trooping the Colour
- Garter Service of the Order of the Garter
- Royal Edinburgh Military Tattoo

Sport

- Boat Race
- Henley Royal Regatta
- Guards Polo Club
- The Championships, Wimbledon
- Cowes Week
- Lord's Test cricket match

23. DRIVING ON THE LEFT

In America (and most of the world), right-hand drive seems a perfectly natural thing to do. This is how many of us learned to drive and still do today. However, a few places on the globe are just a little bit different – and the United Kingdom is one of them. Left-hand drive is the norm for Britain, Ireland, Australia, South Africa, India, and about a dozen or so other nations throughout the world. The question to be explored today is how this came to be and how it plays out still, especially in situations where you leave the confines of the UK and its left-hand drive for the Continent, which is exclusively right-hand.

The history of left-hand driving goes back well before there were cars – hundreds of years, in fact. During the time of the Middle Ages, traveling the roads on horseback could be a dangerous proposition. Who knows what stranger passing you on the other side might be a robber ready to pounce and ride away with your valuables? Since most people are right-handed, traveling on the left side of the road left their sword hand free to defend them should they be beset by my ruffians. The United Kingdom wasn't the only place where this was the standard practice, and most of Western civilization followed the rule.

The first steps towards turning a custom into policy came courtesy of the Vatican. Pope Boniface VIII issued a decree for "rules of the road" that recommended pilgrims traveling to Rome for the Jubilee should do so on the left side. This was a form of early traffic calming meant to help control the flow of people into the city. Britain would turn the practice into law in 1773 when Parliament introduced the General Highways Act, which encouraged riders and farmers taking their produce to market to ride on the left-hand side of the road. The Highway Act 1835 further solidified the policy along with other safety measures against obstructing the road, negligence towards other travelers, and even playing football in the roadway.

Things changed on the Continent thanks to Napoleon Bonaparte. Napoleon preferred riding on the right-hand side of the road, and everywhere he conquered, that became the rule. In 1792 he ordered that all traffic keep to the "common" right and enforced this rule for all French territories. Over a century later, Hitler would force the same rule on countries he conquered, including Austria and Czechoslovakia. Of course, Britain, having held him off, never needed to worry about making a change as neither despot made it across the Channel. At the same time, Napoleon was forcing right-hand drive on much of Europe; Americans were adopting it of their own free will. The Federal Highway Administration conducted a study in which it stated the reason for this was both a rejection of British customs after the American Revolution as well as making it easier to control a wagon.

As cars were developed, the nations that made them cemented where they preferred the steering wheel to be. For Henry Ford and other American manufacturers, it was situated on the left. For British car makers, it was placed on the right. This has remained the case for most former British territories even today, and while Britain has considered switching as Sweden did in 1967, it has remained steadfast in its dedication to left-hand drive. In situations like the Chunnel, British drivers exit on the left from the Eurotunnel train as they would in Britain, but a series of gates helps get them on the right side of the road before they hit the French streets.

Britain has been driving on the left side of the road for so long that they are unlikely ever to change. As some might be inclined to say, if driving on the left-hand land is wrong, Britain doesn't want to be right.

24. BRITISH NEWSPAPERS AND IDENTITY

The character Jim Hacker from the classic British Comedy "Yes, Minister" said it best when talking about the differences between the popular British newspapers:

> Don't tell me about the press. I know exactly who reads the papers: The Daily Mirror is read by people who think they run the country; The Guardian is read by people who think they ought to run the country; The Times is read by the people who actually do run the country; The Daily Mail is read by the wives of the people who run the country; The Financial Times is read by people who own the country; The Morning Star is read by people who think the country ought to be run by another country, and The Daily Telegraph is read by people who think it is.

So, humor aside, if you're an Anglophile, you need to pick a favorite paper. I used to love them all, but as I've become more familiar with England, I've hardened in my choices and prefer a certain few.

What are our choices?

THE DAILY TELEGRAPH AND SUNDAY TELEGRAPH

The Daily Telegraph is a broadsheet newspaper that was founded in 1855. It has a sister paper, The Sunday Telegraph that was founded in 1961. According to recent reports, the Telegraph is the highest-selling British quality paper.

The Daily Telegraph takes a politically conservative slant and is popular with that audience. Oddly enough, the links between the paper's editors and the leadership of the Conservative Party lead the paper to sometimes be called the Torygraph. The current Prime Minister, Boris Johnson, used to write a popular column for the paper.

THE DAILY MAIL AND THE MAIL ON SUNDAY

The Daily Mail is a tabloid-style British newspaper. First published in 1896 by Lord Northcliffe, it is the United Kingdom's second biggest-selling daily newspaper after The Sun. Its sister paper, The Mail on Sunday, was launched in 1982. The Daily Mail was Britain's first daily newspaper aimed at the 'middle-market' and is known to sell a million copies a day.

According to the Wikipedia:

> The Daily Mail considers itself to be the voice of Middle England speaking up for conservative values against what it sees as a liberal establishment. It generally takes an anti-EU, anti-mass immigration, anti-abortion view, based around what it describes as "traditional values," and is correspondingly pro-family, pro-capitalism (though not always supportive of its aftereffects), and pro-monarchy, as well as, in some cases, advocating stricter punishments for crime. It also often calls for lower levels of taxation. The paper is generally critical of the BBC, which it argues is biased to the left.

The Daily Mail is a bit of a joke in many realms because it takes itself rather seriously while reporting on sensationalist, sometimes absurd stories. They wear their conservative values on their sleeves and have no qualms about it. I used to think it was fun to read for the cultural exercise, but I've come to hate this newspaper; it's a cancer on Britain and especially the internet as it's the worst that 'churnalism' has to offer.

THE DAILY MIRROR

The Daily Mirror is a British tabloid newspaper founded in 1903. It's commonly referred to as The Mirror. It is the only UK national daily to have consistently supported the Labour Party at each General Election since 1945. It's not really a 'serious' newspaper, it reports on many of the same stories as the other tabloids, but it is just that a tabloid newspaper.

THE TIMES AND THE SUNDAY TIMES

The Times is a daily national newspaper published that has been published in the United Kingdom since 1785 when it was then known as The Daily Universal Register.

The Times and its sister paper The Sunday Times are published by Times Newspapers Limited, a subsidiary of News International – which is owned by Rupert Murdoch. It's traditionally a center-right newspaper and a supporter of the Conservatives, but it broke with that and supported the Labour party in the 2001 and 2005 general elections.

The Times is the original "Times" newspaper, lending its name to many other papers around the world, such as The New York Times, The Times of India, and The Irish Times.

The Times is considered the UK's 'newspaper of record,' The Times is generally seen as a serious publication with high standards of journalism, which puts it a few rungs above rag sheets like the Sun or Daily Mail.

THE SUN

The Sun is a tabloid daily newspaper and is one of the highest-circulating newspapers in the world. It's as tabloid as you get with the Sun. They'll report garbage and sensationalize stories likes it's second nature. They used to publish naked pictures of women just to sell papers. They're the worst of the British newspapers in that they have no qualms about publishing lies or taking down people they don't like. Their Sunday version 'The News of the World' was forced to shut down due to the dirty tricks they used to employ under former editor Piers Morgan. You cannot even buy The Sun in the city of Liverpool because they tried to blame the Hillsborough disaster on the football fans.

THE INDEPENDENT

The Independent is a British compact newspaper. It's nicknamed the Indy, with the Sunday edition, The Independent on Sunday, being the Sindy. Launched in 1986, it is one of the youngest UK national daily newspapers. The Independent is politically left-leaning. It's a pretty good newspaper and a great place for British news.

THE GUARDIAN

The Guardian (until 1959, The Manchester Guardian) is published Monday to Saturday in the Berliner format from its London and Manchester headquarters. There are many stereotypes, but perhaps the most prominent from the Wikipedia article:

> is that of the Labour-voting middle-class Guardian reader with center-left/left-wing politics rooted in the 1960s, working in the public sector or academia, sometimes eating lentils and muesli, living in north London (especially Camden and Islington), wearing sandals, sometimes believing in alternative medicine and natural medicine though more often atheistic or non-religious and rational.

It has been claimed that the majority of university students in the UK who read a newspaper read The Guardian. It's a non-profit cooperative and one of the most popular and respected newspapers in the world journalistically.

THE EVENING STANDARD

The Evening Standard is a tabloid-style regional local newspaper published and sold in London and the surrounding areas of southeast England. It is the dominant London local daily paper, with a strong financial emphasis as well as carrying national and international news. It's been published since 1827. This is THE paper to read when you are in London. Has excellent local news coverage, TV listings, and movie/theater times. It's now a 'free' newspaper and given out at Tube stations every weekday.

WHAT'S MY FAVORITE BRITISH NEWSPAPER?

My personal choice out of all these is the Times, especially the Sunday Times (which, they are technically separate papers entirely). When I'm in London, I love the Evening Standard and buy it every day. For some reason, the Sunday Times is no longer available in most newsstands in my area, so I try to read the electronic version in their great iPad app. It's become very difficult to buy print versions of British newspapers here in the USA, so usually, we have to rely on the websites and digital apps to read them.

25. THE ROYAL LINE OF SUCCESSION

The Royal line of succession is a source of endless fascination with those in Britain and outside of it. It's a continually changing thing... but it actually doesn't change that often. Even as I write this, there was a new Royal Baby and a new addition to the list, pushing others down.

Succession to the British throne is determined by descent, sex, legitimacy, and religion. Under common law, the Crown is inherited by a sovereign's children or by a childless sovereign's nearest collateral line. The Bill of Rights 1689 and the Act of Settlement 1701 restrict succession to the throne to the legitimate Protestant descendants of Sophia of Hanover who are in "communion with the Church of England." A Roman Catholic or a member of any other religion simply cannot ascend to the throne. Spouses of Roman Catholics were disqualified from 1689 until the law was amended in 2015. Protestant descendants of those excluded for being Roman Catholics are eligible.

The British sovereign is also the head of state for 16 Commonwealth realms, and they all have the same identical rules on succession to prevent any issues that might cause the Crown to go to someone else. This means that when minor changes are made – like giving female heirs the same precedence as male in 2015 – it has to be agreed in all 16 countries and parliaments.

As of June 2021, here is the current Royal Line of Succession, the first twenty-five people (the full list has thousands of people on it by recent count; there are almost 5,000 living descendants of Sophia of Hanover).

1. Prince Charles, The Prince of Wales
2. Prince William, The Duke of Cambridge
3. Prince George of Cambridge
4. Princess Charlotte of Cambridge
5. Prince Louis of Cambridge
6. Prince Harry, The Duke of Sussex
7. Master Archie Mountbatten-Windsor
8. Lilibet Mountbatten-Windsor
9. Prince Andrew, The Duke of York
10. Princess Beatrice, Mrs. Edoardo Mapelli Mozzi
11. Princess Eugenie, Mrs. Jack Brooksbank
12. Master August Brooksbank
13. Prince Edward, The Earl of Wessex
14. Viscount Severn
15. The Lady Louise Mountbatten-Windsor
16. Princess Anne, The Princess Royal
17. Mr. Peter Phillips
18. Miss Savannah Phillips
19. Miss Isla Phillips
20. Mrs. Michael Tindall
21. Miss Mia Tindall
22. Miss Lena Tindall
23. Master Lucas Tindall
24. David Armstrong-Jones, 2nd Earl of Snowdon
25. Charles Armstrong-Jones, Viscount Linley

26. A BRIEF GUIDE TO BRITISH ACCENTS

It's easy to say that someone has a 'British accent.' But that phrase is inaccurate and more of an umbrella term. There are actually several different types of British accents. Dozens, in fact. They blur the lines between dialect and accent. Some are regional; some are class-based.

The most common accent that foreigners think of in the U.K., and more specifically England is Received Pronunciation. Are you sitting there thinking, "Received Pronunciation – what the hell is that?" Basically, it is what most non-Brits are used to hearing as a British accent. It's called the Queen's English, or BBC English, and it's accepted as the standard. It evokes the feeling of drinking tea in a sitting room looking out at the grounds, with a steely posture and one's pinky raised. It's considered the clearest and most understandable of accents.

Now that I have imparted that particular tidbit of info, here's what I was aiming to show: there is no such regional dialect. Sure, it's clear and sounds oh so posh, but it isn't from any one part of Britain. There are, in fact, so many different dialects and accents throughout England and the rest of the United Kingdom that it almost seems like every city – maybe even every neighborhood – in the U.K. has its own particular accent.

The difference in the accents stems from the difference in pronunciation of, well, every letter in the alphabet, frankly. Most English accents do not pronounce the "R" unless it is followed by a vowel (and only if you're lucky), while Scottish accents do. Each different area pronounces letters and words differently, and the difference between them creates a most beautiful mosaic of accents.

There are too many to list, but here are a few "famous" ones.

The Cockney accent – It isn't exactly a regional accent as much as that of the working class, but I think it may be one of the more recognized ones after Received Pronunciation. We've all heard Eliza Doolittle and Michael Caine speak, and lest we forget, they brought us rhyming slang!

The "Brummie" – Another oft-heard accent is the "Brummie," or Birmingham. Ozzie Osbourn's accent is probably heavier than most but still recognizable.

Estuary English – A third, and quite recognizable, is Estuary English. A London accent, it is becoming one of the most popular forms of pronunciation in the 21st century. Katie Price (Jordan) speaks this dialect. And for those who don't know or refuse to acknowledge her, the tenth incarnation of the Doctor spoke in Estuary English. Not David Tennant – he is, in fact, Scottish.

Liverpool – And, of course, there is the Liverpudlian accent. Ah, John Lennon and Paul McCartney...

Cornish – This is the accent you'll hear in Doc Martin, a lilting dialect influenced by the sea.

West Country – Closely related to Cornish, the greater West Country accent is spoken in the West Country and is distinct from a 'regular' British accent.

Yorkshire – A distinct dialect spoken throughout Northern England, with even its own words that aren't used anywhere else (and heavily influenced by the area's Viking heritage).

These are only a few of the many, many different accents and dialects spoken throughout the United Kingdom. Each area differs in vowel pronunciation, emphases of parts of the word, and spacing of words within a sentence. More than that, the language itself has been molded differently. There is different vocabulary and different slang, colloquialisms, and idioms, each distinctive to specific areas or communities, innit?

There are more than 37 separate regional dialects, and even those break down further within their area. There are so many different accents that there really isn't one "real" British accent. While there used to be a class distinction made based on one's accent, this is no longer the case.

The Queen herself has changed the way she speaks, less RP-ish. If you listen carefully, you can catch all the lovely diversity, and after a while, maybe even place the speaker. Now when I watch BBC America or even speak to someone from the U.K., I try to see if I can spot where they come from. Nine times out of ten, I can! (OK, maybe more like four out of ten).

27. WHAT THE BRITISH REALLY MEAN

The British are masters as circumspection and not saying what they mean. It's a cultural trait that probably originates in the oppressive Victorian era when people weren't supposed to show emotion or how they felt. This legacy lives to this day, and it can be difficult for foreigners to pierce through. Here's a handy list of common phrases the British use that doesn't mean exactly what you think they do. English is a very opaque language when wrapped in a complicated culture!

What the British Say: Sorry.
What the British Mean: Not sorry.
What Others Think the British Mean: Sorry.

What the British Say: I hear what you say.
What the British Mean: You're wrong, and I don't want to talk about it anymore.
What Others Think the British Mean: They accept my point of view.

What the British Say: With the greatest respect ...
What the British Mean: I think you're an idiot.
What Others Think the British Mean: They're listening to me.

What the British Say: That's not bad.

What the British Mean: That's good.
What Others Think the British Mean: That's poor.

What the British Say: That is a very brave idea.
What the British Mean: You're insane.
What Others Think the British Mean: They think I have courage.

What the British Say: Quite Good.
What the British Mean: A bit disappointing.
What Others Think the British Mean: Quite Good.

What the British Say: I would suggest
What the British Mean: Do it or be prepared to justify yourself.
What Others Think the British Mean: Think about the idea, but do what you like.

What the British Say: Oh, incidentally/by the way
What the British Mean: The primary purpose of our discussion is...
What Others Think the British Mean: This is not very important.

What the British Say: I was a bit disappointed in that.
What the British Mean: I am annoyed at that.
What Others Think the British Mean: It doesn't really matter.

What the British Say: I'll bear that in mind.
What the British Mean: I've forgotten it already.
What Others Think the British Mean: They like the idea/thing.

What the British Say: I'm sure it's my fault.
What the British Mean: It's your fault.
What Others Think the British Mean: Why do they think it was their fault?

What the British Say: You must come for dinner.
What the British Mean: It's not an invitation; I'm just being polite.
What Others Think the British Mean: I will get an invitation soon.

What the British Say: I almost agree.
What the British Mean: I don't agree at all.
What Others Think the British Mean: We're on the same page.

What the British Say: I only have a few minor comments.
What the British Mean: Please re-write completely.
What Others Think the British Mean: They only found a few typos.

What the British Say: Could we consider some other options.
What the British Mean: I hate your idea.
What Others Think the British Mean: They're indecisive.

What the British Say: Very interesting.
What the British Mean: That's nonsense.
What Others Think the British Mean: They are impressed.

What the British Say: How are you?
What the British Mean: I'm just being nice; I don't want to know other than 'fine.'
What Others Think the British Mean: That they want your life story and your problems.

What the British Say: Cheers!
What the British Mean: A toast, thank you, signing off.
What Others Think the British Mean: Just toasting a drink.

What the British Say: It's a bit dear.
What the British Mean: It's bloody expensive.
What Others Think the British Mean: It's adorable.

28. MARRIAGE IN BRITAIN

Marriage is available in England and Wales to both opposite-sex and same-sex couples and is legally recognized. Marriage laws have historically evolved separately from marriage laws in other jurisdictions in the United Kingdom (Scotland has separate rules). There is a distinction between religious marriages conducted by an authorized religious celebrant and civil marriages conducted by a state registrar.

The legal minimum age to enter into a marriage in England and Wales is sixteen years, although this requires the consent of parents and guardians if a participant is under eighteen (there is talk of changing this). Certain relatives are not allowed to marry. For foreign nationals, there are also residency conditions that have to be met before people can be married. Same-sex marriage was introduced under the Marriage (Same-Sex Couples) Act in March 2014 (civil partnerships are also still available).

Marriage in Britain does not have all the benefits that marriage has in a place like the United States – the tax benefit is not as generous. As a consequence, many Brits will actually never get married and simply cohabitate their entire lives instead. The main reason for this is that it is extremely hard to get a divorce in Britain (you still have to prove something like infidelity or wait a certain amount of time), and it takes a very long time. So, a lot of young people simply don't bother.

Wedding ceremonies in Britain can either be conducted by "authorized celebrants" (usually, but not always, a minister of religion) or by an "authorized registrar." To be legally binding, they must take place with at least two other competent people present as witnesses. The marriage register is signed by the couple, the celebrant, and two witnesses. Civil marriages may not take place in religious venues, but since the Marriage Act 1994 may take place in other licensed venues. If you want to get married in a particularly special place, you must check that it has a license to hold weddings first.

Priests of the Church of England and the Church in Wales are legally required to marry people, providing one of them is from the local parish, regardless of whether the couple is practicing. Special permission may be granted for out-of-parish weddings. Since the Church of England Marriage Measure 2008 and Marriage (Wales) Act 2010, the right to marry in a church was extended to churches that their parents or grandparents were married in or if they were baptized or confirmed in it.

For civil marriages, notices must be posted for 28 clear days at the appropriate register office. Church of England marriages require the banns to be read out three times at the appropriate church or churches unless a Special Licence has been obtained. In most cases, the appropriate churches will be the parish churches where the parties reside and the ones where the ceremony is to take place. Getting married in a church is a very complicated procedure. Many Americans have the fantasy to go to England and have a destination wedding, but this is actually not allowed unless you're willing to stay for several weeks. You're better off having a 'real' wedding at home first, then doing a fake ceremonial wedding in England.

In Scotland, marriage rules have always been different. In fact, it was common for English couples who didn't want to wait to marry to run off to Scotland and elope – often to Gretna Green, just over the border from England, which was a bit like Vegas in that you could get married on the spot.

Royal Marriages are a bit different and are exempt from the rules and regulations on Civil Marriages. The Queen must consent for marriages within the Royal Family, and special permission must be given to marry a Catholic (and this could jeopardize their position in the line of succession). When Prince Charles finally married Camilla in 2005, they had to be given special consent based on their position as divorced people.

29. A FEW KEY THINGS TO KNOW ABOUT BRITAIN BEFORE MOVING THERE

Over the years, we've had lots of chats with people who've made the move to Britain, and there's no shortage of tips on making a life for yourself there. Here are a few nuggets we've learned. Despite the similarities in language, Britain is a completely foreign country and they do many things completely differently than Americans are used to. This applies to simple things like the fact they don't refrigerate their eggs or that traffic drives on the opposite side of the road. It can all very very confusing for people who have just moved to the UK. Here's a few things that we've noted, or that others have noted, that is very different in the UK compared to the USA and other countries. We hope you find this list very useful.

1. Don't expect any kind of closet space; there isn't any.
2. You can't declaw your cats in England; it's illegal.
3. You can't get large quantities of OTC meds, so stock up if you want them. If you try to buy too much, you will get A LOT of questions from the pharmacist.
4. There is a dampness here that gets in your bones and makes you colder than the actual temperature.
5. They don't refrigerate the eggs at the store!
6. Another thing about the eggs: they're brown.
7. You don't have to tip nearly as much, or as often. Tipping is not

the norm in Britain (but it is still done, which can be confusing).
8. Brussel sprouts are mandatory Christmas table garnish.
9. Dry cooking ingredients are measured by WEIGHT, not volume.
10. Toilet handles are on the opposite side and there are often two different buttons for light waste and heavy waste. Also, why are some toilers square? The bum is not square!
11. Light switches operate the opposite way.
12. Pants are trousers and underwear are pants.
13. "Bitch (female dog)," "tit (a type of bird)," and "pussy (a cat)" are acceptable animal terms.
14. A "fanny pack" is something you do not discuss in polite company.
15. Nudity and swearing is common on regular TV.
16. The British school year is divided into three terms: Autumn term (and they don't EVER call it Fall here, by the way) – September-December; Spring term – January-Easter; and Summer term – Easter-till the flippin' END of July! Every term has a week-long break called half-term. There are two weeks off for Christmas and Easter. And the Summer holiday is about six weeks long. Of course, if you're using private schools, the vacations are longer.
17. Electric sockets have on/off switches
18. A Fortnight = two weeks. They use that term a lot.
19. Don't bring many summer clothes. I haven't worn them at all in 3 years up here. Don't bring many pairs of shorts (nobody wears them here) and so many hot weather clothes; they're just sitting around taking up space (which there isn't a lot of).
20. You have to pay a tax to own a TV (the license fee), and TVs have radios built-in.
21. Don't bother bringing your pans; they won't fit in British ovens.
22. Research use of your small appliances on British Voltage. Many people take appliances (including computers) thinking they will work, and they don't. Cheap voltage converters don't always work right either.
23. While it's okay to bring over some of the foods you'll miss, you can find the same or equivalents in British grocery stores.
24. They don't have extreme hot or extreme cold. It stays mild year-round, thanks to the Gulf Stream waters from the Caribbean. They have been known to have a cold spell occasionally. A white Christmas in London is VERY rare. It gets much colder in Scotland. Very much colder.
25. Traffic always comes from the RIGHT in the UK. So, always look right. Also, always stand to the right on escalators.
26. Houses are usually smaller than American houses.
27. It's harder to get a driving license and requires taking actual lessons from a teacher.
28. The UK immigration system is very hard to navigate, and it's

difficult to get a visa.

29. Only talk about politics or religion with friends you know would be comfortable talking about it.
30. Sometimes plugs have to be switched on to use, and voltage is 220 volts compared to American 110 volts. Use American appliances/electronics with care!

30. RANDOM THINGS BRITAIN DOES BETTER

One thing that will hit the wayward Americans hard when they arrive in Britain for the first time is that it will be unlike any place they have been before. Despite the familiarity of shared heritage and language, Britain is, and always will be, a foreign place.

That said, on our many travels there, we've observed things that the Brits do that just make more sense – that we simply don't do. So, we thought it would be fun to put together a list of things the Brits do better than us.

LETTING RETAIL EMPLOYEES SIT DOWN AT THE TILL

When I first went to a British grocery store – the thing that shocked me the most wasn't the variety of different foods – it was the fact that the people who work the check-out lanes get to sit down.

I have never seen this in a grocery store in the USA.

It just makes sense – why do they have to stand? It's a job that could be perfectly well done sitting down, with the occasional standing up to scan an item that won't fit on the conveyor belt. It just seems more humane than having someone stand on their feet for their whole shift. This would be especially nice for older employees and pregnant women who are forced to work.

TRAINS

Dear Britain: Your trains are awesome.

While the Brits might disagree with this statement, I'm writing from a land with few trains at all.

We have a national train network, but it's slow, expensive, and not a very good way to get around the country. It can take up to a WEEK to get from one end of the country to the other by train.

That's why we love to fly.

In Britain, you can get to every corner of Britain by train. Not only that – the trains are FAST compared to their US counterparts (I'm not talking about High-Speed Bullet Trains here).

While Britain's rail network does have its problems (and we've experienced them), the mere fact they exist should be enough to be grateful.

GOVERNMENT

One thing I admire most about Britain is its form of government. In America, we have three branches of government that divide power. In theory, this is a great way to keep the government in check. In practice, it's simply become a recipe for permanent political deadlock.

In Britain, there is ONE branch of government. Parliament. All power, laws, legal force come from Parliament. It is Britain's legislature and executive branch all in one.

When a government wins an election (whatever party), it is guaranteed the ability to actually exert power and get things done. In America, when a President wins an election, he can do nothing without a cooperative Congress and judiciary branch (which almost never happens anymore).

My favorite aspect of the British government is Prime Minister's Question Time. Every week, the head of government, the Prime Minister, has to stand in front of Parliament and answer every question that is thrown at him (often in a hostile environment). Can you imagine how different our political system would be if our President had to do the same?

PUBLIC TELEVISION

We love the BBC. We love their shows, their stars, and their way of doing things.

Most of all, we love what the BBC stands for – it's a public service broadcaster.

While we have PBS here in the USA – PBS is a weak organization dependent on the largesse of donors wishing it to continue. In Britain, if you own a TV, every year you have to pay a tax that funds the BBC in its entirety. The perk of this is a public broadcaster that is unbiased in its news coverage and doesn't air commercials.

Even PBS airs commercials these days.

The BBC model is definitely something to be admired.

SPELLING

Adding the extra U to a lot of words just adds an extra bit of flourish to spellings and seems all the more refined.

THE HOUSE OF LORDS

While most consider the House of Lords to be an anachronism with no place in modern Britain, I would argue that it's an institution that protects British democracy despite the fact it's most certainly not a democratic institution.

I won't get into the merits of a body with hereditary members; I would like to say that there's something to be said about having an upper house that has members appointed for life so that they can be above day-to-day politics and focus on the bigger picture.

We thought we got it right with the US Senate (they have six-year terms), but the realities of running elections mean that Senators only care about re-election, not serving their constituents.

I really like the idea of an impartial upper house that is a check on the power of the lower house (which should always have more power and the ability to overrule the upper house).

BUDGET DAY

Budget Day is a yearly event that we marvel at. Every year, the Chancellor of the Exchequer announces his budget plans for the next year. He makes a big speech to Parliament, and Brits like to take stock of how their taxes will change for the next year.

What's amazing about this rather boring-sounding event is that Parliament passes the budget the very same day.

Coming from a country where the government hasn't had a functioning yearly budget in many years, this is astounding.

HOLIDAY TIME

Like the rest of Europe, Britain gets a lot of time off. Here in America, we usually get two weeks of paid vacation, and that's if we get any time off at all (that's ten paid days, plus the weekends). Most people don't even take that as they're afraid of leaving their jobs for any amount of time.

By law, UK workers get 28 days of paid vacation time. BY LAW. There is no law in the USA mandating vacation.

This does not include the 9 Bank Holidays where most workers get the time off as well (though employers can count these in your 28 days, most don't, however).

On top of that, it's common practice for most 'white collar' businesses to shut down for the two weeks between Christmas and New Year's (and not have it taken out of those days). Don't even get me started on sick days or maternity leave (not part of the 28 days either).

British people work just as hard as Americans do; they just get more time to enjoy themselves or take care of themselves if they get sick.

LIMITED SUNDAY RETAIL HOURS

On Sunday, retail stores are limited to being open only 6 hours. Though this might change soon, it's a great way to encourage people to relax a little more on Sunday. There are places in the US that don't allow business on Sundays, but it's very rare nowadays.

CURRENCY

Britain has successfully gotten rid of the £1 paper note and replaced it with a £1 coin. This just makes complete sense, especially in this day in age where the dollar isn't worth as much as it's used to.

They also have a £2 coin which is even better.

PLUGS HAVE SWITCHES

It's a minor thing – but it rather makes sense; all plugs in the wall have a switch. When you're not using it, you turn it off. Such a simple way to save energy. It's also much safer than having open live plugs everywhere.

Also, many hotels nowadays make you insert your key into a special switch when you're in the room and when you leave, it shuts off the lights in the room. Another great way to save energy.

THE WASHER AND DRYER IN ONE MACHINE

I always wondered by a washer and dryer had to be separate machines, and now I realize the reason: corporate America simply wants us to buy two machines instead of one, so they can make more money.

Most households in Europe have one washer and dryer combo unit – they're compact and are often located in the kitchen (this also makes more sense). It works for an entire continent!

Much less work when doing the wash!

31. BOXING DAY 101

When Americans first try to read up on British Christmas traditions, they're often confused by Boxing Day, which always falls the day after Christmas. It's not a religious holiday, and there's nothing to actually celebrate. So, what exactly is it, and what is it for? Well, fear not, we will try to lift the shroud of mystery and show you what it's all about.

IT'S BASICALLY AN EXTRA DAY OFF

The main thing that sets Boxing Day apart from all the other holidays is that it's basically another day off after Christmas. In Britain, Boxing Day is always a Bank Holiday which means banks are closed and most retail stores are required to have limited hours (usually up to 6 hours open by law). In the USA, many people go right back to work the day after Christmas. Having another day to recoup the madness of the holidays is so much more civilized.

IT STARTED OFF AS A SERVANTS HOLIDAY

There are competing theories for the origins of the term "Boxing Day", none of which is definitive. The Oxford English Dictionary gives the earliest appearances from Britain in the 1830s, defining it as "the first week-day after Christmas-day, observed as a holiday on which post-men, errand-boys, and servants of various kinds expect to receive a Christmas-box." In Britain, it was a custom for tradespeople to collect "Christmas boxes" of money or presents on the first weekday after Christmas as thanks for good service throughout the year. This custom is linked to an older British tradition: since they would have to wait on their masters on Christmas Day, the servants of the wealthy were allowed the next day to visit their families. The employers would give each servant a box to take home containing gifts, bonuses, and sometimes leftover food. Now, it's a holiday for everyone, but gifts are no longer exchanged.

FAMOUS FOR ITS SALES

In America, we have Black Friday Sales; in Britain, they have Boxing Day Sales, which is usually the biggest shopping day of the year in the UK as people rush to the stores to snag great deals and return the gifts they didn't want. It's a great way for retailers to clear out the stock they have leftover from the Christmas shopping binge. The deals have moved online in recent years, but you will find Britain's stores and malls (shopping centers) heaving on Boxing Day, but only for the 6 hours they're allowed to be open. Deals can be had if you can brave the crowds.

BOXING DAY LUNCH

Sunday Roast is a venerable British tradition, and many families will extend it to include Boxing Day, even if it's not on a Sunday. Sometimes they'll eat a roast, or they'll eat a lunch of leftovers from the previous day's Christmas Feast. Pubs are usually open, so you can go get a nice meal as well. It's a time for families and friends to spend the day together without the pressures of work and school.

A DAY FOR A STROLL

Many of Britain's tourist attractions that are usually closed for the winter will open up for the period between Christmas and New Year's. This includes many famous Stately Homes that will have special opening hours. So, Boxing day is a great day to go out for a walk in Britain's beautiful countryside and enjoy some famous buildings while you're at it.

A DAY FOR HUNTING

Boxing Day is also one of the main days in the hunting calendar for hunts in the UK and US, with most hunts (both mounted foxhound or harrier packs and foot packs of beagles or bassets) holding meets, often in town or village centers. It's not an uncommon sight to see the hunts streaming across the English countryside on this day, and many people will watch the meets as spectators. Though fox hunting is now illegal, they are still able to practice the tradition as long as no foxes are harmed or killed (usually, the dogs are sent after a scented dummy).

Simply put, Boxing Day is a day to enjoy the joys of the mid-winter break from the rat race. To eat good food, get a good deal or spend time with your friends and family. It's certainly a lesson we can all learn from!

ASPECTS OF CULTURE

32. BRITISH HONORS SYSTEM

Do you know your Knights from your Dames and your OBEs from your MBEs? Here is a breakdown of the current British honors system.

In the United Kingdom, the Queen is the "Fountain of Honour" and is responsible for recognizing the achievements of men and women across the Commonwealth. The honors may be awarded for achievements in science, math, the arts, charity, and other activities that benefit the kingdom. Queen Elizabeth II typically awards honors twice a year, once on New Year's Day and again on her official birthday in June. Birthday Honours have been around since 1865, while New Year's Honours have been awarded since 1890, both begun during the reign of Queen Victoria and carried on by her successors.

There are different processes for selecting honors. The first and most common means is to make a recommendation to the Cabinet Office, and the recommendations are managed by the Honours Committee. Nominations may be submitted by government departments or members of the public. Various government agencies then pour over each candidate to determine his or her suitability for the award. The Queen will then informally approve the list, and award letters will be sent to the nominees. Once the nominees have accepted, the list of honors is finalized and published in the London Gazette (the official newspaper of record).

The second and less common means is for the monarch to confer honors personally, which is reserved mostly for chivalric honors. These include: the Order of the Garter, the Order of the Thistle, the Order of Merit, the Royal Victorian Order and the Royal Victorian, the Royal Medal of Honour, and the Royal Medal for Long Service. The orders of chivalry are made on a personal order of the Queen and, in some cases, may be granted on special days separate from New Year's or the official birthday.

When it comes to the Orders of Knighthood, the first and most prominent is the Most Noble Order of the Garter. This is the oldest chivalric order, founded by King Edward III in 1348. The reason for its selectiveness is that the order is limited to the Sovereign, the Prince of Wales, and twenty-four "Knights Companion" or "Ladies Companion." There are also supernumerary members who do not count towards the twenty-four, which includes members of the Royal Family who are designated "Royal Knights and Ladies of the Garter." Foreign dignitaries may also be included in the order and are known as "Stranger Knights and Ladies of the Garter."

Second comes the Most Ancient and Noble Order of the Thistle, which was founded by King James II (VII of Scotland) and relates primarily to Scotland, and the Garter relates more to England and Wales. As with the Order of the Garter, the Order of the Thistle is a limited one reserved for the Sovereign and sixteen Knights and Ladies, who are known as "Knights and Ladies of the Thistle." There are also an unlimited number of "extra" knights and ladies. The order was suspended after James II was deposed in the Glorious Revolution, but revived with Queen Anne. This is the last order that invests women with the title of "Lady," with lower orders instead of using the title "Dame."

Since the Order of St. Patrick has long since fallen dormant, the next chivalric order in precedence is the Most Honourable Order of the Bath, which was founded in 1725 by King George I. The name itself doesn't come from the City of Bath but from the ancient method of awarding knighthood that required the candidate to bathe as part of the ceremony. The order has three grades and absolutely limits the number of members, with "Knight/Dame Grand Cross" set at 120 members, "Knight/Dame Commander" at 355, and "Companion" at 1,925 (Companions are not considered knights or dames). Further, while the Order of the Garter and Order of the Thistle are at the Sovereign's own selection, the Order of Bath is the first on which the nominations are made on the recommendation of the government.

The Most Distinguished Order of St. Michael and St. George, which is awarded primarily to diplomats, also has three levels of "Knight/ Dame Grand Cross" (125 members), "Knight/Dame Commander" (375 members), and "Companion" (1,750 members). It was created by the Prince Regent, later King George IV, in 1818 and recognized the contributions of those who work overseas. Foreigners may be appointed as "honorary" members, but despite this status, they are still considered full members of the order. Another order dedicated to service is that of the Royal Victorian Order, which is awarded to persons for service to the Crown. It ties for the most grades of any order at five: 1) Knight/Dame Grand Cross, 2) Knight/Dame Commander, 3) Commander, 4) Lieutenant, and 5) Member. Since Queen Victoria created the order in 1896, it remains one of the only honors that is personally granted by the Sovereign and does not require a recommendation from the Cabinet.

Male knights get to use the title 'Sir' (as in Sir Patrick Stewart) with their name, and women get to use 'Dame' (as in Dame Judi Dench).

One of the most publicly known chivalric honors is that of the Most Excellent Order of the British Empire. King George V founded it in 1917 as he realized that no specific honor existed for ordinary citizens who rendered great service to the British Empire. As such, this is the largest of the orders as the most public honors are admitted to this order, with thousands of people admitted every year. The Order of the British Empire is divided into two types: recognition for public service and recognition for military service. As with the Royal Victorian Order, it has five grades: 1) Knight/Dame Grand Cross, 2) Knight/Dame Commander, 3) Commander, 4) Officer, and 5) Member. Those who receive an MBE can use 'MBE' after their names (i.e., David Beckham MBE).

There are further honors that may be granted, though they confer no title. The Order of Merit acts similarly to the Order of the British Empire in that it may be rewarded for services in the arts or the military. The Distinguished Service Order is granted to administrative and clerical workers on the completion of twenty-five years of public service. The Distinguished Service Order is presented to military officers in wartime for meritorious or distinguished service. The Victoria Cross is the highest military award a member of the armed forces can receive and is forged of metal recast from Russian cannons that were captured during the Crimean War. Meanwhile, St. George's Cross is the highest decoration for civilians, awarded for "acts of the greatest heroism or of the most conspicuous courage in circumstances of extreme danger."

While this is by no means the extent of the honors one may receive, the orders and awards covered above represent a wealth of distinguished service to Britain. Twice a year, these people receive the acknowledgment they so richly deserve. The men and women recognized by the Crown and the Government of the United Kingdom have helped to protect the county, nurture its culture, and serve its people.

33. BRITISH PEERAGE SYSTEM

In Britain, the peerage comprises a number of legal hereditary, life, and representative titles. The system dates back to the 11th Century and the Anglo-Saxons. It began as a means to protect England from invaders, with earls being appointed over various shires, which continued after the Norman conquest, though the administrative duties shifted to appointed sheriffs. Over time, a series of various titles evolved, including Duke/Duchess, Marquess/Marchioness, Earl/Countess, Viscount/Viscountess, and Baron/Baroness.

Further, there are five co-existing peerages. The three oldest are the peerages of England, Scotland, and Ireland. With the Acts of Union of 1707, the English and Scottish peerages became the Peerage of Great Britain. After the Acts of Union of 1801, future peerages were made under the Peerage of the United Kingdom, including those from Ireland and now Northern Ireland. Traditionally, most of these peerages have been hereditary.

In the past, a hereditary peerage could only pass from fathers to sons. If the peer had no children, the title would pass to his brother. If he only had a daughter, it would pass to her husband. To this day, women are still not entitled to inherit most hereditary peerages. At one point, there were over 800 hereditary peers in the UK, and a majority of them were entitled to sit in the House of Lords. However, under Tony Blair's government, the House of Lords Act 1999 removed all but 92 of these seats.

The Life Peerage Act of 1958 created titles that only last for the life of the person appointed. The Prime Minister typically appoints life peers from his or her own party, though he or she may also appoint life peers from the opposition. These peers are expected to attend sessions of the House of Lords, and they now make up the majority of the seats in the chamber. Representative peers, on the other hand, are peers chosen by the peers of Scotland and Ireland to represent those nations in the House of Lords. These peers were introduced after the Acts of Union 1707 and ended for Ireland when it became a free state in 1922, while Scottish peers continued until 1963 when all Scottish peers were permitted to sit in the House of Lords. The remaining representative peers were among the ninety-two hereditary peers under the 1999 act (they hold an election amongst themselves to decide which 92 sit in the Lords).

DUKE/DUCHESS

King Edward III created the first dukedoms of Cornwall, Lancaster, and Clarence in 1337. Dukes are the highest rank of peerage below the sovereign. At present, there are roughly 30 dukedoms in the United Kingdom, with 10 of them being Royal Dukedoms, which are held by members of the Royal Family. For non-royal dukes, the rank goes in order of creation, meaning that the oldest non-royal duke is the most senior. The form of address for most dukes and duchesses is "Your Grace."

MARQUESS/MARCHIONESS

King Richard II created the first Marquess when he appointed Robert de Vere, 9th Earl of Oxford, as the first Marquess of Dublin in 1385. The title of marquess is below a duke, but one level higher than an earl. King George V styled most of his relatives as Marquess after they relinquished their German titles during World War I, and the last Marquess created was the Marquess of Willingdon in 1936. No other such titles have been created since, with the most recent honor above an earl being the Duke and Duchess of Cambridge in 2011. A marquess or marchioness is addressed as "The Most Honourable" or "My Lord Marquess/Madam."

EARL/COUNTESS

As mentioned, "earl" is the oldest form of peerage dating back to pre-Norman times. The Norman equivalent was a Count, though that was not continued under King William I. However, the female title of countess is a holdover from the Normans. After William, succeeding kings continued to reduce the power of earls. Even so, they still had enough power to depose King Edward II. Over time, the earldoms came to be less associated with shires and more with towns, local landmarks, or surnames. The proper address for earls and countesses is "The Right Honourable Earl/Countess" and "My Lord/Madam."

VISCOUNT/VISCOUNTESS

The fourth rank in the British peerage system, a viscount or viscountess, is typically named in association with a place. The title originated under the Carolingians in France and was carried over to Britain by the Normans, though the use of it wasn't recorded until 1440 when King Henry VI created John Beaumont as Viscount Beaumont. It was a title created by the monarch, and while it was similar to a life peerage at first, eventually, it became a hereditary peerage. Viscounts and viscountesses are often addressed as "My Lord" or "Madam" rather than by their title. It's pronounced 'VY COUNT' not 'VIS COUNT (as in discount).

BARON/BARONESS

Baron or baroness is the lowest rank of the peerage and were created by the Normans as a mostly administrative position within the "barony," or feudal tenure. In Scotland, the title became that of "thane," prominently remembered now from the play Macbeth. Barons were expected to be loyal to the king and serve as military commanders at the monarch's command. It was the barons who forced King John I to sign the Magna Carta, and it was the barons who formed the first parliament. Over time, baronies became less tied to land and more products of royal creation. Further, all of the above titles also typically carry the title of baron. The proper title is typically "Lord" or "Lady," and the form of address is "My Lord" or "Madam."

Of course, this information represents only the basics of the peerage system, and it is, in practice, very complex with a rich history, and we have inevitably left some things out – this is meant to be an overview.

34. HOW TO GET A KNIGHTHOOD (OR DAMEHOOD)

During Medieval times, becoming a knight was a method of social mobility – beginning as a page, then moving up to squire, and finally becoming a knight. The position was one that was granted for service to a monarch, almost always for military service. Knights became their own social class, though still divided between noble and non-noble knights, and developed their own code of honor known as chivalry. Knights as a military order began to die out around the 15th Century when nations started to form professional armies. Since that time, what it means to be a knight and how one achieves this honor has changed.

Several orders of knighthood have existed, including the Most Noble Order of the Garter, the Most Noble Order of the Thistle, and the Most Distinguished Order of St. George and St. Michael, amongst others. However, these orders were very exclusive. Modern knighthood really came about thanks to King George V, who formed the Most Excellent Order of the British Empire in 1917. George felt that the honors system of the time needed to be expanded to recognize the many individuals who had fought and contributed to the British Empire during World War I. A year later, the OBE would be expanded to include both military and civilian categories, honoring not only contributions during wartime but peacetime also.

Regardless of whether the honor is earned for military or civilian contributions, there are five grades: 1) Knight/Dame Grand Cross

(GBE), 2) Knight/Dame Commander (KBE/DBE), 3) Commander (CBE), 4) Officer (OBE), and 5) Member (MBE). The two most senior ranks of the Order grant their bearers the titles of "Sir" or "Dame," though "honorary appointees" or appointees whose citizenship is not with the United Kingdom, do not receive this title, such as Irish musician and activist Bob Geldof (KBE). However, this can change for honorees who become British citizens, such as Sir Terry Wogan. Regardless of their grade or citizenship, the honoree can still put the initials on their name.

The reigning monarch is the Sovereign of the Order and the person responsible for making appointments, but the process does not typically begin with Queen Elizabeth II. For reasons of practicality, the list of honors to be given out on New Year's Day and the Queen's Birthday begins with the Cabinet Office Honours and Appointments Secretariat. The Honours Committee receives recommendations from many avenues, including members of the public, previous honorees, and Her Majesty's Government. The committee has several sub-committees to review applications which are organized by the type of achievement such as Community, Military, Arts and Military, Education, Political Service, and so on.

Committee and sub-committee members are often not civil servants and are tasked with ensuring the nominated individual meets the requirements for knighthood. The person nominated must "have made a major contribution to the country at a national or international level; their work and achievements will be viewed as an inspiration to others; and they may have influenced their peers, industry or the nation through their sustained and outstanding commitment to their chosen area." It is not required or up to the nominator to recommend a grade for the knighthood as that is decided on by the Honours Committee. The committee's recommendations are then provided to the Queen through the Prime Minister.

Her Majesty will then informally accept the recommendations, and letters will be sent to the nominees to inform them that they will receive a knighthood honor. Not everyone who is nominated chooses to accept, however, for various reasons, including disagreements with the government or with the system itself. Some notable individuals to turn down an honor include actor John Cleese and musician David Bowie (twice). Others who have accepted have returned their honor later on, such as John Lennon, and some have given up their honor on taking citizenship in a country that does not permit its citizens to hold titles, such as Anthony Hopkins when he became a United States citizen. Individuals can also be stripped of their knighthood following the conviction of a crime, such as jockey Lester Piggott for tax fraud in 1987 and Rolf Harris in 2015 for indecent assault.

Following the notification to the honorees, the list of honors will be published in the Crown's official newspaper, the London Gazette.

The Central Chancery of the Orders of Knighthood at St. James's Palace arranges the investitures of medals that take place on New Year's Day and on the Queen's official birthday in mid-June. The Queen herself may not host the investiture ceremony, and other members of the Royal Family, including Prince Charles and the Duke of Cambridge, have hosted the ceremonies in the past.

While one doesn't really need knighthood for social status anymore, the honor does confer other benefits. In addition to using the initials or calling yourself "Sir" or "Dame" for the higher grades, members of the Order may wear their badges on their chests. Membership also grants a position in the British order of precedence for state dinners and other ceremonial events. The order of precedence not only includes the honoree but also their partner and their children. What's more, it is possible for an individual to move up in grade as they gain further achievements, meaning that a Commander could move up to become a Knight or Dame and gain that extra title.

While the honor has changed over the centuries, the most important aspect of it is that knighthood still denotes accomplishments that have benefited Britain and the world. Whether one has made an accomplishment on the battlefield, in a laboratory, or on the stage, they have contributed something to make this world a better place. Such achievements will continue to deserve and receive recognition from a grateful Sovereign.

35. BRITISH PATRIOTIC SONGS

In addition to the national anthem, there are several songs that are important to the British people and act as unofficial anthems. Most of these songs can regularly be heard during the Last Night of the Proms, a yearly BBC concert where songs like this are performed with much audience participation at Royal Albert Hall. The concept of a 'Proms' is very popular in Britain, and there will be hundreds of events across the country where similar classical music concerts are held, and this music is played (like the Battle Proms concerts). Here's a rundown of the most popular and important ones.

God Save the Queen

This is Britain's official anthem. Like most things with British culture, no one really knows who wrote it originally; it's one of those things that has evolved over the years. The tune also has unclear origins, though John Bull is sometimes credited. Americans would recognize the tune as we sing the song 'My country tis of thee' to the same tune.

The standard version has three verses, but in most cases, the first one is the only one performed or sung. Though sometimes, the second verse is omitted, and the third is sung. It's one of those things with British culture where you shrug your shoulders and say, 'it depends.'

Here are the lyrics of the standard version:

God save our gracious Queen!
Long live our noble Queen!
God save the Queen!
Send her victorious,
Happy and glorious,
Long to reign over us:
God save the Queen!

O Lord our God arise,
Scatter her enemies,
And make them fall:
Confound their politics,
Frustrate their knavish tricks,
On Thee our hopes we fix:
God save us all.

Thy choicest gifts in store,
On her be pleased to pour;
Long may she reign:
May she defend our laws,
And ever give us cause,
To sing with heart and voice,
God save the Queen!

Jerusalem

This is widely considered the unofficial anthem of England. Based on a poem by William Blake, the song has come to represent England's own idea of itself as an Arcadian Utopia. The poem was not widely popular or known until it was set to music as a hymn by composer Sir Hubert Parry (with orchestration by Elgar). It's England's most popular patriotic song. The Women's Institute members famously sing the song at their meetings. It's deeply embedded in English culture but is a relatively recent addition to it.

Here are the words:

And did those feet in ancient time,
Walk upon Englands mountains green:
And was the holy Lamb of God,
On Englands pleasant pastures seen!

And did the Countenance Divine,
Shine forth upon our clouded hills?

And was Jerusalem builded here,
Among these dark Satanic Mills?

Bring me my Bow of burning gold:
Bring me my Arrows of desire:
Bring me my Spear: O clouds unfold:
Bring me my Chariot of fire!

I will not cease from Mental Fight,
Nor shall my Sword sleep in my hand:
Till we have built Jerusalem,
In Englands green & pleasant Land.

Land of Hope and Glory

Land of Hope and Glory is a British patriotic song, with music by Edward Elgar written in 1901 and lyrics by A.C. Benson later added in 1902. It's often performed alongside Jersusalem and other British patriotic songs. The tune will be familiar to most Americans as it's the tune used in our "graduation marches." It's very popular, and most British people would know the words to it.

Here are the lyrics:

Solo
Dear Land of Hope, thy hope is crowned,
God make thee mightier yet!
On Sov'ran brows, beloved, renowned,
Once more, thy crown is set.
Thine equal laws, by Freedom gained,
Have ruled thee well and long;
By Freedom gained, by Truth maintained,
Thine Empire shall be strong.

Chorus
Land of Hope and Glory, Mother of the Free,
How shall we extol thee, who are born of thee?
Wider still and wider shall thy bounds be set;
God, who made thee mighty, make thee mightier yet,
God, who made thee mighty, make thee mightier yet.

Solo
Thy fame is ancient as the days,
As Ocean large and wide:

A pride that dares, and heeds not praise,
  A stern and silent pride;
Not that false joy that dreams content
  With what our sires have won;
The blood a hero sire hath spent
  Still nerves a hero son.

Chorus

Rule, Britannia!

Rule, Britannia! is a British patriotic song, originating from the 1740 poem "Rule, Britannia" by James Thomson and was set to music by Thomas Arne in the same year. It is strongly associated with the Royal Navy, but is also used by the British Army. It's a song that is rather inappropriate in modern usage because of its association with British Imperialism. The song makes a major point about 'Britons never being slaves,' but it was also written at the height of the British slave trade. There are quite a few people in the world who were not pleased to be ruled by Britannia (and resent the colonial history). Still, it's a popular song that is still sung at events along with the other patriotic songs mentioned in this chapter.

Here are the lyrics:

When Britain first, at Heaven's command
Arose from out the azure main;
This was the charter of the land,
And guardian angels sang this strain:
"Rule, Britannia! rule the waves:
Britons never will be slaves."

The nations, not so blest as thee,
Must, in their turns, to tyrants fall;
While thou shalt flourish great and free,
The dread and envy of them all.
"Rule, Britannia! rule the waves:
Britons never will be slaves."

Still more majestic shalt thou rise,
More dreadful, from each foreign stroke;
As the loud blast that tears the skies,
Serves but to root thy native oak.
"Rule, Britannia! rule the waves:
Britons never will be slaves."

Thee haughty tyrants ne'er shall tame:
All their attempts to bend thee down,
Will but arouse thy generous flame;
But work their woe, and thy renown.
"Rule, Britannia! rule the waves:
"Britons never will be slaves."

To thee belongs the rural reign;
Thy cities shall with commerce shine:
All thine shall be the subject main,
And every shore it circles thine.
"Rule, Britannia! rule the waves:
"Britons never will be slaves."

The Muses, still with freedom found,
Shall to thy happy coast repair;
Blest Isle! With matchless beauty crown'd,
And manly hearts to guard the fair.
"Rule, Britannia! rule the waves:
"Britons never will be slaves."

I Vow to Thee, My Country

I Vow to Thee; My Country is a British patriotic hymn, created in 1921 when a poem by Sir Cecil Spring-Rice was set to music by Gustav Holst (adapted from the Jupiter section of his orchestral suite The Planets. It's a popular song, but it's also notable for its use in funerals, private and public. It was played at the funeral of Sir Winston Churchill in 1965.

I vow to thee, my country, all earthly things above,
Entire and whole and perfect, the service of my love;
The love that asks no questions, the love that stands the test,
That lays upon the altar the dearest and the best;
The love that never falters, the love that pays the price,
The love that makes undaunted the final sacrifice.

And there's another country, I've heard of long ago,
Most dear to them that love her, most great to them that know;
We may not count her armies; we may not see her King;
Her fortress is a faithful heart, her pride is suffering;
And soul by soul and silently her shining bounds increase,
And her ways are ways of gentleness, and all her paths are peace.

36. THE IMPORTANCE OF REMEMBRANCE DAY

In British History, World War I is just a seminal moment that World War II is. WWI in America is a bit of a historical afterthought because we entered it so late. But for Britain, it was an existential struggle that saw slaughter that did not discriminate along class lines. Almost no one was untouched. So, to this day, even over 100 years later, Remembrance is a key event in British public life.

The eleventh hour of the eleventh day of the eleventh month marks the signing of the Armistice, on 11 November 1918, to signal the end of World War I. At 11 am on 11 November 1918, the guns of the Western Front fell silent after more than four years of continuous warfare. Remembrance Sunday is held on the second Sunday in November, which is usually the Sunday nearest to 11 November. Special services are held at war memorials and churches all over Britain.

A national ceremony takes place at the Cenotaph in Whitehall, London. The Cenotaph stands in the middle of the road in Whitehall (part of London for those who are wondering). It was designed by Sir Edward Lutyens and erected in 1919. It is a bare stature save for the carved wreaths on each end and the words "The Glorious Dead" as chosen by the author Rudyard Kipling. The Cenotaph in the middle of the road paying homage to the war dead is certainly a stark reminder of the destruction man can cause. Many tourists will have walked or driven past it and not even noticed it.

The first such modern ceremony was held on 11 November 1919, following a suggestion by King George V for a two-minute silence across the United Kingdom and a ceremony to take place in London. Thousands had gathered around the wood-and-plaster Cenotaph in Whitehall, where Prime Minister David Lloyd George walked from Downing Street to place a wreath. Every year the Queen lays the first wreath at the Cenotaph.

Of course, the most enduring symbol of Remembrance is the poppy, adorned by public figures and politicians in the lead up to Remembrance Day. The poppy symbolizes hope and life. Flanders Fields, which is located in the western part of Belgium, saw some of the bloodiest and concentrated fighting during World War I. Complete and utter devastation as buildings, homes, roads, trees, and everything in its path were decimated. Where homes once stood there was a sea of mud, the graves of the dead although men still lived and fought among their fallen comrades. Ironically, the poppy was the only living thing that survived in that area. Therefore a symbol of survival, life, hope, and reassurance to the brave men still fighting.

A Canadian doctor serving with the Canadian Air Force was so touched by what he witnessed he penned a poem called Flanders Fields. Dr. John McCrae published his poem, and the poppy soon became a popular symbol for those who perished in battle.

In Flanders Fields:

In Flanders fields, the poppies blow
Between the crosses, row on row,
That mark our place; and in the sky,
The larks, still bravely singing, fly
Scarce heard amid the guns below.
We are the Dead. Short days ago
We lived, felt dawn, saw sunset glow,
Loved and were loved, and now we lie In Flanders fields.
Take up our quarrel with the foe:
To you from failing hands we throw
The torch; be yours to hold it high.
If ye break faith with us who die
We shall not sleep, though poppies grow
In Flanders fields.

Remembrance Day is a moment for Britain to stop and remember those who came before and sacrificed their lives so that Britain could endure. World War I was a foundational moment for 'modern' Britain as directly after the war, many changes came to society – like the right to vote for all – including women. Never again was an aristocratic elite going to sacrifice the lives of everyone without them having a say in it first. Almost every British family that can trace their roots that far back will have a relative that fought in the Great War. They don't forget. And the country does not forget.

37. QUESTIONS NOT TO ASK A BRITISH PERSON

As a general rule, most Brits are more than willing to answer anything and everything that comes their way, and why not? Over the years, we've been asked everything from the rules of cricket and driving on the left to the frankly bizarre question of whether the British have the internet (yes, incidentally. Tim Berners Lee, anyone?). While the British are happy to while away the hours waxing lyrical about their green and pleasant land, there are a few questions that should probably be avoided if you want to avoid a tutting or even, heaven forbid, a raised eyebrow!

DO YOU LIKE SOCCER?

Let's start with an easy one, shall we? Not necessarily a question to avoid so much as to reword. I know that this is simply a point of linguistics, and yes, admittedly, soccer is considered the proper term, but honestly, they neither play, watch or even like soccer. To them, it is football and to call it otherwise requires us to undertake a swift and painful retaliation, explaining in detail why it should not now, nor ever be soccer. It's bizarre that it's even an argument. They invented the game, after all!

HOW MUCH DO YOU MAKE?

Ooh, steady on, now we are in the potential offense-causing territory. Understandably, there are many places where your take-home pay is as open for discussion as your daily commute or working hours. And why not? It is, after all, just another aspect of your job. Not for the British, though! To be asked what you earn is overly familiar, to say the least, and they generally go to great pains to avoid such talk. They might say the pay is not bad or might say that they can finally afford to shop at Molton Brown, but what they won't give you is a sterling amount. It really comes down to not wanting to appear crass. The British are happy to complain about their bosses, their hours, no tea bags, and off milk in the break-room, but pay is strictly off-limits.

WHO DO YOU VOTE FOR?

Ah! Another one! Similar to your wages in many respects, very few Brits, in my experience, are comfortable openly talking about who they voted for. Of course, there are those who are super partisan and will quite happily extol the virtues of the Tories/Labour/Greens/Monster Raving Loonies. Plenty more might even admit their choice with a sniff of 'they were the best of a bad bunch,' but on the whole, the British don't ask, and they don't tell. It's not out of any principle to a particular political ideology; more, it's rather an in-built English embarrassment for not wanting to take responsibility for those idiots in office (and it doesn't matter which party!).

HOW FAR IS IT FROM LONDON?

American knowledge of the geography of Britain is rather limited – it's not like we're taught the English shires in school! So instinctively, our view of the geography of Britain is how something relates to London, our only point of reference (and apparently the same for most British politicians, but I digress here). But Britain is a massive place with huge cities spread out across the Isle, and the people that live in them are rather proud of their cities. Comparing them to London irritates them to no end, and many hate their capital – some have never even visited! It's like a Brit asking someone from Iowa how far away from Washington DC it is. It doesn't matter! Look at a map instead!

WHY DON'T THE BRITISH SPEAK ANY OTHER LANGUAGES?

This one is changing by the day, but then stereotypes are hard to shed, particularly if that stereotype is of a lobster-pink British man in a Spanish restaurant talking FAR TOO LOUDLY and ending every other word with an 'o'. Of course, there are plenty of Brits with connections to other countries who speak a multitude of languages. It always comes as a bit of an embarrassment when chatting to someone with a half a dozen languages in their head while we can barely remember the basics. Speaking English is quite enough for most Brits, especially since English now has more global speakers than English people!

WHY DO THE BRITISH HAVE SUCH BAD TEETH?

Well, if the former was a stereotype that stops us talking, this one ensures they won't even crack a smile. Possibly from the bad old days of the 1950s and 1960s when dentistry was considered an offshoot of dry stone walling, British teeth have run the gamut from 'Hollywood starlet' all the way down to 'poorly kept medieval graveyard.' Again, this is something that is improving to the point where now, we aren't much different from anyone else, and yet still, this stereotype persists. There are several reasons why the British historically had bad teeth. Many of those things are no longer relevant. Sometimes they even sneer at our perfect American smiles.

HAVE YOU MET THE QUEEN?

There are almost seventy million British people. And while the Queen seems to have existed forever, she has not been on this earth nearly long enough to have met them all. Give the poor old lady a bit of a break. Granted, millions HAVE met her. But usually, to meet the Queen, you have to be 'special' in some way – have done a great public service, be very famous, or important in some other way. The closest most British people get to meeting the Queen is waving at her as she drives by in her Rolls-Royce.

WHY ARE THE BRITISH ALWAYS DRUNK?

Have you ever tried to spend your entire life polite, reserved, and ever so slightly awkward socially? No? Well, if you had, you might also need some kind of social lubricant to make things a little less … well … stuffy! Of course, this is a massive generalization, but I don't know too many Brits who don't enjoy a tipple, and of course, they all have their own reasons for it. Admittedly there are way too many who seem to think that the volume of vomit and the magnitude of a hangover is directly proportional to the amount of fun they (forgot they) had the night before, but before you start assuming they're all binge drinking nut-cases, they aren't, the majority are social drinkers at best. They do like a drink, these people. And it does raise an eyebrow when you tell them you don't drink at all.

WHY DO THE BRITISH ALWAYS TALK ABOUT THE WEATHER?

Anyone who has read Kate Fox's Watching the English will know by now that it is far more subtle than that. Having a maritime climate for the entire country means that the weather changes from one minute to the next, and so it's a relatively safe topic of conversation. Not having the luxury of an annual dry season or a rainy season, weather chat is a great leveler. But it is so much more than that. A casual nod to the prevailing conditions of the day to someone at the bus stop is not mere observation, but more a coded way of beginning a friendly (albeit meaningless) way of engaging in a brief conversation in a way that is both non-threatening and overtly polite, two things that the common or garden Brit will respond to! A little travel tip? Rather than pointing out their obsession with the weather, talking to a Brit about it will find them opening up in no time! After all, it's a bit chilly out today, isn't it?

WHY IS ALL BRITISH FOOD TERRIBLE?

British food, on the whole, is not terrible. Seriously, this reputation came (in part) in the post-war years as a consequence of rationing, but things have changed, and British cuisine has undergone a major reinvention! I promise! The West Midlands have given the world the mighty balti as well as the gift of the pork scratching (perfect with a pint of black country ale!), Cornwall has delicious pastries, Somerset has the best cider you've ever tasted, and Welsh rarebit is food fit for a king (or Queen). Real Scottish porridge is magnificent, so too are the single malts, kippers, and scotch eggs they've graced British menus with. Every region has something to celebrate; from tangy blue stilton and cheddar sharp enough to cut you to gently fried whitebait anointed with a dollop of homemade tartar sauce, you really can not go wrong. Friends, I urge you, don't ask why our food is terrible; instead, get yourself a ticket and make a reservation! Table for two at 8 o'clock? Not a problem! Empty bellies welcome! Breakfast is served 7-9, tipping welcome but not expected, and don't forget ... try the fish!

38. A GUIDE TO UK ELECTIONS

UK general elections are interesting to watch. The British didn't invent elections, but they certainly have introduced a uniquely British flair to the proceedings. They are not like American elections at all. Personally, I'm a British politics junkie (I usually watch the election night coverage until the winner is announced). And while it's not my place to share an opinion on matters relating to British politics (we're not British), I thought it would be helpful to put together a quick guide to the British political system for those that want to learn the process.

While the American system of Government has its roots in British parliamentary democracy, there are fundamental differences in practice – many of which we fought a war to achieve.

I will try to keep this as simple as possible. This is meant to be an overview of UK politics; I have left lots of things out. It's not comprehensive; it's only a guide. There are plenty of other resources out there to explore each topic in more granular detail (I've read quite a few good books on the subject).

DOES THE UK HAVE A CONSTITUTION?

Yes and no. It has a constitution, but it is largely unwritten. It's more of an idea. There is not a single codified document that lays out Briton's rights or their structure of Government. UK government evolved based on precedent, tradition, and conflict. That being said, many 'rights' that Americans hold dear are also codified rights in the UK – like Freedom of Speech (though the British interpret it differently and have more restrictions – famously in libel). You'll hear British political commentators talk about a man named Walter Bagehot (usually they'll just say his last name – pronounced Badge-it); he wrote a book called the English Constitution that sets out the frameworks and ideas behind the unwritten constitution. The book explores the nature of the constitution of the United Kingdom, specifically the Parliament and its relationship to the monarchy.

THE SOVEREIGN

At the top of the British political system is Her Majesty The Queen. She's the Head of State and the authority from which all power resides. The Government in the UK is called Her Majesty's Government, and it operates in her name. The Queen, in practice, has no actual power. It's been stripped away during 500 years of parliamentary democracy. But she's an important symbol of Government (and continuance of governance – PM's come and go, the Queen and her Government does not). The Prime Minister also meets with her weekly in private to discuss issues facing the nation. The contents of these meetings are confidential. The Queen has a right to advise and to warn but not to act politically. She is apolitical. The Sovereign also formally dissolves Parliament and calls an election (after asked to do so by the PM).

PARLIAMENT

In America, we have three branches of Government that share power equally (with a powerful executive that also acts as the Head of State). In the UK, Parliament is sovereign (Parliamentary sovereignty was an issue in the Brexit debate); there is no higher authority. Parliament is all branches of Government – it is the Executive, Legislative and Judicial branch, all wrapped into one. There is no formal separation of powers like in our system. In practice, it's a little more complicated, but I'll try to break it down.

Houses of Parliament

There are two houses of Parliament, and they meet in the Palace of Westminster.

House of Commons

The House of Commons is the fully elected body and has full

governmental power – it is more powerful than the House of Lords (it used to be the other way around, but this changed slowly over hundreds of years and after a civil war). Members of the House of Commons are elected to represent 650 constituencies which have a population of roughly 70,000 people. The House of Commons is elected for a five-year term (but this is a new thing – terms used not to be fixed). However, the Prime Minister can now call an election anytime with the support of the majority of the house. The Conservative Party has pledged in their Manifesto to abolish the Fixed Term Parliament Act and revert to the old system. As of 2021, this appears likely to happen soon.

House of Lords

The House of Lords, or Upper House, is a hereditary and appointed body that is more focused on long-term governance and refining laws. It used to be the more powerful house, but now it's more of a consultative body. The Lords takes the dirty laws written in the Commons and refines and rewrites them into proper laws. It rarely stops legislation, and if it tried to, the House of Commons has the power to override it (see Parliament Acts). Most of the hereditary Lords were abolished in 1999, but there are still about 100 left. There is talk of abolishing the House of Lords altogether and replacing it with an elected Senate, but it's an issue that rarely gets discussed anymore because, honestly, no one really cares. The status quo works. Only when the Lords agitate (like they did during the Brexit debate recently) does the Government threaten to get rid of it. It never does.

THE GOVERNMENT

The Government consists of two parts, the party that has the most seats in the House of Commons and the actual machinery of Government.

POLITICAL GOVERNMENT

The political party that is elected with the largest majority of MP's forms the Government. The UK has a first past the post voting system, which means that the winner takes all. If any political party can command a majority in the House of Commons, it can form a government. This is where things get interesting. Sometimes the party with the most votes doesn't win a majority, and then it has to govern in a coalition government (as in the 2010 election).

The leader of the largest party in the Commons is called the Prime Minister, and he or she is the de facto Head of State – meaning they are the one that actually wields power. The Prime Minister forms a government of ministers – political appointees who are given power over specific areas and run various government departments.

Some key ministers:

Prime Minister – First Lord of the Treasury and the de facto Head of state. The Prime Minister is not technically 'elected' by the British people; Theresa May was selected by the Conservative Party as leader after David Cameron resigned (and then she lost the election and was forced into a coalition). Calling an election is a chance for a PM to be officially elected by the British people and have a mandate.
Chancellor of the Exchequer – The person in charge of the treasury and puts together the yearly budget, the second most powerful figure in Government.
Foreign Secretary – The British equivalent to Secretary of State.

CIVIL GOVERNMENT

Outside of the political system, there is a vast government apparatus that operates for the British Government to function. Britain's civil servants are apolitical servants of the Crown whose job it is to enact government policy, whoever is in charge. Oftentimes, the civil service has its own views on how things should be done and can often 'house train' ministers to do their bidding (something lampooned in Yes, Minister). The civil service does not like to draw attention to itself, but they're the people responsible for the Government working in Britain (and they do like it to actually function even if they don't agree with the policies). The Head of the Civil service is the Cabinet Secretary, and he's the highest-ranking non-politician in Government.

LOCAL GOVERNMENT

The UK has a strong central government. Local Government as a corollary is weak but becoming more important. Local elections are usually held on a different cycle than a general election, which is primarily concerned with the national Government. Most localities have a district or city council. They don't have as much power as Parliament and only function in roles that have been clearly defined. They are most Britons direct contact with Government, so often they are what people complain about the most. These are the organizations responsible for picking up the trash, road maintenance, etc. On a town and village level, there are parish councils and town councils. Politics there can be just as bloody as they can on the national level!

POLITICAL PARTIES

When you vote in a British election, you're not voting for a particular Prime Minister. You're voting for the party you want to be in power and thus the leader of their party. The leader of the party who winds up with a majority in the House of Commons forms the Government. The current party in power is the Conservative party, led by Boris Johnson.

The UK has three main political parties and several smaller ones. We'll try to break down all of the most important ones (and let us be clear, we do not support any particular party – this is for informational purposes).

We will discuss these parties in the context of the Left/Right political scale.

Conservative Party – AKA The Tories – Right Wing

The Tories are the traditional right-wing conservative party in the UK. They've been around for hundreds of years. Their full name is the Conservative and Unionist Party. It's hard to define what they stand for without sounding political. They're very much like the Republicans in the USA in some regards, but actually, they're nowhere near as conservative (with a small c). Think of them as a party of socially liberal and fiscal conservatives. They are not religious at all. Religion does not play as much of a public role in British politics as it does in the USA. Many people view the Tories negatively; they call them the 'Nasty Party.' Many have not gotten over the Thatcher years. The hard truth, though, is that England is generally conservative, and the party is very strong right now. Basically, people complain about them, yet they keep winning elections.

Labour Party – AKA Labour – Left Wing

The Labour party is the traditional left-wing party in the UK. They used to be more centrist under Tony Blair, but since then have moved much further to the left. The previous leader, Jeremy Corbyn, was often called essentially a Communist (he's not popular except amongst his rabid supporters). The current leader, Sir Kier Starmer, is returning the party back to the Blairite center. The closest analog in the USA would be the Democratic party, except they're much further to the left than the Democrats would ever be. They haven't been in power since 2010 and are very politically weak right now. The 'Opposition' in the House of Commons is an official title, and the leader of the Opposition is accorded special respects, and he has his own 'shadow cabinet' of people who would be ready to take up the same positions in Government if they found themselves in power.

Liberal Democrats – AKA Lib Dems – Somewhere in the middle

The Liberal Democrats are a much harder party to define, which is why I suppose they haven't had the electoral success they would have liked. The party's reputation has been tarnished with its participation in the Coalition Government from 2010 to 2015, and it has yet to recover. They currently only have a handful of MPs; they used to have 70.

Minor Parties

Plaid Cymru – Party of Welsh Nationalists. They often align with Labour.

Scottish National Party – Party of Scottish Nationalists. They made headlines in 2015 by attempting to gain Scottish independence. They're very left-wing and would work with Labour, but it comes with strings attached (another independence referendum – which they've officially called for). They currently break Westminster Politics. Their only goal is Scottish Independence, so they don't want a UK-wide Parliament to function well.

UKIP – The UK Independence Party. They're hard to classify on the left/right scale, but essentially they're against membership in the European Union and against almost all forms of Immigration into the UK. They're considered a spent political force. They only had one reason to exist: to get the UK to leave the EU. Now that they've done that, there is no reason for UKIP to continue to exist, and this has been shown in recent local elections; they were completely wiped out. The natural home for UKIP supporters is the Tory party, and many have simply returned now that Brexit has happened.

Green Party – This very left-wing party is the party for environmentalists. They only have one MP and a handful of council seats throughout the country. They're not taken seriously as a party except by their own supporters.

Sinn Fein – Irish nationalists. Often elected from Northern Ireland but refuse to ever take their seats because they refuse to swear the loyalty oath to The Queen. They want Ireland to be unified into one country.

Democratic Unionist Party – Northern Irish right-wing conservatives who want to stay in the United Kingdom. Natural allies with the Tory party, though they're generally religious fundamentalists, which is rather un-Tory.

SELECTION PROCESS

UK elections are quick affairs, lasting just five weeks once they're called. In the USA, the election cycle pretty much never ends. We're already in the 2024 election cycle, and it's only 2021. It's 2021, and our current President is technically already campaigning for the 2024 Presidential Election. In the UK, there is no campaigning before the election is called (though there are many unofficial things that LOOK like campaigning but aren't).

Once the election is called, Parliament is dissolved. This means there are no MP's. Current government ministers maintain their posts – the UK is not without a government during this time, but this is when the Civil Service really takes over to ensure the smooth operation of Government. However, there are rules of what government ministers can do during an election cycle so as not to unduly influence the election (like no new policies, etc.).

There is no TV advertising during an election campaign. No negative commercials. Nothing. There are party political broadcasts, and the major parties are all given allotted time to get their message out.

There is a cap on spending. It's an election on a budget. Money does not play a huge role in the result of the election though politicians can be bought anywhere; the UK is no exception.

If a candidate wants to be an MP, they need to be selected by their local party organization (the process differs for each party). Candidates for MP have to place a £500 deposit to get on the ballot; if they do not get enough votes (5% of votes), they lose the deposit (which is considered an embarrassment).

PARTY MANIFESTOS

We're not going to get into the details of what each party stands for in any election. In the weeks leading up to the election, each party publishes a manifesto. This Manifesto essentially lays out everything they plan to do during their term in office. It's considered a somewhat binding promise with the electorate that if you vote for this party, they plan to try and do these things. As always with politics, manifesto promises are routinely broken. But it gives the party in power a mandate, and you will often see that the UK Government will avoid big issues that it did not have a mandate for in its Manifesto. If the issue is big enough, another election could be called to decide the matter.

ELECTION DAY

Election Day is a sedate affair in the UK. It's been held on a Thursday for every election since 1935. It has been suggested that this tradition arose as the best of several circumstances: Friday pay-packets would lead to more drunken voters on Fridays and weekends; having the election as far after a Sunday as possible would reduce the influence of Sunday sermons; many towns held markets on Thursdays; thus the local population would be traveling to town that day anyway. Polls open at 7:00 am and close at 10:00 pm. The media is not allowed to discuss issues, exits polls, and individual candidate performance until after the polls have closed at 10:00 pm. The news during election day will often show footage of the party leaders voting, but that's usually it. It's almost as if the election is not happening. Polling places are in a variety of locations and sometimes in the oddest of places – like a fish and chips shop. Electioneering is not allowed.

ELECTION NIGHT

When polls close at 10:00 pm, the counting begins. Counting is done at a central location in each constituency. Counting is done by hand. Some places will count faster than others (and some even compete to complete the count soonest). Once all the ballots are counted, the 'returning officer' for the constituency will announce the winners, along with a count on how many votes each candidate received.

The BBC will begin its election coverage at 10:00 pm sharp and will often have early exit polling data to share. They will talk and analyze the day until the first results start being called. The first few will probably have live coverage, but as each constituency result starts to flood in, they'll simply start filling in the electoral map. Within a few hours, it will be pretty clear who's going to win and when that point happens, the BBC will declare who they think will win. Most results will be in by 3 or 4 am. Political junkies in the UK will stay up all night (and the TV presenters will stay on the air until the results are clear). The rest of the UK will wake up to the results in the morning. The traditional host for election night is David Dimbleby, but he's getting on in years, and it's quite a feat for an older man to stay up so late!

If the current party in power wins the election, their leader remains the Prime Minister. They will usually go to Buckingham Palace as soon as possible to ask HM The Queen to be allowed to form a new government. It all happens very quickly. If the current party LOSES power, then the current PM will go to Buckingham Palace and resign, and then the new PM will arrive shortly after that and ask to form a new government. MP's will be sworn in a few days later.

And then the job of governing begins (or resumes in the case of a returning government).

39. WHAT IS MORRIS DANCING?

Morris dancing is one of England's stranger cultural quirks. It almost died out completely but has had a revival in recent years. Full of pretty eccentric men (and sometimes women) wearing traditional clothing that is certainly eye-catching, Morris dancing has a mysterious and rich history that cements it as a cultural icon of the United Kingdom. From ancient times to the present day, it's more than just an activity that makes people scratch their heads; this is a type of dancing that connects the dancers and the audience with another time. If you looked at Morris dancing with anything other than respect, you might find yourself tapping to a different tune by the end of this piece.

The actual origins of both the name and the style of dancing are so old that they've been forgotten by history. It is speculated by some that it began as part of Celtic rituals around the monolithic sites of Britain. Places such as Stonehenge and the barrow at St. Weonards in Hertfordshire could have been some of the original sites of Morris dancing, done to praise nature and ask for a fruitful harvest. Another idea is that the dancing was brought back to England in the 14th Century by John of Gaunt after his time in Spain. The origin of the name is equally mysterious, but it's speculated that Morris derives from "Morisco," "Morisk," or "Moorish," and goes back to the supposed nature of the dancers to blacken their faces with soot so as to not be recognized by the local priest (due to the believed Pagan origins of the dances). However, none of these potential origins can be substantiated.

It's about this time that the first references start appearing, from a Morusk dance at Lanherne, Cornwall in 1468 to a stained-glass window in a house in Betley, Staffordshire originating in 1470. If the Church didn't care for the Morris dancing, it didn't show much as the dancing started being incorporated into Christian festivals. From there, it became a part of village festivals as well May Day celebrations during the 16th Century. Even Shakespeare makes reference to it in several plays such as Henry VI, Henry V, and All's Well that Ends Well. In 1599, Shakespearean actor William Kemp performed what he called his "Nine Days Wonder," Morris dancing from London to Norwich for nine total days over several weeks.

By the 19th century, the practice was beginning to die out across the country, fueled by changes from the Industrial Revolution. D'Arcy Ferris, a music teacher, took it on as his personal mission to bring Morris dancing back, organizing festivals. Cecil Sharp experienced Morris dancing for himself in Oxford in 1899 and set about collecting songs and dances from all over the country to preserve the tradition. Moving into the 20th Century, six sides (or dancing groups) formed the Morris Ring in 1934, one of three larger organizations that still support the practice today, including the Morris Federation and Open Morris. While Morris Ring is essentially men-only, the other two include women's and mixed sides.

It really has to be seen to be believed.

The style of Morris dancing is similar to other folk dances around the world, focusing on rhythmic stepping and choreographed routines. Dancers may also use several accessories, including handkerchiefs, swords, and sticks. Several different styles exist, from North West Morris, which is more precision-based and military in style, to Border Morris that is looser and more energetic. Morris sides tend to practice during the winter months and put on their performances in the summer once warmer weather festivals begin. Accompanying music is usually provided by a melodeon, a fiddle, or a pipe and tabor, and the sides could be joined by either a single player or a whole band. Depending on the style of Morris, the music ranges from traditional to innovative.

From the brink of extinction, Morris dancing is just as alive today as it was in past centuries. Whatever style and side you're watching, you better believe it will be full of movement, color, and music. You can take in a Morris dance anywhere from village festivals to concert halls and everywhere in-between. If you ever want to experience this British cultural tradition for yourself, the Morris Ring, Morris Federation, and Open Morris provide links and calendars for the various sides, or you can check the local council's calendar to see when their next major festival is.

40. PATRON SAINTS OF THE BRITISH ISLES

Every country has its own unique symbols. They can be places, things, and even people that represent the country. Patron saints are in many ways an extension of this symbolism, each an important figure not only for Christianity but specifically for the country which he patronizes, his history and lore tied to the land and its culture. The countries of the British Isles each have their own patron saint who acts as an advocate and protector over England, Scotland, Ireland, and Wales, and we're going to take you on a journey to discover each one and his importance to each land in Great Britain and Ireland.

ST. DAVID (WALES)

Not too much is known about St. David and his early life aside from that which was chronicled by Rhygyfarch, the son of the Bishop of St. David's. David was born the descendant of Welsh royalty, and during his life, he founded twelve monasteries (including Glastonbury and Minevia), traveled to the Holy Land, was consecrated as a bishop, and ultimately became the Archbishop of Wales in 550 AD. Pope Callistus II canonized David in 1120 and he subsequently became the patron saint of Wales. David died on March 1st, 589, and that date is reserved for his feast day. On an interesting note, St. David is said to have been a strict vegetarian and would sometimes stand in water up to his neck and recite scripture as penance. St David's Day is March 1st.

ST. ANDREW (SCOTLAND)

Unlike David, Andrew is the first saint in this article who wasn't from the country he patronizes. Andrew, along with his brother Simon Peter, was a fisherman who gave up his livelihood to become one of Jesus Christ's original twelve disciples. Following Christ's death, Andrew traveled far, spreading the word of Christ and died in Patras, executed on an X-shaped cross (now known as St. Andrew's Cross) because he felt he was not worthy to die in the same manner as Jesus. Legend has that his travels brought him as far as Scotland, where he founded a church at Fife. His feast day has been celebrated in Scotland as far back as 1000 AD, and he became the patron saint of Scotland in 1320 with the Declaration of Arbroath when the country announced its independence. St Andrew's Day is November 30th.

ST. GEORGE (ENGLAND)

Perhaps the most legendary figure among Great Britain's patron saints, Saint George is the one on this list about whom we know the least. It is believed he was once a high-ranking Roman soldier in the 4th Century, and the Emperor Diocletian tortured him in an attempt to get George to renounce his Christian faith. George's resiliency and the strength of his faith led to stories of his courage spreading throughout the Christian world, including the legend of him fighting a dragon (dragons also represented Satan in serpent form during the Middle Ages). Despite never having visited England, English Crusaders began to evoke his name, and King Edward III made him the patron saint of England in 1350 when Edward founded the Order of the Garter. St George's Day is April 23rd.

ST. PATRICK (IRELAND)

Arguably the most famous amongst the four, St. Patrick's celebrity is owed in part to his feast day being as much a representation of all things Irish as it is his ministry to the island of Ireland. Patrick grew up in lowland Scotland or possibly Wales, the son of a Roman officer and a deacon. Young Patrick had little interest in Christianity until he was kidnapped at the age of sixteen and sold into slavery in Ireland. He considered these events a punishment from God for his lack of faith and became increasingly more religious. Patrick eventually had a vision that aided in his escape back to Britain and, after studying to become a priest, had another vision that led him back to Ireland as a missionary. For twenty years, he traveled throughout the island, baptizing believers and constructing churches and monasteries. Several legends sprung up about Patrick in the wake of his death, including that his walking stick transformed into a living tree and that he banished all snakes from Ireland. While not the first missionary to Ireland, he was by far the most successful and, as a result, became the country's patron saint.

41. BRITISH POLICE RANKS

"Rank has its privileges," as they say, and in any military or police organization, you can find quite a lot of them. Ranks exist to create order and a clear chain of command between officers with different levels of experience. In the UK, ranks tend to be fairly standardized from jurisdiction to jurisdiction, with some minor differences. Watching any mystery show or police procedural, you may be a little lost trying to determine what's what. Well, have no fear, Anglotopia readers, because here is your guide to the basic ranks of the British police services!

POLICE CONSTABLE

The lowest rank on the totem pole of the police service, the Police Constable (also called "PC"), is the foot soldier in the fight against crime. As such, they have the most direct contact with the people they serve at the local level, not just arresting baddies but also conducting community outreach, collecting information at the scene, submitting reports, and working crowd control. On a TV program, they're most often the officers who discover the initial crime, keeping onlookers from interfering with the scene, doing office work, or running errands for the higher-ranking officers.

SERGEANT

A Sergeant is the first supervisory rank and oftentimes the first "Detective" rank in many TV programs. The rank is senior to "Constable" and junior to "Inspector." Sergeants are largely operational officers, both supervising constables and managing the day-to-day administration of the division. Though the rank of "Detective Constable" exists, these officers are mostly training to become detectives, and often the first detective rank you'll see in a program is that of "Detective Sergeant." These plain-clothed officers are not necessarily superior to other Sergeants, but their rank identifies them as members of the Criminal Investigative Division (CID) or the Special Branch.

INSPECTOR

Inspector is the second supervisory rank. Like Sergeants, they are mainly concerned with operational duties, and a uniformed Inspector is often responsible for supervising a duty shift of Constables and Sergeants. Most protagonist detectives in police programs tend to be this rank, including Inspector Endeavour Morse and Detective Inspector Sam Tyler of "Life of Mars."

CHIEF INSPECTOR

The next supervisory level, a Chief Inspector, is the senior officer in command of a district, usually of one or more local authority areas. In a larger town, the rank has often replaced that of Superintendent, such as Chief Inspector Frank Butterman in the film "Hot Fuzz." Detective Chief Inspector tends to be the Senior Investigating Officer in a CID branch. Notable examples include DCI Gene Hunt from "Life on Mars" and "Ashes to Ashes," DCI John Luther from "Luther," and DCI Greg Lestrade from "Sherlock." Typically, these are the highest officers one will see as a regular character.

SUPERINTENDENT/CHIEF SUPERINTENDENT

Every once in a while, the Superintendent will make an appearance on a program if they are not already a recurring character. In the past, Superintendents were in charge of each division. A Detective Chief Superintendent is senior to the Detective Chief Inspector and the Detective Superintendent. A Chief Superintendent is the highest rank below the Chief Officer Level. Chief Superintendents will command the largest areas of supervision. The Detective Chief Superintendent is the highest rank possible in the CID, often serving as the senior detective and commanding officer.

CHIEF OFFICERS

These highest-ranking officers are rarely seen in any police or mystery program unless something very big is happening. A Commander is a chief officer rank for the City of London and the Metropolitan Police. They are senior to Chief Superintendents but junior to Deputy Assistant Commissioners. The Deputy Assistant Commissioner rank is equivalent to Deputy Chief Constable and Assistant Constable in forces outside of London. A Chief Constable is the chief officer for a territorial police force outside of London. The Deputy Commissioner, as you may imagine, is the second-in-command of London's Metropolitan Police Service, while the Commissioner is over the entirety of the City of London or the Metropolitan Police Service.

42. BRITISH ARMED FORCES RANKS

The military of any country is a vital part of keeping the people safe from external threats. In Britain before the 17th century, military forces were usually formed when there was a need to attack someone else or whenever the land itself came under attack, with the soldiers and sailors conscripted from the local populace. The English Army formed as a standing military force in 1660, and in 1707, the English and Scottish armies combined into one operational command. The first rank insignia for the British Army weren't introduced until 1760, and badges for field officers came about in 1810.

ARMY RANKS

For the most part, British ranks are very similar to their American counterparts, which is not surprising considering American ranks and military culture were based upon the British. The first enlisted rank is that of Private and actually has no insignia. The next up is Lance Corporal or Lance Bombardier (a Bombardier designating someone in artillery), followed by Corporal or Bombardier, with the former's insignia being one chevron and the latter having two chevrons. At three chevrons, one is designated a Sergeant. The next level up presents a difference as a Staff Sergeant has four chevrons and a crown. At this level, the Royal Marines designate this rank as a Colour Sergeant. The highest two enlisted ranks are Warrant Officer Class 2 and Warrant Officer Class 1; the former includes a Quartermaster Sergeant. Class 2 rank insignia is a crown, and for a Quartermaster Sergeant, a crown encircled with a laurel. Warrant Officer Class 1 insignia features the Royal Coat of Arms with a laurel as these warrant officers are appointed to the Royal Logistics Corps.

On the officer side, Officer Cadets are the first rank for Officer Candidates and have shoulder boards with a single white stripe across them. They are referred to as "Mister" or "Miss" rather than by rank, and this is true for both the British Army and the Royal Air Force. The first rank of a commissioned officer is Second Lieutenant, and its insignia is a single Bath star (more commonly referred to as a "pip"). A Lieutenant has two pips, and a Captain has three pips. At the rank of Major, the insignia is a single St. Edward's Crown, while a Lieutenant Colonel has one crown and one pip. Colonel has a crown and two pips, and a Brigadier has a crown and three pips. After that, you get into the General ranks, with the first being a Major General whose insignia features a pip over a crossed sword and baton. A Lieutenant General keeps the sword and baton, but the pip is replaced with a crown. A full General has all three symbols: Crown, pip, and sword, and baton. At the top is a Field Marshal, an appointed position that is designated by a crown over two crossed batons on a red field surrounded by a yellow leaf. On appointment, a Field Marshal receives a gold-tipped baton that he must carry with him on formal occasions.

ROYAL NAVY RANKS

Meanwhile, despite the fact that they were both formed in 1660, the Royal Navy's formation before the Army designates it as the "Senior Service." As stated, Royal Marines, even though they are part of the Navy, have roughly the same ranks as the Army. Enlisted sailors' ranks begin with Able Seaman with an insignia that simply says "Royal Navy." The next rank is Leading Rate, the insignia of which features an anchor. Following that is the rank of Petty Officer, which features a crown over two crossed anchors. A Chief Petty Officer, meanwhile, features a crown over an anchor encircled with a gold leaf. Lastly, much like the Warrant Officer classes for the Army, Class 2 features a crown inside a gold leaf, while Class 1 also has the Royal Coat of Arms.

Naval officers begin with Officer Cadet at the Britannia Royal Naval College before formal training begins, then ascend to the rank of Midshipmen for the remainder of their time at the college. Their first rank on graduation is Sub Lieutenant, and the insignia features one gold braid stripe with an executive curl. A Lieutenant features this curl with an additional gold stripe under it, while a Lieutenant Commander has both a thin gold stripe as well as a medium stripe. A full Commander has the curl with two medium stripes, and a Captain has the curl and three medium stripes. Meanwhile, a Commodore's insignia features a gold loop with a very wide gold lace stripe. At the Admiralty level, a Rear Admiral's sleeve features the executive curl with the wide stripe while also having shoulder boards with a crown and sword and crossed baton over two stars. A Vice Admiral is similar but with three stars, and an Admiral has four stars, while their sleeves include a curl and wide stripe with one and two medium stripes, respectively. Lastly, Admiral of the Fleet, much like Field Marshal, featured a crown over a sword and crossed baton encircled with silver leaf, while the sleeves have a curl, wide stripe, and three medium stripes.

RAF RANKS

The Royal Air Force was founded in 1918 and is the most junior service. Its enlisted ranks begin with Aircraftman/woman, which has no insignia, while the next rank up, Leading Aircraftman/woman, features a two-bladed propeller. Next is Senior Aircraftman/woman, which features a three-bladed propeller, and if one is a Senior Aircraftman/woman Technician, the propeller is encased in a circle. Chevrons begin to be used at the rank of Lance Corporal, which features one chevron, followed by Corporal at two. Sergeants get three, but depending on rank and position, may include an eagle for Sergeant Aircrew, a four-bladed propeller for Chief Technician, and a crown for Flight Sergeant with an eagle added for Flight Sergeant Aircrew. Warrant Officers are the same as in other services.

For Air Force Officers, an Acting Pilot Officer has one thin, light blue stripe flanked by two black stripes until an Acting Pilot Officer is promoted to Pilot Officer, which has the name insignia. The next rank, Flying Officer, receives a thicker medium stripe. A Flight Lieutenant receives two medium stripes, while a Squadron Leader has two medium stripes with a thin stripe between them. Moving up the chain, a Wing Commander has three medium stripes, and a Squadron Commander has four. Air Commodore is the first to have a thick stripe, Air Vice Marshal has a thick stripe and one medium stripe, while Air Marshal has a thick stripe and two medium stripes, and Air Chief Marshal has three medium stripes. Lastly, the Marshal of the Royal Air Force, the top position in the RAF, has a thick stripe with four medium stripes as well as shoulder boards featuring an eagle surrounded by a wreath, two crossed Marshal's batons, and a crown above it all.

43. UNUSUAL BRITISH FESTIVALS

Britain can be a strange place sometimes. Underneath the prim and proper attitude with which it's associated is a world that is both weird and wonderful. This oddness can be found in many festivals that take place throughout the country. Of course, many of these events are ancient and deeply rooted in tradition, though the original meanings might be lost on most people today. Nonetheless, they add color and fun and involve everything from the oddest competitions to the most outlandish fancy dress. We've made a list of ten of our favorite unusual British festivals.

DUNMOW FLITCH TRIALS

Taking place every four years, the Dunmow Flitch Trials are so old that they're mentioned in Chaucer's Canterbury Tales. During the trials that take place in the Town of Great Dunmow, Essex, couples compete to convince a panel of judges that they have not fought in the past year and a day since they've been married. To this day, couples that can convince the panel of "six bachelors and six maidens" are awarded a flitch of bacon, which is essentially the entire side of the hog.

KETTLEWELL SCARECROW FESTIVAL

Scarecrows have been used for years to drive away birds from feeding on crops, but the Village of Kettlewell has turned this ancient farming tool into an art form. Throughout the villages of Yorkshire, scarecrows are done up in colorful costumes or made to look like famous figures. Past well-known scarecrows have included Queen Elizabeth II with her corgis and Jeremy Clarkson in the village stocks. The festival began as a fundraising event in 1994 but has really taken on a life of its own.

WORLD TOE WRESTLING CHAMPIONSHIPS

While most people are familiar with thumb wrestling, this competition in the Town of Wetton in Derbyshire features wrestling with a very different set of digits. George Burgess created the competition in the 1970s because he wanted England to have a sport that it could unquestionably win. Opponents interlock their toes and try to force one another off the "tedium." England has won more often than not, and the current champion is Mr. Alan "Nasty" Nash with fourteen wins.

HUNTING OF THE EARL OF RONE

The Village of Combe Martin has one of the most unusual traditions in the United Kingdom. Every year, villagers in fancy dress beribboned and playing "Grenadiers" spend days searching for the "Earl of Rone," another villager dressed in sackcloth and wearing a mask. The Grenadiers might occasionally catch and shoot him, but a wooden hobby horse will appear to revive him, and the chase begins anew. Naturally, they catch him on the final day of the festival, mount him back-to-front on a "donkey," and parade him through the village, eventually dumping him into the sea. Local legend bases the tradition on the supposed hunt for and capture of the Earl of Tyrone, Hugh O'Neill.

PADSTOW 'OBBY 'OSS

Supposedly the oldest dance festival in Britain, the 'Obby 'Oss in Padstow may have its foundations in Pagan rituals for the god Bel, who was believed to make the days longer and help crops grow. The festival comes with some of the traditional May Day trappings such as the maypole and the village decked out in greenery, but at the center of it is the 'Obby 'Oss, a black horse costume that parades through the streets while music and dancing take place around it. There's also a Blue 'Oss, and people will wear either red or blue depending on which one they support.

INTERNATIONAL WORM CHARMING FESTIVAL

It may seem a bit daft, but there's a very well-grounded reason for this annual festival in the Village of Willaston. Worm charming is actually a way of getting worms to come above ground so they can be harvested to use as fishing bait. Tom Shufflebotham organized the first championship in 1980 and managed to conjure 511 worms in half an hour. Each contestant is given a 3×3 meter area and can use any means or liquid (except drugs or water, which is considered a stimulant) to conjure the worms. Music and cider tend to be the most popular methods.

UP HELLY AA

The last Tuesday of January features one of the largest Viking-themed celebrations in the UK as the townspeople of Lerwick don horned helmets attributed to the ancient invaders. Days in this Shetland Islands town are filled with performances and marches, while evenings treat visitors to burning Viking longboats held aloft amongst the torches. The festival is effectively Europe's largest fire festival, and though it features many Viking trappings, there isn't much evidence to support that Vikings were the origin of the celebration, as it began in the 19th Century, though the islands did once belong to Norway.

WORLD GRAVY WRESTLING CHAMPIONSHIPS

Wrestling competitions take place across the world in a variety of odd substances, but the World Gravy Wrestling Championships of Rossendale is certainly one of the more interesting. Taking place at the Rose n' Bowl pub, opponents of both sexes wrestle in a pool of gravy for two minutes, with points awarded for performance, comic effect, fancy dress, and sheer entertainment. For the last ten years, the competition, which draws visitors from around the world for only £1.50 to £2.50, has raised money for the East Lancs Hospice.

STRAW BEAR DAY

While Yorkshire might dress up their scarecrows as people, Whittlesea dresses up its people as scarecrows, or "straw bears", every year on the Tuesday following Plough Monday (or first Monday after Twelfth Night). No one really knows what inspired the first person in Whittlesea to dress himself entirely in straw on Plough Monday, 1882, but he gave birth to a tradition that continues to this day. The straw bear parades through town, dancing for people in the hopes of earning food, money, or beer. The festival also includes concerts, storytelling, and dances, amongst other fun activities.

44. STRANGE BRITISH SPORTS COMPETITIONS

A country that has existed in various forms over the last several thousand years is bound to create some strange sports competitions. Britain has many. Here is a list of the most interesting. I'm sure we've left something off – but for now, he's a list of unique British sports competitions.

CHEESE ROLLING

A passion for cheese is a must for this annual event, which involves daredevils hurling themselves down the steep, grassy slopes of Coopers Hill, near Gloucester, in pursuit of Double Gloucester cheeses. There are downhill races throughout the afternoon, including ones for men and for women. The race starts with the master of ceremonies rolling a 7- 8 lb (4kg) Double Gloucester cheese down the hill. Dozens of competitors run, roll and somersault down the hill after it. It's impossible not to fall over due to the rough, uneven slope with a 1:2 gradient. The winners take home the cheeses as well as a few cuts and bruises.

The event is very popular with international competitors, and nothing deters them – hot, cold, wind, wet, or any other combination of British weather – in fact, it all adds to the sense of spectacle. Hundreds of people gather to watch this unique event, which dates back to medieval times. Common theories about the origin of cheese rolling include the idea that it began as a pan festival celebrating the onset of summer, while others maintain the festival is related to ancient fertility rights and hopes for a successful harvest.

SHIN-KICKING

The Cotswold Olimpicks were started by a local barrister, Captain Robert Dover, in 1612 at Dover's Hill, above Chipping Campden. The annual event attracts thousands of spectators and features some well-known countryside games such as tug-of-war, obstacle races, and wrestling, as well as a few bizarre ones, with the highlight being shin-kicking. The shin-kicking competition involves two contestants who first fill their trouser legs with straw to help reduce the pain. The players then hold arms and kick each other using steel-toe capped boots until one of the contestants is so bruised that he cannot stand the pain and gives in. The festivities close with a huge bonfire and fireworks display followed by a torchlight procession to the town square of Chipping Campden, where Morris dancing and other entertainment takes place. The Olympicks are over 400 years old.

SWAMP SOCCER WORLD CHAMPIONSHIPS

The rules of swamp soccer are similar to regular soccer, with a number of exceptions. Each team has just six players, a goalkeeper, and five outfield players, with unlimited substitutions. Games last for 24 minutes total, and costumes are allowed.

FACE GURNING

The Egremont Crab Fair – one of the oldest fairs in the world – takes place on the third Saturday of September on the Cumbrian coast in North West England. The events end with the World Gurning Championships, where contestants compete to make the most grotesque and silliest facial expressions possible. 'Gurning' is the name for such face-pulling. It is thought the sport comes from the faces the locals made when they tried to eat the sour crab apples. Contestants frame their face with a horse collar known as a braffin.

HUSKY RACING

The parkland surrounding the house, built for a visit by Henry VIII in 1541, will host 400 dogs competing along a timed route, pulling sleds and their owners. The imposing country house sits amongst rolling Lincolnshire countryside that is surrounded by formal gardens, extensive woodland, and a 50-acre lake, which provides a stunning setting for the race.

ANNUAL NETTLE EATING CONTEST

An annual contest in which around 30 challengers are encouraged to eat more nettles than the current champion nettle-eater. Contestants are given two-foot-long stalks of stinging nettles and have one hour to eat as many leaves as possible. The winner is the person with the longest length of empty stalk. The competition stems from a contest between two farmers in the mid-1980s as to who had the longest stinging nettles. A longest nettle night was established. One day, a contestant called Alex Williams brought in a nettle over 15-foot long and said if anyone had a longer nettle, he would eat his. His nettles were subsequently beaten, and he duly ate them, giving rise to the annual nettle-eating contest. Now people come from all over Europe to watch or take part.

MAN VS. HORSE RACE

The race, which has up to 500 entrants competing each year, is run over 22 miles of mixed and very hilly terrain, including farm tracks, bridle paths, forestry roads, and open moorland. The Man vs. Horse Race was the brainchild of local man Gordon Green, at the time when he was the landlord of Neuadd Arms, after a discussion over a pint about the relative merits of man and horse.

The race has been run each year since continually attaining new levels of entry and challenges. It took 25 years before a man finally beat a horse, when, in 2004, Huw Lobb won in two hours and five minutes, finishing two minutes before the fastest horse.

WORLD BOG SNORKELING CHAMPIONSHIPS

The World Bog Snorkeling Championships are an international sporting event that takes place annually on August Bank Holiday in Waen Rhydd peat bog on the outskirts of the smallest town in Britain, Llanwrtyd Wells in Powys, Mid Wales. The aim of the championships is to swim two lengths (about 115 meters) of a peaty, murky trench, which has been dug out of the Waen Rhydd peat bog, in the quickest time possible. Competitors wear snorkels and flippers. Wet suits are optional but strongly recommended. Snorkeling across the smelly and dirty bog is popular with hardy individuals from all over the world. Competitors come from as far afield as Australia, America, and Europe as well as from Britain for the pleasure of taking part. The snorkeler with the fastest time wins a small cash prize. Organized by 'Green Events,' the novel event was originally thought up by a local pub landlord, Gordon Green, in 1986 in a bid to boost tourism to the area.

INTERNATIONAL WORTHING BIRDMAN

The Birdman is a flight competition for human-powered flying machines held each summer in the picturesque seaside resort of Worthing on England's south coast. Many flyers take part to raise money for charities; others design complex machines to aim for the distance prizes. A substantial prize of £30,000 is offered for the furthest flight in excess of the challenge distance of 100 meters. The event attracts contestants from as far away as Germany, Switzerland, and America. The Birdman competition started in 1971 along the coast in Selsey and then spent 29 years in Bognor Regis before relocating to Worthing in 2008.

CARRYING TAR BARRELS

On Guy Fawkes Night, there is the ritual of carrying the blazing tar barrels, which dates back to 1688. Men carry the flaming barrels on their shoulders until the weight or heat becomes too much for them and another person takes over. This carries on until the barrels start to break up, and then they are allowed to burn out. Preparation of the barrels and coating them with tar starts early in the year, and some can weigh over 50 pounds (22.68 kg). A gigantic bonfire over 30 feet (10 meters) high forms an impressive background to the occasion together with a fairground and many other attractions.

45. THE CHURCH(ES) IN BRITAIN

Religious observance in the United Kingdom is on the decline across the board, but the main religions still play an important role in the structure of British society even if people don't worship in the numbers that they used to.

THE CHURCH OF ENGLAND

Unlike America, Britain has an official state church – the Church of England. This was founded during the Reformation when King Henry VIII wanted to divorce his wife in order to sire an heir. This very personal reason to separate from Rome and the Catholic Church led to hundreds of years of religious instability as Britain yoyoed between Catholicism and Protestantism (and one point a group of people called the Pilgrims were so fed up, they left for America to found the Plymouth Colony).

The Church of England won the day, and it's the official state religion in Britain. The Queen is the official head of the Church, while the Archbishop of Canterbury is the de facto head of the Church. Many rites and traditions of the CofE (as it's colloquially called) have a basis in Catholicism but in a more streamlined fashion. It's the most 'Catholic' of the various Protestant denominations. The CofE isn't just a British institution; the Anglican Communion has hundreds of millions of adherents around the world (Americans call this 'Episcapolianism').

Bishops of the Church sit in the House of Lords and vote on laws.

While the Church is functionally part of the State, it doesn't receive state funding, so it has to fend for itself and the care of Britain's big cathedrals and iconic churches on its own. There is a priesthood that manages it all. Anglican priests, however, can marry and have children.

Pretty much every village, town, and city will have at least one church or a series of churches. Most are sparsely attended these days, and the most common adherents are elderly. The CofE also plays a key role in British education as it runs a shadow network of church schools. And most of these are very good schools. Churches attached to good schools will find themselves better attended as parents seek to get their children places in these choice schools (and houses, where they're located, are more expensive).

THE CHURCH OF SCOTLAND

The Church of Scotland, also known by its Scots language name, the Kirk, is the national Church of Scotland. It is of the Presbyterian denomination, having no head of faith or leadership group, and adheres to the Bible and Westminster Confession. According to the Church of Scotland, in 2013, its membership was 398,389. It has been in existence since the 1500s. It is a much different form of Protestantism than the Church of England.

Monarchs have sworn to maintain the Church of Scotland since the sixteenth century. The duty to "preserve the settlement of the true Protestant religion as established by the laws made in Scotland" was affirmed in the 1707 Act of Union between England and Scotland. The Queen is not the head of this Church but is represented on its governing council. When she is resident in Scotland, such as at Balmoral, she will attend Church of Scotland services.

CATHOLICISM

Despite the destruction of the Catholic faith in the English Reformation, there are still millions of Catholics in Britain. They have their own separate churches and governance, and the Queen has no role in this at all. The Catholic Church has separate national organizations for England, Wales, and Scotland, which means there is no single hierarchy for the Catholic Church in the United Kingdom. Catholicism is the second largest denomination in England and Wales, with around five million members, mainly in England. A large number of these Catholics are of Irish descent as there is a huge Irish population throughout Britain.

PROTESTANTISM

Britain pretty much has absolute religious freedom, despite having a state-sponsored church. This means that you can have no faith or whatever faith you like. As a consequence, there are many different threads of Protestantism active through the UK – including Baptists, Methodists, Evangelicals, and the list goes on. Despite this, the Church of England is still supreme in the land and the focus of national discourse on religion.

JUDAISM

The Jewish faith has a long history in Britain. Currently, British Jews number around 300,000, with the United Kingdom having the fifth largest Jewish community worldwide. They have played a key role in British society. Benjamin Disraeli, an important Prime Minister during the Victorian age, was of Jewish descent (though a converted Christian). Jews in the East End of London invented one of Britain's most famous dishes – fish & chips.

OTHER RELIGIONS

Due to Britain's history of immigration, there are large numbers of Muslims in Britain – the last estimate was almost 3 million. There are almost a million Hindus and half a million Sikhs. There are also a few hundred thousand Buddhists. The entire panoply of human religion generally exists in some form in Britain. You can believe what you like. The British no longer like to make a fuss out of religion even though it's always in the background of daily life.

46. THE CONCEPT OF THE CROWN

The Crown in the UK is both a concept and an object. The object sits on the head of the reigning Monarch. The Crown of State is kept in the Tower of London when not in use (the Queen only wears it on special occasions).

The Crown as a concept is more complicated.

The Crown, in the simplest terms, is the State of the United Kingdom and everything in it.

In legal terms, a type of corporation, the Crown is the legal embodiment of executive, legislative, and judicial governance in the monarchy of the United Kingdom. The concept of the Crown developed first in England as a separation of the literal Crown and property of the kingdom from the person and personal property of the Monarch. It spread through English and later British colonization and is now rooted in the legal lexicon of the United Kingdom, its Crown dependencies, and the other 15 independent realms.

The term is also found in various expressions such as "Crown land," which some countries refer to as "public land" or "state land,"; as well as in some offices, such as minister of the Crown, Crown attorney, and Crown prosecutor.

The Crown is immortal. It never dies. It is eternal. Even if the current Monarch dies, the Crown immediately passes to the next heir, in an uninterrupted line. The Crown can never cease. The reigning

Monarch is the living embodiment of the concept of the Crown and the personification of the State.

The concept of the Crown took form under early feudal systems in the British Isles. Though not used this way in all countries that had this system, in England, all rights and privileges were ultimately bestowed by the ruler. Land, for instance, was granted by the Crown to lords in exchange for feudal services, and they, in turn, granted the land to lesser lords.

The body of the reigning sovereign holds two distinct personas in constant coexistence: that of a natural-born human being and that of the British State as accorded to him or her through law; the Crown and the Monarch are conceptually divisible but legally indivisible, the office cannot exist without the officeholder.

The reigning king or Queen is the employer of all government officials and staff (including the viceroys, judges, members of the armed forces, police officers, and parliamentarians), the guardian of foster children (Crown wards), as well as the owner of all state lands (Crown land), buildings and equipment (Crown-held property), state-owned companies (Crown corporations), and the copyright for government publications (Crown copyright). This is all in his or her position as sovereign, not as an individual; all such property is held by the Crown in perpetuity and cannot be sold by the sovereign without the proper advice and consent of his or her relevant ministers.

The Crown also represents the legal embodiment of executive, legislative, and judicial governance. While the Crown's legal personality is usually regarded as a corporation sole, it can, at least for some purposes, be described as a corporation aggregate headed by the Monarch.

For example, the Queen does not need to carry a passport or get a driving license because they are all issued in her name. She is above the State, above the citizenry. It's a bit bizarre. To make it even more confusing, HM The Queen has her own property portfolio and collections that she owns personally and is not part of the Crown Estate.

The Crown Estate is a collection of lands and holdings in the territories of England, Wales, and Northern Ireland within the United Kingdom belonging to the British Monarch as a corporation sole, making it "the sovereign's public estate," which is neither government property nor part of the Monarch's private estate. It cannot be sold or divided by the Monarch. Now, the Crown Estate used to be under the control of the Monarch, but this was given up several hundred years ago when a monarch was deep in debt. In exchange for a yearly subsidy to run the Royal household and affairs, control of the estate was given to the British government. However, the Monarch still has possessions in their personal capacity that are not part of the Crown Estate.

As I said, it's very confusing but endlessly fascinating.

47. THE BRITISH CLASS SYSTEM

The class system in operation is probably the most complicated aspect of British life that's confounding to outsiders. It's something that has evolved over thousands of years but has really been cemented in the last century. Britain likes to consider itself a meritocracy, and while in some cases, that is true, there are many varying cultural attitudes at Brits towards each other in play. Class isn't necessarily a rigid structure with clear borders and rules, and it can be transcended, but your position in British society is decided by your birth and becomes your identity. As with all things like this, there is overlap between the classes.

THE POOR/UNDERCLASS

In the United Kingdom, this the lowest rung on the ladder and the group that engenders the most resentment in media. In America, the equivalent would be white trash (the Brits call them 'chavs'). Generally, a group of people who are uneducated, unskilled, and exhibit anti-social behavior. Often, they live on poor and crumbling housing estates that create generations of poverty. Very few people leave this class, and if they do – it's because they got wealth through hard work and/or graft (or luck like winning the lottery). The stereotype from the high classes is that these people live off government benefits and choose not to work (this is not wholly true). A lot of this is obviously stereotypes and not true, but attitudes in Britain are just as strong as class lines. Many poor work their bums off but just can't get ahead like in any other country.

THE WORKING CLASS

This is the segment of the population that would traditionally have been manual labor in Britain's industrial machine. Usually, they leave school as soon as possible and don't go into higher education. They're trained to do a job and usually do it their whole lives. This class is proud to work and wants to work. This class has faded in power as Britain has de-industrialized over the last 50 years. This has turned many working-class folks into members of the poor underclass, and many will live in the same communities. There is still a large working-class population as Britain does still make things.

MIDDLE CLASS

This is 'middle England.' The England that we all envision when we think of England. It's the people who work in cities, who live in the countryside. They work with their minds, not with their hands. They often live in the suburbs of Britain's cities and commute in (usually by rail). In fact, Britain created the idea of middle class 'suburbia.' Middle-class England is typified by Napoleon's crack that Britain was a 'nation of shopkeepers.' Middle-class people have a level of pretension that the classes below them do not have – such as an appreciation for the finer things in life like Classical music, fine food, foreign travel. They're usually politically conservative, but a large chunk will also swing left – with a desire to bring the lower classes into the middle class. It's rare for someone to transfer into the middle class – usually, an English family will have been middle class for generations. They will also speak differently than lower classes – with their own middle-class English accents (that will vary by region). There is stratification in the middle classes, but we won't go much into it here. But the upper-middle class is usually wealthier and more likely to send their kids to 'private' public schools (and their wealth lets them skirt aristocracy, but not quite).

THE RICH

These are the people who have managed to have success. This class will be made up of people who started out in all the other classes – a poor person can become rich. A working-class person can become rich. The middle classes can become richer still. But wealth on paper in Britain doesn't buy you 'class.' This category is for people who have made wealth in the world and have been successful. You could also apply it to sports and entertainment personalities who got rich for being famous (and stayed that way) though many celebrities will have upper-class pedigrees. Sometimes, this class is more prone to brash displays of wealth like mansions or fancy cars.

THE ARISTOCRACY

This is the landed gentry. You are born into this class. You can marry into it, but you cannot 'join' the aristocracy by getting rich. There are rich families that have been rich since the Victorian era that are still not considered part of the aristocracy. These people are the lords, ladies, earls, dukes, etc., that feudally ruled Britain for over a thousand years. Many are 'old money.' Many don't actually have any money anymore but still have that 'breeding.' There are a few that still own their old stately homes, but many haven't for a long time. Britain didn't behead their aristocracy as France did; they simply taxed them into oblivion instead. Despite the decline in Britain's aristocracy, many of the prominent families in this class still rule Britain through their financial power. Central London is mostly owned by the same few families it has always been owned by (that and the Crown). When we think of this class, we think of Downton Abbey. It's not a fantasy; there are still people who live like that, though it's becoming rarer and rarer.

ROYALTY

The top of the pyramid that is the British class system. Royalty can also only be born into. The 'central' Royal Family is quite small, but the Royal blood extends all over Europe. There are thousands of people who could be considered Royal. At the head is the reigning monarch. They exert a special kind of power over their own family – for example, The Queen has to give permission for marriage in the Royal Family (though not to everyone). You can marry into the Royal Family, but this is rare, though less rare these days. Usually, royal spouses are found in the 'proper' landed aristocracy. As an interest group, Royalty often takes their hobbies, social cues, attitudes from the aristocracy and the upper middle classes. They usually like the same things – like hunting on the weekends and driving Land Rovers to the shires.

48. PRIVATE MEMBERS CLUBS

Private members clubs are more popular than ever in London, with fashionable new venues such as Dryland Business Members Club in Kensington, Searcy's on top of the Gherkin, and One Alfred Place in Fitzrovia replacing the old guard as the places to network and socialize with the business elite. Although long-established sites such as Whites (founded in 1693) and Boodies (founded in 1762) still persevere as a bastion for London's more affluent inhabitants, the private members club has undergone a significant transformation over the past two decades, replacing the glasses of port and smoking rooms of the aristocracy with the iPhones and high-tech space favored by creative directors and online entrepreneurs.

Exclusive private members clubs have existed as hubs of business and networking, socializing and solicitation, and even more nefarious activities since the dawn of civilization. From the Mithraic Mysteries of ancient Greece and Rome to the Masonic Lodges of the Middle Ages and the Skull and Bones society at Yale University, the private members club has always been a place for those hungry for wealth and power to meet and conspire.

The modern incantation of the members club was established by the English aristocracy in London's West End, particularly around St. James's Park, in the late 19th century. The illegal activities which went on in these exclusive clubs for London's rich and nouveau rich, included gambling and prostitution, were largely ignored by the newly formed Metropolitan Police Service, creating an air of mystery and scandal among those who could only speculate about what went on inside. The English Parliament began introducing legislation that gave more citizens the right to vote and assemble, leading to a boom in new clubs in London during the early 20th century. Although the aristocracy fought to prevent the unwashed masses from entering their enclaves, the newly enfranchised citizens simply started their own private clubs, often based around members' interests such as politics, leisure activities, sports, art, literature as well as occupations and professions.

The gentry's attempts to rebrand members clubs as "gentleman's clubs" in order to keep out anyone who was deemed "unclubbable," a phrase first coined by the writer of the first English dictionary Samuel Johnson (also the creator of "The Club," a famous social group made up of some of London's most influential citizens who met each week in Soho), were unsuccessful in preventing the proliferation of similar clubs designed for members of the middle and lower classes.

During the 20th century, the clubs in London existed primarily as retreats for men, allowing them to escape from their families and jobs to a place where they could smoke, drink, relax, socialize and network in comfortable surroundings with like-minded gentlemen. Their role also quickly expanded to provide places for newly qualified or graduated young men to make connections and rent a room before they could afford to pay for a house or flat in London.

Up until the 1950s, membership in the clubs of London remained extremely exclusive, prohibiting people of certain races, nationalities, and the female sex from joining. As a way of accommodating pressure to liberalize their membership policies, some clubs began opening up public spaces where non-members could dine and socialize. Several women-only clubs were also formed over the years, with the University Women's Club on Bond Street being the oldest and most famous, having being first established back in 1883!

In recent years the traditional gentleman's club was forced to change in order to keep up with the times and, in doing so, enjoyed an increase in popularity among those who wanted to be socially and professionally connected. Nowadays, members are still often from professions that have traditionally been associated with the London clubs such as finance, politics, law, and medicine but also include a growing number of young entrepreneurs, graduate students, start-up business owners, and others who want to be part of the "London business scene." One of the most noticeable changes has been the transformation of the very meaning of the phrase "gentleman's club." As clubs started to open their membership to women, this name has been dropped and has instead become associated with exotic dancing.

The new private clubs no longer exclude people based on race or sex but nonetheless will often keep their clientele exclusive by setting high membership fees or requiring a current member's recommendation to join. The traditional splendor of the old members clubs have been replaced by the high-tech and modern, substituting drawing rooms and gambling with inspiring post-modern architecture, flat-screen monitors, wi-fi, and networking events. Without a rich history to use as a draw, many of the new private clubs have taken advantage of innovative selling points in order to attract new members. For example, members of Searcys, situated atop the landmark "Gherkin" building in London's central business district, enjoy unparalleled views of the city from the highest private club in the city.

From ancient secret societies and fraternities to the ultra-modern venues of today, the exclusive private members club seems it will always exist in some shape or form. Although the air of exclusivity and mystery remains, particularly in the older West End institutions, the face of private members clubs have changed with the times, becoming far more accessible to people from all walks of life and focusing more on providing places of business and socializing than retreats from family life and pressures. Many are purposely quite inconspicuous from the outside, but a quick Google search will provide you with address and contact information for private clubs of all varieties in every London borough if you are interested in finding out what really goes on in the member's only areas.

49. BRITISH HUMOUR 101

The British sense of humor is one of the most talked-about irksome points of relations between Britain and the rest of the world. Namely that most other countries have difficulty in getting their heads around it, except perhaps ex parts of the Empire, such as Australia, New Zealand, etc. This is often assumed to be the fault of the inhabitants of that country. However, nothing could be further from the truth.

I will use the example most known to myself, and that would happen to be the differences in American and British humor. May I first say that some American comedies are pure pieces of gold; I can name some that have me laughing on the floor for hours on end. Programs such as Family Guy, The Simpsons, South Park, Scrubs, and so on. However, I have noticed that the main selling point of good old American laughter is that it tends to be both fairly blunt and rather obvious. Often making the viewers laugh out loud rather than merely chuckle or snigger.

This here is the main difference; British humor has five cornerstones that you will rarely find in any other country except perhaps the ones listed above. Now before I start, I am not saying that British humor is impossible to understand for all foreigners, merely that it is quite radically different and therefore difficult to pick up. However, once you get it, undoubtedly, it is fabulous.

The first cornerstone is undoubtedly that of an understatement. Without us knowing it, many Brits will be continually understating the current situation or state of affairs. A rather classic example is that of Captain Eric Moody, who in 1989 piloted a Boeing 747, which had lost ALL of its four turbofans. 99% of the passengers were either British or Australian; this is the statement made by Captain Moody.

"Ladies and Gentlemen, this is Captain speaking; we currently have a small problem. All four engines have stopped. We are doing our damnedest to get them working; I trust you are not in too much distress."

A masterpiece, there was no screaming or shouting, nobody tried to jump out of the door, and the plane landed safely with no ill health present. All British comedies and people understate almost everything in life. Don't try and figure it out; trust me, just go along with it. Eventually, it will become almost second nature should you stay in Britain long enough.

The second cornerstone is that great mystery, irony. This is nigh on impossible to explain; however, rest assured that the British constantly find the ironies in life, and they are a source of enormous amusement to them.

Here's an example in story form:

> "My friend recently said to me that he was tougher than a wall of bricks, rather ironic that later that day, a brick fell off a construction site duckboard and knocked him senseless. I should have probably called the ambulance quicker than I did, but the fact was that both all my friends and me were paralyzed with laughter, almost on the floor. He was fine before you all call me a heartless soul."

The third is undoubtedly that of the macabre. The Brits have a unique sense of humor when it comes to death and mortality. British funerals often contain a great deal of jokes and laughter, alongside the more somber moments. They often find the pain of others a constant source of amusement. Laughter is their unique way of coping with the tragedy of death and suffering, so much so that after a terrible event, a great deal of very macabre jokes will be inevitably circulated by the public that would probably be considered in very bad taste by many foreigners. The fact is, though, that Brits find them incredibly funny; although many of them feel ashamed that they laugh, they cannot seem to help it.

The fourth is perhaps a tad unsanitary, but to Brits, it is part of everyday life. I am talking about the world of sexual innuendo. The British love innuendo and have the ability to see it in even the most innocent statements. In fact, to many foreigners, their bluntness about innuendo is quite shocking, and many of them perfect it before they are even adults.

The fifth and final pillar is self-deprecation. A British person will never take themselves too seriously and will be the first to criticize themselves or make a joke at their own expense. That's what we find so charming in

British romantic comedies. British people will spend a lot of time playing down their achievements, actives, and successes while saying unflattering things about themselves – but often as a joke. In British film, pretty much every character played by Hugh Grant in the 1990s illustrates the traits of self-deprecation.

It is difficult to explain why they do all this, but the simplest answer would have to be that it is part of the British national psyche. To laugh at others, themselves, the absurd, and even illness as a source of humor. Even in the darkest hours, British humor will find something to laugh about.

50. THE UNION JACK

Nothing says Britain like the Union Flag – also known colloquially as the Union Jack. The flag has a long history, and within that history are many interesting nuggets of information.

LONG HISTORY

The flag was first proclaimed by James I (aka James VI of Scotland) in 1606 when he inherited both the thrones of England and Scotland and sought to create a flag combining the two crosses of the respective nations. Ireland was later added in 1801 when it joined the United Kingdom. Despite Ireland's independence, the flag was not changed.

IT'S ACTUALLY THREE FLAGS IN ONE

The flag is actually made up of the three flags of England, Scotland, and Ireland, which are the crosses of each country's patron saint.

England: Cross of St George – Red Cross
Scotland: Cross of St Andrew – White Saltaire
Ireland: Cross of St Patrick – Red Saltaire

WALES IS MISSING

While there are four constituent countries that make up the United Kingdom, only three of them are actually represented on the Union Flag. Why is this? Well, technically, Wales is a principality and has legally always been considered a part of England until recently when it was given more devolved powers. If Scotland votes to leave the Union, it's highly likely Wales will get a place in whatever flag replaces the Union Flag. A dragon is a pretty cool thing to put on a flag!

IT'S ACTUALLY NOT CALLED THE UNION JACK

While pretty much everyone calls it the Union Jack, it's technically called the Union Flag unless it's being flown at sea. Well, this is the tradition anyway. Everyone calls it the Union Jack these days.

THERE'S A RIGHT WAY TO DISPLAY IT

If you look closely at the flag, you'll notice that it's actually not symmetrical in its shapes, which means that there is a proper way to display the flag. This little graphic should clarify how to properly display the flag.

THERE'S A US STATE FLAG WITH THE UNION FLAG

Despite fighting a lengthy war for independence, there is still a US state flag with the Union Jack on it – the Hawaii State flag still features it in the upper left corner. Why is this? It's a relic of Hawaii's colonial past when it was more associated with the British empire when Hawaii was still a monarchy. The King of Hawaii at the time sought to placate both British and American interests by creating a hybrid flag, and it's stuck ever since. When America took control of the islands, they opted to stick with the hybrid flag.

THERE ARE 23 COUNTRIES USING THE UNION FLAG

There are still 23 countries around the world – many small territories or islands – that use some form of the Union Flag in their design. But there are big ones that still do, like Australia and New Zealand.

NEW ZEALAND TRIED TO DITCH THEIRS

Recently, New Zealand voted on a referendum on whether or not to change its flag. They even went as far as to ask the public to submit designs (leading to rather humorous submissions). A few designs were voted on, but New Zealand just decided to keep their old flag.

CANADA DITCHED THEIRS IN THE 1960S

After much debate, in the 1960s, Canada decided to discard their 'Red Ensign' flag, which was never actually its 'official' flag, and adopt the Maple Leaf as their national flag. There was a huge public debate, but in the end, public support was behind adopting a new national symbol to represent the independence of Canada.

THEY DON'T HAVE A 'FLAG CODE' AND NO MODERN CONCEPT OF FLAG DESECRATION

The United States takes its flag very seriously and has an entire code dedicated to the proper treatment of the flag. The UK doesn't have any of this, and they have no legal concept of flag desecration. There is also no specific way in which the Union Flag should be folded as there is with the United States Flag. It should simply be folded, ready for the next use. Which I guess, explains why no one makes any noise over the availability of Union Jack underwear or seat cushions.

HISTORY

51. 10 EVENTS IN BRITISH HISTORY TO KNOW ABOUT

There are a few major events that anyone interested in Britain should absolutely know about. Whittling it down to just ten is a challenge, but here are the ten most important events in British History, starting with the Norman Invasion in 1066. We've decided to keep Roman and Medieval Britain out of it and focus on ten events that have a more direct role in making Britain what it is today.

THE NORMAN INVASION

In 1066 England suffered a series of upheavals that changed the course of British History. The death of the old King led to a power struggle for his throne that resulted in two invasions by separate foreign armies. The Anglo-Saxon army successfully fought off the first threat but failed to defeat their second foe. Invasion ultimately turned to conquest, and the Anglo-Saxons were forced to accept their new masters, the Norman French. England would never be the same, turning from a small-time satellite of the Scandinavian kingdoms into a European power in her own right. It completely changed the ruling class of Britain, brought new technologies like Castles, and led to the first full inventory of the British Isles in the Domesday Book (written records for many places in Britain begin here).

THE REFORMATION

During Henry VIII's reign, England started on a journey of religious change. The old faith, Roman Catholicism, was pushed aside in favor of a new Protestant Church of England. It was neither a seamless nor a peaceful transition. Both sides suffered during the reigns of Henry and his children, but by the close of the House of Tudor, the Church of England was firmly established and remains so today. It started with Henry VIII seeking to divorce his wife Catherine of Aragon, and when this was refused, he broke away from Rome. This led to decades of internecine warfare between those that didn't think the break went far enough and those that thought Catholicism should return. To this day, the throne of the UK cannot be held by a Catholic.

THE DISSOLUTION OF THE MONASTERIES

While this event is considered part of the Reformation, it deserves its own entry because it was one of the biggest wholesale changes in property ownership in history. Once he was Head of the Church in England and in possession of a new wife, Henry cast his eyes covetously on a new prize: the wealth of the country's many religious houses. He stripped away not only the land, money, and privileges amassed by the religious orders over the centuries but also the aid and shelter they gave to the common people. With the monasteries swept away, England saw a redistribution of wealth and power and had to deal with the problem of how to help the poor. Over the years, Britain's laws to deal with the poor evolved into the modern Welfare State.

ABOLITION OF SLAVERY

By the middle of the 18th Century, Britain was the leading slave-trading nation. Vast wealth had been accumulated by individuals and companies involved in the trade. For many people at the time, the benefits brought by the trade to the nation far outweighed the personal misery of those whom it enslaved. Public opinion swung behind the abolitionists when the economic, political, and social climate in Britain changed. First, the slave trade and then slavery was outlawed throughout the British Empire in 1833. Compensation was paid to the slave owners (the slaves received nothing but their freedom) has ensured that many have been able to cling to their influence centuries later. Many great stately homes in Britain were built on the backs of slavery wealth, and many great fortunes still around can be traced back to this time period. Britain is still reckoning with this dark legacy.

ENGLISH CIVIL WARS

In the mid-seventeenth Century, tensions between King Charles I and Parliament reached a head. War broke out between the King's supporters and those who favored Parliament. In fact, it was not just one war, but several, and it lasted almost a decade. It became a conflict with several different factions – not just those against the King – but also those who didn't think the Reformation went far enough. It tore the country apart, and many of the ruins scattered across Britain can be traced to this time period of strife. The King lost not only the war but also his head. He was replaced by a military dictatorship led by Oliver Cromwell. The Commonwealth did not last long, the English deciding that a monarchy was preferable to a Republic. Three hundred and fifty years later, that view has not changed.

BATTLE OF TRAFALGAR

The Battle of Trafalgar was a bittersweet moment for Britain; victory and tragedy wrapped up in one memorable day. The nation won the battle but lost its hero. Although Horatio Nelson did not live to see what he had achieved, it was more than the defeat of the enemy's ships. After Trafalgar, Britain had no effective rival on the high seas. Napoleonic France would no longer be a great naval power. Although Napoleon did not acknowledge it, his plans for European domination had been dealt a decisive blow. Britain, on the other hand, could continue her empire-building without effective opposition, allowing her to take her place as one of Europe's leading nations. It cemented Britain's sea supremacy that would last for another 150 years and help with victory in World War II.

BATTLE OF WATERLOO

Napoleon had waged war in Europe for 25 years, building an empire that stretched from Spain to Russia. Across the English Channel, Britain remained free, protected by her navy after the victory at Trafalgar. Her army had been unable to decisively defeat the French Emperor on land, but an allied army had forced his abdication and exile in 1814. In early 1815, Napoleon escaped his island prison and gathered his armies once more. It was to be his final campaign, culminating in a close-run defeat at Waterloo, which ended his political ambitions and allowed Europe to enjoy nearly half a century of peace and a wholesale reordering of European power.

THE ABDICATION

In 1936, the charismatic new King, Edward VIII, announced to his advisors his intention of marrying his American mistress, Wallis Simpson. Not since Henry VIII resolved to marry Anne Boleyn had a royal marriage threatened to wreak such havoc on the country. Henry was able to force his will on the kingdom. Four hundred years later, Edward found that his personal desires were no match for the State's, and he was obliged to abdicate, opening the way for a new royal family who would endear themselves to the nation. If it had never happened, there would not have been King George VI to lead the nation through World War II, and Princess Elizabeth would never have been Queen. The world would be very different!

WORLD WAR I

On August 4th, 1914, after a turbulent decade, kick-started by the assassination of Archduke Franz Ferdinand, Britain declared war on Germany. Allied with France and Russia, Britain fought Germany, Austria-Hungary, and their partners in a war that affected people across the globe, hence the colloquial title 'The Great War. Fought primarily in trenches on the Western Front, an area around important industrial regions in France, the war led to a number of significant costly offensives that led to the deaths of millions. By the time Germany signed an armistice on November 11th, 1918, fighting during the war had killed approximately 17 million individuals and wounded 25 million more. The legacy of war had devastating consequences across the world and led to a wave of long-lasting political repercussions that shaped global History as we know it today.

WORLD WAR II

History has written much about World War II and the man who led Britain through it, Sir Winston Churchill. It was, to borrow his words, Britain's 'finest hour.' Centuries of empire building and world domination culminated in an existential crisis that affected every level of British society. There are a thousand stories from the war. The war devastated Britain's cities and led to a wholesale reordering of British society. After the war, it was never the same again. It won the war, with help from its American and Soviet allies, but lost its empire and its expansive global influence (supplanted by American power and a Cold War against those same Soviet allies). If there is one event that affects the daily lives of Brits today, it is this, even almost 80 years later. Some would argue that it's time for Britain to get over it and move on, but they're all living in a society created by the fires of World War II.

52. FIVE OF BRITAIN'S OLDEST BUSINESSES

Transacting business is something that goes back centuries, if not millennia, to the first time humans began to trade with one other. In Britain, the oldest businesses stretch back to before the Norman Conquest and represent some of the island's oldest professions. While some are still owned by the original families that formed them, others have made the transition to corporate entities owned by shareholders. While you may have heard of these businesses, others are so small you'd never suspect that they are amongst the oldest in the United Kingdom.

THE BINGLEY ARMS – 905 AD

The Bingley Arms in Bardsey, Yorkshire, claims to be both the oldest business and the oldest pub in the United Kingdom. Evidence in the pub suggests that it has been around since the year 905, which is 45 years before the nearby All Hallows Church. Well before it was The Bingley Arms, the pub was called The Priests Inn and was a popular stop for clergymen between Kirkstall Abbey and the Abbey at St. Mary's. The pub was also a popular place to hold court, and during the Dissolution of the Monasteries, priest holes were added to hide the holy men from King Henry VIII's forces. The pub was renamed when it was purchased by Lord Bingley in 1780.

OTTERTON WATER MILL – 1068

The River Otter became a popular Saxon settlement in pre-recorded British history, and the oldest document that mentions the Otterton

Mill is the Domesday Book in 1068. William the Conqueror granted the Otterton estate to the Monks of St. Michel, and later, King Henry V gave it to the nuns of Syon Abbey. After the Dissolution of the Monasteries, it was sold to Richard Duke, who kept it in the family for 200 years before it passed to a series of owners. The building stopped being used for milling in 1959 but was restored by Desna Greenhow in 1977, who still operates it today as a mill, bakery, and shop.

THE OLD BELL – 1135

Another inn, The Old Bell in Hurley, was opened as a coaching inn in 1135, and much like The Bingley Arms, it began as a guest house for those visiting the Benedictine Priory. There is actually a secret passage built into the pub that connects it with the priory. The inn has also seen its share of famous guests over its history, including Boris Karloff, Winston Churchill, Dwight Eisenhower, Elizabeth Taylor, Richard Burton, and more. It has passed to a number of owners over its history, but The Old Bell still lives by St. Benedictine's belief that "true hospitality be provided to travelers and strangers."

ABERDEEN HARBOUR BOARD – 1136

The oldest functioning harbor in Britain, the Aberdeen Harbour Board, was founded by the Scottish King David I in 1136. While others may not have such formal recognition, the Guinness Book of World records actually recognizes Aberdeen Habour as the oldest continually operating business in the UK. The harbor has had a long and interesting history, including attacks by both Vikings and pirates. Over its 900+ year operation, Aberdeen Harbour has been expanded as necessary, and the last attack on it came from the Luftwaffe during World War II. Today it remains a busy port for Scotland.

HALYDEAN CORPORATION – 1138

Halydean is the oldest dairy corporation in the United Kingdom, founded by the Crown in 1138 but owned by the Catholic Church. It's from the Church that the corporation got its name, which was originally "Holy Dean," with the agricultural and grazing lands becoming known as "The Barony and Lordship of Halydean." Halydean is in some incredible company as many of the oldest corporations working in tea, sake, and metalworking were also formed around the same time. Parliament divested itself of the company in 2004, and it reincorporated as an American firm in 2014.

53. NORMAN INVASION 101

In 1066 England suffered a series of upheavals that changed the course of British History. The death of the old King led to a power struggle for his throne that resulted in two invasions by separate foreign armies. The English army successfully fought off the first threat but failed to defeat their second foe. Invasion ultimately turned to conquest, and the Anglo-Saxons were forced to accept their new masters, the Norman French. England would never be the same, turning from a small-time satellite of the Scandinavian kingdoms into a European power in her own right.

In the first week of 1066, the English King, Edward the Confessor, died. His death created a power vacuum since, being childless, he had no obvious heir. However, there were three powerful men who were each eager to claim the Crown as their own.

Harold Godwinson succeeded to the throne on Edward's death. His claim appeared strong. Harold was the Earl of Wessex, a nobleman whose influence, wealth, and authority was second only to the King's, so he was ideally placed to take over the reins of power. More importantly, according to Harold, the dying King had named him as his successor on his deathbed. Accordingly, the day after Edward's death, the noblemen of the Witan, or King's council, acknowledged Harold as their King, and he was crowned at Westminster Abbey.

Harold had managed to maneuver himself smoothly into power, but he was soon facing a rough ride to keep his Crown as events from the past returned to haunt him.

Tostig Godwinson was Harold's younger brother and the Earl of

Northumbria. Unlike Harold, Tostig was an ineffective and unpopular leader, and by 1065 the nobles of Northumbria had had enough of him. They raised a rebellion resulting in Tostig being driven out of his stronghold and his men killed. A group of the rebels traveled south to demand that Tostig was outlawed. They were met by Harold, who was acting as the King's representative. Harold realized that his brother had no hope of holding on to his earldom and that the peace of the kingdom was threatened, so he advised the King to do as the rebels asked. Tostig blamed his brother for the loss of his power. Taking his family abroad, he began plotting against his brother, and by the spring of 1066, he staged a series of unsuccessful raids on the coast of England before sailing to Norway. Tostig went to the King, Harald Hardrada, and persuaded him that he should pursue his distant claim to the English throne by invading England and ousting Harold.

While Tostig and Harald Hardrada were discussing attacking England, plans for an invasion were already underway in Normandy. The young Duke of Normandy, William, was convinced that he was the rightful heir to the English Crown and he was prepared to take it by force.

William claimed that King Edward had promised him the throne years before in 1051. Furthermore, William stated that Harold Godwinson had sworn an oath in 1064 in which he not only acknowledged William's right to the throne but promised to support him. William and his court were outraged that Harold had failed to keep his oath and instead taken the throne for himself. A petition was sent to the Pope, and he declared his support for William's cause. The Duke now felt that he had right, might, and God on his side, and by the spring of 1066, he was busy assembling an invasion force.

THE VIKINGS ATTACK

In the event, it was Harald Hardrada's Vikings who were the first to invade. In September, he and Tostig assembled around 300 longships, packed with around 15,000 men. Initially, he sent a force to the English Channel to await Duke William's men. However, many of his soldiers were ordinary men who were needed to gather the harvest back in Norway, so he had to allow them to sail home. He and Tostig then concentrated on the North of England. By September 20th, 1066, Harald's Vikings had defeated the army hastily assembled by the local Earls and taken control of the City of York. News of the invasion soon reached King Harold, and he set off on the long march north, gathering more men along the route.

Harold set a punishing pace for his army, covering around 25 miles a day. Their reward was that they took the Norwegian King and his forces by surprise. At dawn on September 25th, Harold's English army destroyed their enemy at the village of Stamford Bridge. Both Harald Hardrada and Tostig were killed, and the surviving Norsemen submitted to a truce.

Whereas they had arrived in 300 longships, they needed only 24 to sail home, and the bones of their fallen comrades were said to have turned the battlefield white for the next 50 years. It was the end of the Viking era; the end of the Anglo-Saxon era would follow swiftly.

THE NORMAN INVASION

While King Harold was away in the north defeating the Vikings, Duke William was finally launching his invasion. He had gathered around 700 ships and about 7,500 men. Although they were ready to invade in August 1066, strong winds put off their attack until September. William landed in England, at Pevensey, on September 28th. He built a wooden castle and gathered supplies for his army by raiding the surrounding villages. For the Anglo-Saxons, it was a taste of how their future would unfold.

Harold was already returning south when he received the news of the invasion. Again, he made rapid progress, but this time his men were already exhausted, and he had to leave many behind. Once he reached London, he rested for a week, then marched for the south coast. Unlike the Battle of Stamford Bridge, he did not have the element of surprise, and the two armies met face to face at Senlac Hill, near Hastings, on October 14th.

Although Harold did not have the benefit of surprise, he was fortunate to occupy the high ground at the top of Senlac Hill. This was a serious problem for William since his heavily armored knights were unable to charge up the hill. Instead, his foot soldiers labored up the hill where they were repeatedly repulsed by the Anglo-Saxon shield wall. Norman casualties began to mount steadily, and some of William's troops began to panic and flee. The English cavalry seized the opportunity to pursue and cut them down too. Fear was growing amongst the Normans, and rumors spread that the Duke had been killed. William responded by pulling off his helmet to show that he was still alive, which rallied his troops. Watching the English response to his men's flight had also given William an idea; it was an idea that would turn the battle in his favor.

Once his troops were back in check, William sent out orders that they should feign another retreat. The ordinary and inexperienced soldiers in Harold's ranks were delighted to see their enemy running away, broke the ranks of the shield wall, and ran down the hill in pursuit. Once the English had broken ranks, William turned his cavalry on them, cutting them down. His archers then picked off what remained of the shield wall.

Harold was left with his housecarls, his bodyguards. They formed a ring around him, but he eventually fell. He may have been hit by an arrow in the eye, as suggested in the Bayeux Tapestry, but there is no definitive account of his death. His body was left on the battlefield, and William refused to release it to Harold's mother, even though she offered the weight of the body in gold. Legend has it that Harold's long-term mistress, Edith the Fair, secretly visited the battlefield, found Harold's corpse, and had it buried at Waltham Abbey.

After such a decisive victory, William had expected to be accepted by the Anglo-Saxons as their King. He was not. The Witan declared 15 year old Edgar the Aetheling, the last male member of the House of Wessex, as their King. Edgar did not get the chance to be crowned. William marched from Hastings towards London, and by the time he had crossed the River Thames at Wallingford, support for Edgar began to melt away. By December, the Witan resolved to set Edgar aside in favor of William. Finally, on Christmas Day 1066, William was crowned King of England in Westminster Abbey.

There were pockets of English resistance to the Normans for a few years. The largest rebellion broke out in the north in 1069, led by Edgar the Aetheling, with the aid of allies from Scotland and Denmark. William's response was brutal. Not only were the armies defeated, but he ordered that villagers, their animals, and their crops were to be destroyed. Those who survived the "Harrying of the North" were left destitute and starved to death. The Norman invasion had turned to Norman Conquest; the age of the Anglo-Saxons was over.

THE NORMAN LEGACY

The arrival of the Normans touched every aspect of English life. An obvious physical sign of the arrival of the Normans was their buildings, notably their castles. These mighty strongholds allowed the Norman lords to rule their new lands without fear of recrimination. Eventually, their great castles also emboldened these great lords to rebel against their kings. The Normans didn't just build castles, though; many churches, cathedrals, and monasteries were erected.

England's place in the world changed too. For centuries, England had been linked to Scandinavia, sharing with the Norse many customs, laws, and even kings. The many quarrels, rebellions, and disputes between competing Danes, Norwegians, and Anglo-Saxons kept England relatively unstable. Once the Normans arrived, England became tied to Normandy and Europe. The old order was swept away. The Norman aristocracy, whilst often ruthless, were also ambitious, and perhaps it was their drive, administrative ability, and military power that pushed England to become a world-class power.

The richness and variety of the English language also owes a debt to the Normans. For many years there were two languages being spoken in England: French for the ruling classes, Anglo-Saxon English for the peasants. Hence, modern English often has two words for the same thing. For example, from the French, we have mutton, phantom, and purchase, whilst we still use the Anglo-Saxon equivalents sheep, ghost, and buy.

54. 10 WORST BRITONS

There have been plenty of terrible Britons over time. They robbed, cheated, and murdered. They've committed such heinous crimes that they've gone down in the history books as not only the most horrible people in the UK but the world as well. But who are the worst of the worst? What ten people belong on this list the most? Of course, this list is only our opinion, and they appear in no particular order. What's more, as noted, there are plenty of terrible people throughout the country's history, so feel free to add your own favorites in the comments.

KING JOHN

Quite possibly the least popular man who ever sat the throne on England, he was already doomed when he had a hard act to follow in his brother Richard. Like his brother, he continued to fight wars but was far less successful, leading him to raise taxes on the nobility to such an extent that his barons rebelled and forced the Magna Carta on him. John promptly broke the charter as soon as it suited him and had to be forced into it again. It's probably a good thing for him that he died of illness before someone killed him.

GUY FAWKES

The most infamous member of the Gunpowder Plot, Fawkes, was part of a group of Catholics who apparently felt King James I wasn't Catholic enough for their liking (due in part to his conversion to Protestantism and subsequent persecution of Catholics in Britain). They decided to blow him and the rest of Parliament to bits, but an ill-conceived letter got everyone caught, with Fawkes being the first arrested. While several more people were involved in the plot, Fawkes being the one caught with the powder made him History's scapegoat to be burned in effigy every November 5th.

QUEEN MARY I

"Bloody Mary" earned her terrible nickname after she took the throne by force when her brother, King Edward VI, chose Lady Jane Gray to succeed him. Since Mary didn't agree with King Henry VIII's break from the Catholic Church, she opted to undo everything he'd accomplished, ruthlessly suppressing any Protestants who defied her. She further complicated matters for Britons by marrying King Phillip II of Spain, giving rise to a belief that Spain and the Pope would be in full control of England. Mary's foreign and domestic policies were utter disasters, making her even more unpopular.

THOMAS BECKETT

Certainly, a controversial choice for the list, though historians have argued that a number of the problems during King Henry II's reign were a result of Beckett's actions as Archbishop of Canterbury. The carefree courtier he was, Henry gave way to a man who was a very autocratic Church figure and split English society by siding with Pope Alexander II over Henry, moving to make sure the Church did not have to answer to civil authorities. There are also rumors that he misused the court's funds when he served under Henry and was even put on trial for embezzlement, though it was never proven. Some actually see his assassination by Henry's knights as Beckett's just desserts.

OLIVER CROMWELL

While King Charles I may not have been the best ruler, his time on the throne was relatively tame compared to the tyrannical control of Cromwell's Commonwealth and the later Protectorate. Under his leadership, Parliament issued some incredibly Puritanical rule, virtually banning leisure on Sunday (except walking to Church) and seizing any feasts prepared for Christmas. What's more, he led a very bloody campaign against Ireland that resulted in his troops massacring a village of 2,000 people. It's not much of a wonder that people were more than happy for King Charles II to come back and reclaim the throne not too long after Cromwell's death.

JACK THE RIPPER

Perhaps the most notorious killer in British History, the Ripper earns the distinction of having never been caught. His six canonical murders (with possibly more tied to him) have gone down as one of Britain's greatest mysteries. Despite Scotland Yard utilizing several new police methods to capture him (including crime scene photography, bloodhounds, and psychological profiling), no murderer was ever uncovered. It also wasn't just the number of murders the Ripper committed, but the other savagery and skill by which he sliced up the six Whitechapel women and even removed their organs.

HENRY VIII

While King Henry VIII's breaking from the Catholic Church was one of the seminal moments in British History, his Dissolution of the Monasteries was a particularly violent affair that resulted in the deaths of many loyal Catholics and the seizure of Church assets. Then there's Henry's violent temper and his tactic of divorcing or executing his wives on trumped-up charges for failing to give him a son. Henry's actions had negative ramifications for decades after his rule ended, and it was only during his daughter Elizabeth's time on the throne that everything settled down and Britain experienced a golden age.

OSWALD MOSLEY

In these modern times, it becomes much easier to understand how a populist spewing hate speech can gain such public attention. Mosley was originally a Conservative member of Parliament before founding the British Union of Fascists after meeting Benito Mussolini. Mosley's protectionist economic proposals were popular with many, but they came with a heavy dose of anti-Semitism. He and his party followers caused several major riots, which resulted in him being banned from the 1934 election and even more violent riots following his marches into Jewish neighborhoods in 1940. Historians consider Mosley the founder of many modern far-right groups, and his influence remains to be seen in the present day.

DUKE OF CUMBERLAND

Prince William, the Duke of Cumberland and son of King George II, is a particularly nasty villain if you're Scottish. The leading general of the time, William, was put in charge of quelling the revolt of forces loyal to Charles Edward Stuart, what is known in history as the Jacobite Uprising. William was a little too eager in his job, famously issued an order of "no quarter" against the Highlanders, even going so far as to punish his officers who showed them mercy. He labeled the rebels as "inhuman savages" and dispensed with any pretense of war etiquette, attempting a genocide of the Highlanders and effectively destroying the clan system in Scotland.

NEVILLE CHAMBERLAIN

As Prime Minister before World War II, Neville Chamberlain has become the symbol of appeasement towards Adolf Hitler. Before the war, he negotiated trade treaties with the Republic of Ireland that harmed Britain's economy and later war efforts. Chamberlain was one of those who believed that giving in to some of the Nazi leader's demands would help create a stable Europe when in actuality, it played into Hitler's plans to conquer the continent. Chamberlain's conciliations merely emboldened Hitler and ultimately led to his invasion of Poland in 1939 and the beginning of World War II. Chamberlain was judged ill-suited to run the war by Parliament and was replaced with Winston Churchill.

55. GUY FAWKES AND THE GUNPOWDER PLOT

"Remember, remember the 5th of November." November 5th, 1605 was the date of the infamous Gunpowder Plot, an attempt by several Catholic dissenters to blow up Parliament and assassinate King James I. Their plan was foiled when the plotters sent a letter to William Parker, 4th Baron Monteagle, warning him to stay home that day. A search of the Palace of Westminster discovered the gunpowder and plotter Guy Fawkes guarding it. He and his co-conspirators were tried and executed, while Edward Montague suggested Guy Fawkes Day as a holiday to commemorate the triumph of the monarchy.

Now, every year on November 5th, the British gather and have massive bonfires and set off fireworks. It's the British equivalent to America's Fourth of July. It's an excuse to get together and have a party and celebrate Britishness. Though, celebrating the failure of a terrorist plot and the subsequent executions by burning the perpetrator in effigy is a bit ... dark and odd!

THE SONG

There's a famous poem that has been used ad nauseum, especially since the hit film V for Vendetta:

Remember, remember!
The 5th of November
The Gunpowder treason and plot;
I know of no reason
Why the Gunpowder treason
Should ever be forgot!
Guy Fawkes and his companions
Did the scheme contrive,
To blow the King and Parliament
All up alive.
Threescore barrels laid below,
To prove old England's overthrow.
But, by God's providence, him they catch,
With a dark lantern, lighting a match!
A stick and a stake
For King James's sake!
If you won't give me one,
I'll take two,
The better for me,
And the worse for you.
A rope, a rope, to hang the Pope,
A penn'orth of cheese to choke him,
A pint of beer to wash it down,
And a jolly good fire to burn him.
Holloa, boys! holloa, boys! make the bells ring!
Holloa, boys! holloa boys! God save the King!
Hip, hip, hooor-r-r-ray!

A BIG BOOM

When Fawkes was captured, security found him with 36 barrels of gunpowder. This is the equivalent of 2500kg of explosives. Had the conspirators pulled it off, they would have destroyed everything in a 490m radius, including both houses of Parliament and Westminster Hall. Windows would have been blown out up to half a mile away.

NO CELEBRATION HERE

The only place that officially does not celebrate Guy Fawkes Day is St. Peter's School in York. Fawkes attended the school as a child, and they will not burn him in effigy as a sign of respect for a former pupil.

WHAT'S IN A NAME?

Guy Fawkes is also sometimes referred to as Guido Fawkes, a name he picked up while fighting as a soldier for the Spanish against the Dutch.

WE HAVE WAYS OF MAKING YOU TALK

Guy Fawkes is one of the Tower of London's more famous prisoners. He was taken there after being discovered and tortured for four days until he gave up the names of his co-plotters. The signature on his confession is very weak, as opposed to a stronger signature on a later confession, displaying the physical toll the interrogators exacted on him.

A NOT-SO-QUIET PINT

The five conspirators first met at the Duck and Drake Pub in the Strand, though they were joined by others as the conspiracy grew. While Guy is most well-known, the other plotters were: John Wright, Christopher Wright, Thomas Wintour, Robert Wintour, Thomas Percy, Robert Keyes, Thomas Bates, John Grant, Ambrose Rookwood, Sir Everard Digby, and Francis Tresham.

WARDING OFF GUYS

While bonfires and fireworks are two of the primary ways of celebrating, effigies of Fawkes, also known as "Guys," are also burned on Bonfire Night. Effigies have been burned as far back as the 13th Century originally to ward off evil spirits.

CLEVER ALIAS

When the Yeomen of the Guard caught Fawkes, he tried to give them a fake name when quested – John Johnson.

NOT HELPING YOURSELF

After being caught, Fawkes was taken to James' bedchamber to be questioned by the King himself. When asked why he wanted to blow up King James and Parliament, Fawkes responded calmly that he thought of the King as a disease as the English monarchy had been excommunicated. When asked why the plotters used so much gunpowder, Fawkes allegedly responded, "To blow you Scotch beggars back to your own native mountains!" James was apparently impressed by the response, but not so much that Fawkes wasn't tortured and executed.

A REAL PAGE-TURNER

Ever the savvy publicity hound, King James I seized upon the Gunpowder Plot to write his own account, "The King's Book," along with a published account of Fawkes' and Thomas Wintour's confessions. The book was published less than a month after Fawkes was arrested.

PROTESTANTS-ONLY

As a result of the Gunpowder Plot, Parliament passed anti-Catholic legislation that prevented Catholics from voting, practicing law, or serving as an officer in the Army or Navy. Catholics did not get the right to vote back until 1829.

56. INDUSTRIAL REVOLUTION 101

In the second half of the eighteenth century, life in Britain began to change. Scientific discoveries, agricultural innovations, and technological inventions drew people off the land and into the towns. At the cutting edge of emerging technology and industry, Britain's empire grew, and she became a world leader. Over time, the Industrial Revolution spread out from Britain, changing the lives of people the world over.

In the mid-eighteenth century, the people of Britain lived much as they had done for centuries. The vast majority lived in the countryside, working long hours on the land. There were numerous cottage industries, workshops, and craftsmen. Travel was slow and arduous, along unmade roads, either by foot or with a horse-drawn vehicle. Slowly at first, life began to change. A few new inventions soon became a wave of change, gathering pace and ushering in a new way of working and a new way of life. The seeds of the Industrial Revolution had been sown well before the eighteenth century by the free thinkers and inventors of the previous century, but it wasn't until the eighteenth century, in Britain, that the conditions were ripe for industrialization.

The British Isles in the eighteenth century provided the ideal economic and social climate for industrial innovation. Following the Act of Union in 1707, which joined England and Scotland, the nation was peaceful and stable. The two countries shared an interest in free-market trade, and the legal system made it easy to set up corporations to exploit economic opportunities. Money from the British Empire allowed entrepreneurs who were keen to increase their wealth to push forward with innovations. Hard work and the pursuit of wealth were considered virtues. Besides her financial resources, Britain also had the natural resources, such as coal and metal ores, which would be vital for the emerging technologies. Britain had everything needed to become the cradle of industrialization.

Some of the first changes began on the land. Landlords and farmers had begun transforming British agriculture during the early part of the eighteenth Century. Selective breeding, crop rotation, and the Enclosure Acts were resulting in higher yields and productivity. Greater efficiency was boosted by mechanization. Jethro Tull used scientific principles to design first the seed drill and later the horse-drawn hoe. Tull had successfully demonstrated that mechanization outperformed manpower, a principle that would eventually spread to other industries.

Abraham Darby was another of the early pioneers of the Industrial Revolution. Darby, an enterprising Quaker, was involved in the manufacture of brass. In 1709 he perfected the process of using coke, rather than wood or charcoal, to smelt iron ore. This was an important breakthrough. Iron was used extensively during the Industrial Revolution, and Darby's innovation would allow iron to be produced on a mass scale since manufacturers would be unfettered by the supply of mature timber.

Coal was to play a major part in industry, but in the early eighteenth century, coal mines had a major problem: flooding. In past centuries, coal was extracted near the surface. As demand grew, deeper shafts were sunk to reach richer seams, but water often filled the tunnels. Thomas Newcomen, an ironmonger who supplied the mining industry, set about improving the system for pumping water from the mines and, in the process, discovered that steam power could be used to power engines. The Newcomen Steam Engine, first built around 1712, gradually increased in popularity and was used not only in Britain but in mines abroad too. However, despite refinements, it was not a particularly efficient machine. James Watt, a Scot, began working on improving Newcomen's engine in the 1760s. His principal modification was the use of a condenser, which cut down on waste and improved efficiency. By 1776, with the help of his business partner, Matthew Boulton, Watt was able to market his new engine. One of Boulton and Watt's employees, William Murdoch, also made adaptions to the steam engines, which he worked on whilst installing engines in Cornwall. He went on to invent several other items, including gas lighting, and later worked on steam locomotion. The new, efficient machines were set to become the powerhouses of the age.

While steam engines were transforming the mining industry, the textile industry was undergoing its own transformation. Traditionally, weaving was a cottage industry. Families would have a handloom at home, and they would work together to card, spin, and weave yarn, selling the woven fabric to make a living. Once cotton began being imported from

Britain's growing empire, there was an excess of cotton that could not be processed at home. Increased mechanization was needed, and one of the earliest inventions was the flying shuttle, introduced around 1734 by John Kay. This allowed for faster weaving on the handloom and made it possible for a single loom operator rather than the two required previously. A problem arose. The loom was now twice as efficient, and the simple spinning wheel could not keep pace, so there was not enough yarn being produced to feed the looms. Fortunately, a few inventors were ready to turn this obstacle into an opportunity.

James Hargreaves was himself a weaver, as well as having carpentry skills. In 1764 he introduced a system that allowed the supply of yarn to keep up with the demand created by John Kay's flying shuttle. Hargreaves' spinning jenny was a spinning frame with multiple spindles. Initially, one worker could oversee eight spools, with the number growing to 120 spools over time. The demand for yarn was further addressed by Richard Arkwright, who built a water-powered spinning frame based on a design by John Kay (not the inventor of the flying shuttle). Arkwright's water frame was housed in a cotton mill in Cromford on the River Derwent, making his establishment one of the first purpose-built mechanized factories.

The final refinement to the textile industry was introduced by Samuel Crompton in 1779. The spinning mule was so-called as it was a hybrid, combining the technologies of the spinning jenny with the water frame. Not only did the mule allow thread to be spun faster, it allowed it to be spun finer, producing a superior thread. Sadly, Crompton lacked the funds to patent his invention, and so, despite revolutionizing the textile industry, he failed to profit from his work.

Improved transportation played a major role in the industrialization of Britain. Thomas Telford, The Colossus of Roads, was an early civil engineer who designed many roads (around 1000 miles in total), canals, and bridges across Britain. His London to Holyhead road was built to allow stagecoaches to carry the mail from London to the mailboat to Ireland and therefore needed to be relatively flat throughout. Telford's fellow Scot, John Loudon MacAdam, contributed a new method for smooth, hard road surfaces that allowed for durable roads that allowed vehicles to travel more speedily, whatever the weather. Many roads were financed by Turnpike Trusts, run by investors who charged fees, collected at toll houses and turnpikes for the use of their roads.

Besides roads, canals became the other main form of transport during the early Industrial Revolution, and there was a spate of canal building between 1790 and 1810 that was dubbed Canal Mania. The construction of canals caused the price of goods, such as coal, to fall dramatically, which not only aided further industrialization but attracted more investors, too, stimulating the economy. Even after the birth of the railways, many canals continued to be used profitably.

By the early nineteenth century, Britain was firmly on the path to mass industrialization. Once the railways became popular, the country was transformed. Britain was used to ruling the waves; after the Industrial Revolution, she set about ruling the world – for a time, at least.

One of the major effects of the Industrial Revolution in Britain was on society. As mills and factories opened up in towns and cities and traditional cottage industries died, people were obliged to move to the cities and towns to find work. The pattern of life changed as people worked to the clock, not the rising and setting of the sun. Many saw their standard of living rise, with more manufactured goods available cheaply, but others, including many children, found themselves exploited and living in slums. The growth in trade unions, labor laws, and government regulation of industry all grew from industrialization.

The Industrial Revolution was not long confined to Britain, and the rest of Europe and the USA soon became industrialized, too, ushering in a new era of technology worldwide.

57. 10 Greatest Britons (Men)

Britain is filled with many fascinating historical figures, and it's a bit of a challenge to whittle it down just to the ten most important men – but we're willing to make a go of it. Here are 10 British men you should absolutely know about if you're an Anglophile.

JOHN CHURCHILL, 1ST DUKE OF MARLBOROUGH

This aristocrat is widely considered to be one of Britain's most important military figures – someone who climbed the 'greasy pole' of politics in the 1600s and 1700s and ended up very wealthy and influential. He led the 'allied' British forces to victory against the French at the Battle of Blenheim. He was an ancestor of Sir Winston Churchill and inspired him greatly in his own battles against the Germans.

ARTHUR WELLESLEY, 1ST DUKE OF WELLINGTON

The Anglo-Irish military leader had successes on the battlefield and in the political arena, becoming Prime Minister during the Regency era. He led the allied forces to victory against Napoleon, ending with the Battle of Waterloo. He beat Napoleon on the land.

HORATIO NELSON

Britain's greatest naval leader. He had a creative flair for tactics that no one had ever thought of before, outwitting many enemy forces, culminating in the French and Spanish. What's he most known for? He beat Napoleon on the sea long before he was beaten on land. He died heroically at the Battle of Trafalgar, one of the most important naval battles in world history.

ALAN TURING

It's rare that a single person can have such a massive effect on an event as huge and sprawling as World War II, but Turing definitely did. His theories on codebreaking and leadership at Bletchley Park led to the British breaking the German Enigma encryption, giving the allies a huge advantage in the war. He also set out the basic theories that ended up creating the computer age itself. Every time you use a computer or a smartphone, you're experiencing the legacy of Alan Turing.

ISAAC NEWTON

One of the most important figures in the history of science; his theories and experiments helped create the foundation of the way we think about the world with his laws of motion, light, and more. He even created calculus in his spare time.

ISAMBARD KINGDOM BRUNEL

The 'greatest' engineer in British History, his legacy is visible all around Britain, mostly in railway infrastructure, and most of the things he built are still standing and used today. He was the primary architect of the Great Western Railway, and to travel the rails from London to the West Country is to travel on his legacy. He also had the coolest name in History.

JMW TURNER

Don't let any experts in art tell you that Britain doesn't have any great painters. It has several, but the greatest of them all is JMW Turner, who had a unique way of painting light and landscapes. His paintings are instantly recognizable to anyone who has visited the National Gallery in London or the Tate Britain. Britain's favorite painting is considered 'The Fighting Temeraire' – a lone sailing ship being taken to the breakers by a steamship, showing the passing of the age of sail to the age of steam against a stunning sunset. They even put it on the new £20 note.

SHAKESPEARE

Considered the greatest writer in British History – many of his plays, poems are so well known many people don't even realize he wrote them. Shakespeare is the most performed, most studied, and probably the most hated by students. He also created thousands of words in the English language that were never known before.

CHARLES DARWIN

After Newton, the most important scientist is Charles Darwin. Based on his studies during the HMS Beagle's expedition, Darwin created the theory of evolution, which proved that man descended from a distant ape-like ancestor and wasn't created out of nothingness. His teachings are considered controversial in the religious communities, but they're a simple fact now. The British are quite proud of him; until recently, he was on the £5 note!

CAPTAIN JAMES COOK

One of Britain's greatest explorers. He was an incredibly skilled mapmaker and mapped parts of the world that had never been known before – credited with mapping Australia and New Zealand. He went on several important voyages that led to discoveries of new lands, species, and cultures that had never been known to Europeans.

WINSTON CHURCHILL

The 'Greatest Briton' of them all. Churchill is important for his leadership of Britain during the dark days of World War II. He's most famous for his stirring speeches, but he was also a skilled leader who knew how to take the reins of the British establishment and marshaled the British people to victory in their greatest threat in history. Most historians agree that World War II could not have been won if he had not been the leader at the time.

58. 10 Greatest Britons (Women)

History doesn't just belong to the 'great men' – British history also has just as many important women who changed History. Here are a few of the most important ones that you should know about.

BESS OF HARDWICK

Bess of Hardwick was a woman whose power almost eclipsed that of Elizabeth I. She amassed huge wealth and power from her base in the Midlands – building the iconic Hardwick hall and founding the Cavendish dynasty, which exists to this day (but now lives at Chatsworth).

FLORENCE NIGHTINGALE

Modern nursing can be traced directly to Florence Nightingale. Nightingale came to prominence while serving as a manager and trainer of nurses during the Crimean War, in which she organized care for wounded soldiers at Constantinople. This led to the professionalization of nursing and to many best practices still followed today.

JANE AUSTEN

She only wrote seven finished novels, but her impact on English literature cannot be underestimated. She proved that women could write and write well. Her stories have become just as timeless as the works of Shakespeare, continually adapted, rewritten, and reimagined even today.

ELIZABETH FRY

Fry was an English prison reformer, social reformer, and, as a Quaker, a Christian philanthropist. She has been called the "angel of prisons." Fry was a major driving force behind new legislation to make the treatment of prisoners more humane, and she was supported in her efforts by Queen Victoria. She was depicted on the Bank of England £5 note until she was replaced by Winston Churchill.

ADA LOVELACE

She was a brilliant English mathematician and worked closely with Charles Babbage in the development of his analytical engine. Popular history calls her the 'first computer programmer'; however, the machine was never built, just theorized. It would take another hundred or so years for that to happen. Born the daughter of Lord Byron, Lovelace has had, perhaps, an even greater impact on history.

BEATRIX POTTER

Known as the author of the Peter Rabbit stories, she was also a renowned naturalist in her own right. But in her later years, she was an important advocate for the conservation of the English landscape, using her own wealth to help found the National Trust and protect Cumbria's farmlands and culture from technological change. She is a hero to Cumbrians (and a well-known sheep breeder).

MARGARET THATCHER

Britain's first female Prime Minister – the 'Iron Lady' was a political force to be reckoned with – staying in power for 11 years and dragging Britain out of the malaise of its 1970s economic troubles. She is both respected by some and reviled by just as many today. Her legacy is complicated and huge. She is probably Britain's second most important Prime Minister in British history (the first most important being Churchill).

MARIE STOPES

Marie Stopes was a British author, paleobotanist, and campaigner for women's rights. She was an advocate for contraception and founded the first birth control clinic in Britain. Her sex manual Married Love was controversial and influential and brought the subject of birth control into wide public discourse and changed many attitudes. However, her legacy is checkered by her advocacy of eugenics.

GRACE DARLING

In most instances, a woman like Grace Darling would never have been known much to history. She was a lighthouse keeper's daughter. But one night, she led the rescue of survivors from a shipwreck to safety, becoming a hero and public sensation.

EMMELINE PANKHURST

Emmeline Pankhurst was a very important British political activist. She is best remembered for organizing the UK suffragette movement and helping women win the right to vote in the United Kingdom. It wasn't just a movement in Britain, but around Europe and the rest of the world. Her most famous quote is 'deeds, not words.'

BRITAIN'S HERITAGE

59. THE NATIONAL TRUST

If you watch a lot of British TV or read a lot of British news – you've probably heard the phrase 'National Trust' quite a bit. The truth is the National Trust is one of the most important organizations in Britain, safeguarding its culture and heritage for everyone to enjoy. But how was it founded, and what exactly IS the National Trust?

The National Trust for Places of Historic Interest or Natural Beauty, also known as just the National Trust, is one of the largest charities in all of the United Kingdom. It operates a wide variety of properties throughout England, Wales, and Northern Ireland and has been in existence since 1895. Finding a good guide to the National Trust when you arrive in England can provide you with lots of information on what to see.

The variety of properties that the National Trust cares for is virtually endless, from immense and beautiful castles to small country gardens. You will find that there are factories, workhouses, beaches, lakes, and cottages all owned by the National Trust. When a piece of property is given to or taken over by the National Trust, it's granted inalienable rights to it, which means that the National Trust will own it forever (this is enshrined by an Act of Parliament).

Much like the National Park system in the United States, the National Trust owns and manages a large portion of the natural park areas of the country (but the National Trust is a private charity). From a huge portion of the Lake District to the Peak District National Park, the National

Trust is in charge. It actually owns almost twenty percent of the coast of England, Wales, and Northern Ireland and is constantly trying to gain more of it (the Crown Estate is the biggest owner of Coastline in Britain).

The National Trust does not operate in Scotland, as Scotland has its own version, the National Trust for Scotland, but the two organizations are known to work hand in hand on certain projects and are structured in a similar way.

For a visitor to the United Kingdom, the guide to the National Trust is like a virtual tour guide. They provide many printed materials and online resource guides that can lead someone on a tour of various trees, grasses, animals, homes, or other properties. Interestingly enough, two of the National Trust's most popular attractions are the childhood homes of Sir Paul McCartney and John Lennon.

Other extremely popular National Trust attractions include Waddesdon Manor in Buckinghamshire, which is an extravagant and ancient traditional English castle, the rope bridge at Carrick-a-Rede, and Fountains Abbey in Yorkshire, which was built in 1132.

The National Trust is a pure non-profit organization, which means it relies solely on annual donations and receives no funds from the government. Although it was founded over a century ago, it wasn't until 1993 that it received its formal non-profit status. On top of employing quite a few people, it also has an army of volunteers who work at the various properties.

Its mission statement states that its purpose is for the preservation of lands, tenements (buildings), animal and plant life. It also serves to protect individual pieces of furniture, art, or gifts that have a particular national significance. Its official motto is: "For ever, for everyone." Which is rather beautiful in its simplicity and meaning.

One of the primary benefactors of the National Trust, and for whom its headquarters is named, was Beatrix Potter, who was the British author of The Tale of Peter Rabbit. She was an ardent conservationist and left much of her property and funds to what was then a very young National Trust.

As the big estates in England began to be broken up early in the 20th century to heavy taxes, the easiest way for the landed gentry to avoid taxes was to donate their estates to the National Trust. Oftentimes, the families could continue to live in the properties as custodians, often for generations to come.

If you will be traveling in England, Wales, or Northern Ireland, the guide to the National Trust is an excellent place to start looking for places to see. They will be able to provide you with guidebooks, maps, travel ideas, and the stories behind all of the places you will see along the way.

Here are some examples of more famous National Trust properties:

- Wakehurst Place Garden
- Stourhead
- Waddesdon Manor
- Fountains Abbey & Studley Royal
- Attingham Park
- Polesden Lacey
- Belton House
- Carrick-a-Rede Rope Bridge
- Calke Abbey
- St Michael's Mount

Joining the National Trust

UK residents can join the National Trust for £63 a year. Americans cannot join the Trust directly, but we can join the Royal Oak Foundation. The Royal Oak Foundation is the Trust's official American Partner, and if you join them, you gain all the rights of UK members – including access to all National Trust Properties. They hold fundraisers for National Trust appeals and have a lecture series on things related to British History and design. Join at https://royal-oak.org.

60. HOW TO BEHAVE IN A B&B

One of the best travel experiences you can have as you explore Great Britain is to stay in a Bed & Breakfast. B&Bs are usually small, family-run affairs where you can get a nice room for the night and a hearty breakfast in the morning. It's a great way to get to know locals as you travel and make new friends.

That being said, many people go to a B&B expecting it to be like a hotel – it's not. We've stayed in quite a few B&Bs in our travels, and we've heard owners lament that some of their guests are sometimes the worst part of running a B&B.

So, in an effort to bridge cultural understanding, here's a code of standards of sorts for people planning on staying in a Bed & Breakfast in the UK(or even Europe). Some of these tips may sound like something any child should know, but all of these are things that B&B owners have brought up with us, so they are real problems.

1. YOU ARE STAYING IN SOMEONE'S HOME

Most B&Bs are family-run businesses, and more often than not, the family actually lives there. While it's a business, it is also someone's home. So, provide respect accordingly as if you were a guest in someone else's home.

2. THIS IS OFTEN A PART-TIME JOB

Many people run B&Bs on the side in addition to having full-time jobs or other businesses. So, don't expect them to always be around to cater to your every whim.

3. IT'S ITS NOT A HOTEL. DON'T EXPECT HOTEL-LEVEL SERVICE.

I will probably end up saying this several times in this chapter: B&Bs are not a hotel, so don't expect to be treated like you're in one. And certainly don't treat the B&Bs owners like hotel clerks.

4. RESPECT CHECK-IN/ CHECK-OUT TIMES

B&B owners usually operate on a tight schedule. They have to serve breakfast at set times in the mornings, facilitate checkouts and then turn the rooms over for the next evening. This means that if they've set a time for you to arrive, you would do well to arrive after that time, or else they won't be ready to receive you. If you're going to be later than the time you've agreed on, call ahead to let them know, so they're not waiting around for you.

5. EATING AND DRINKING

I'll leave a B&B owner to give this advice:

> "Tea is at 4 pm. Supper at a pub or restaurant generally between 7-9 pm and breakfast at 8 or 9 am. It seems obvious to us Brits, but I frequently get bemused guests from across the pond who come back from the village pub at 5.30 complaining that it is shut and they aren't serving food. Or when offered a cup of tea on arrival, say "no thanks, I'd rather have a beer"!"

6. NO OUTSIDE FOOD

Bringing outside hot food into your B&B room is a bit of a slap in the face for B&B owners (especially if you bring in your own breakfast!). Most rooms are not equipped to handle food waste, which can lead to smells that permeate the whole place. Most B&Bs have a 'no outside food' rule, and that applies to everyone, including you.

7. DON'T STAY OUT TOO LATE

To reiterate my first point, this is someone's home. Do not stay out too late at night as you're bound to make noise when you come in for the evening and wake up the owners or other guests. I can't tell you how many times I've been woken up in the night by drunken revelers coming in a little too late. You have a key to a person's home, don't abuse it.

8. BREAKFAST IS A GREAT TIME TO SOCIALIZE WITH OTHER GUESTS BUT NOT ALWAYS

Staying in a B&B is a great way to meet people from other countries and learn about other cultures. However, some people just want to eat their breakfast and be left alone. So, if it's clear that someone doesn't want to small talk, leave the poor patron alone.

9. DON'T TALK POLITICS

If you do get friendly with your fellow guests, don't ever fall into the comfortable trap of talking about politics, especially if you're chatting with foreigners. It's just not worth bringing up. You're wrong; they're wrong; let's just leave it at that. Also, don't feel like you need to apologize for America (which some foreigners try to corner you into doing, including Brits).

10. BE QUIET

Silence is golden, especially in a charming bed and breakfast. People come to these places to relax. Try to always use your 'inside' voice. Keep the volume on your TV at a reasonable level. Don't stomp around late at night. If you're being... intimate... keep in mind there are other guests you have to face at breakfast.

11. LEAVE THE YOUNG KIDS AT HOME

We stayed in two B&Bs a few years ago with our young toddler and Mrs. Anglotopia, and I agreed on one thing: we would never stay at one again with young children (we're talking under 5). It was a nightmare. Most rooms only have one bed, ours provided cots, but our toddler refused to sleep in them. We had problems with ... screaming at all hours of the day. At the end of the day, climbing the stairs to the top of the B&B with all our baby gear was just exhausting. We felt so bad for the B&B owners where we stayed even though they put on a brave face. We won't stay in B&Bs again with our kids until they're older. If you have very young children, stick to self-catering or hotels. The owners and your fellow guests will thank you (rather than look at you with derision).

12. DON'T OVERUSE RESOURCES

Again, it's not a hotel. Don't just take and take because it's not a bottomless resource. Don't overuse the towels and ask for more. Don't hog all the breakfast or ask for seconds. Don't steal the soaps and shampoos.

13. GET DRESSED FOR BREAKFAST

This really bothers us when we stay in a B&B. When you come down for breakfast, show some respect for your fellow guests and the owners by putting on some clothes. Despite staying in someone's home, you're not at home. Put some effort into your appearance, and don't look sloppy in your pajamas (or worse, lingerie!).

14. LEAVE MUDDY BOOTS OUTSIDE!

I learned this lesson the hard way – if you go for a hike in the countryside, take your muddy boots off before you come in. Check to see if they have an outside hose where you can wash off the mud. Nothing will annoy the owner more than having to call the carpet cleaners as soon as you leave. One B&B owner we know recommends carrying a towel (not one of theirs!) in your pocket to wipe off the mud before you return.

15. CHECK FOR RULES

This isn't an exhaustive list for all B&Bs, so be sure to check the info book in your room for any special rules that your B&B may have. This will help ensure your stay goes smoothly.

16. BE CAREFUL WITH PROVIDED APPLIANCES

Many rooms will have a kettle for tea – resist the urge to put it on a wooden surface; this is people's furniture, sometimes they're heirlooms. Also, watch out for your curling iron, don't put it on the carpet – the same goes for irons too. Use these tools as if you were at home – carefully!

17. DON'T ABUSE THE TOWELS WITH MAKEUP

Another B&B owner we know kindly asks that you remove your makeup with your own special makeup removal towels – please don't stain up their crisp white towels with your makeup!

18. DON'T RE-ARRANGE THE FURNITURE

According to a good friend of ours, they've had guests actually re-arrange the furniture in the room! Madness! And then they didn't bother to move it back when they left.

19. WEDDING REVELERS

If you've been out to a wedding very late and REALLY enjoyed yourself, perhaps it's best to skip the breakfast part of your stay if you're still drunk in the morning. But at least check out on time.

20. IT'S OK TO ASK FOR ADVICE

B&B owners are a very useful resource for how to spend your time while you're staying there. They will be happy to answer your questions and provide guidance. Most will have maps and brochures for local attractions. More critically, they'll honestly tell you what's worth visiting and what is not. Don't be afraid to ask but do it at a convenient time for them – after breakfast or when you check-in.

21. CLEAN UP AFTER YOURSELF

Don't leave your room a dumpster when you check out. Do the B&B owner a favor and keep things tidy. They will appreciate it when it comes time for them to turn over your room and ensures you get treated well if you return (they'll never forget a bad guest).

61. HOW TO BEHAVE IN SELF-CATERING ACCOMMODATION

Staying in self-catering accommodation in Britain is much different than a hotel or B&B, so we thought we'd put together some tips for how to behave in a self-catering cottage or flat in Britain.

Now that we have young children, we prefer to stay in self-catering accommodation. It's much easier when the kids have their own rooms, and it's much more cost-effective to cook your own locally sourced meals.

YOU ARE STAYING IN SOMEONE'S HOME

First rule – you are staying in someone's home. While it may not be their main home – it is still someone else's home. You are a guest there, and despite paying to stay, it's still someone's personal property.

MAKING INQUIRIES

When guests are first inquiring, remember that holiday cottage owners are not faceless company employees but individuals who are letting their most valuable material possession to complete strangers. Friendly emails are always appreciated. It's a good idea to acknowledge email replies so that the owner knows that their replies have reached you.

BE FLEXIBLE WITH PAYMENT OPTIONS

Pay deposits and balances on time and ensure that bank fees are covered if applicable – it is highly unlikely that owners make very much profit, if at all. The biggest challenge self-catering owners face is processing payments from abroad, which eats into their thin margins once you factor in exchange rates and credit card fees. Consider using a wire transfer service like Wise.com and pay the fees. If you can pay via Paypal, send it as a gift so that you cover the modest fees. Some owners will take Credit Cards directly so you can stay covered under your Credit Card's travel protections, but many will charge a small fee for this.

READ THE INFORMATION PACKET

Most cottages will provide you with an information pack on how to make use of all the facilities. Be sure to read all information packs in advance to ensure that you are fully prepared. If it's not provided in advance, make time to read it when you arrive. That way, if the place has a finicky thermostat – you'll know!

TRAVEL INSURANCE IS A GOOD IDEA

It's a good idea to take out travel insurance that covers weather – if you are prevented from reaching the cottage, the owners shouldn't lose out! With the unpredictability of the self-catering market, they're unlikely to be able to fill your booking at the last minute.

ARRIVE ON TIME (AND NOT EARLY)

Arrive no earlier than the stated time – the owners need all the time they have available to prepare the cottage to the standard that guests expect. It's also important to get yourself good directions there, so you're not frantically calling trying to find the place. Usually, these are provided by the cottage owners when you book. Satnavs can be very unreliable, so it's a good idea to have multiple directions.

TAKE CARE OF THE PROPERTY AND ITS FURNISHINGS

Take every care with the property, the furnishings, and contents, etc. – accidents happen, but excessive breakages are frustrating for owners. Equally, spillages and marks on carpets, bed linen, and sofas are usually avoidable and difficult to clean quickly within the time available during a changeover.

COASTERS ARE YOUR BEST FRIEND

Use coasters! Ring marks on wood and antique furniture are bad news!

LEAVE IT AS YOU FOUND IT

Leave the cottage as you found it – everything in the same place, basically clean and tidy and ALWAYS do the washing up.........leaving a filthy oven with a dirty roasting tray in the oven, which has been left ON for 24 hours is unacceptable! (Yes, this happened to a friend of ours).

TRY TO BE CONSCIOUS OF ENERGY USAGE

Be aware of saving energy – turn lights off when you leave a room and definitely when you go out (this happens ALL the time!) and try not to leave the heating on with all the windows open!

LEAVE ON TIME

Try to leave on time, which is usually in the morning. The poor housekeeper has to get the entire house ready for the next guests in just a few hours' time.

PAY ATTENTION TO WASTE MANAGEMENT

Pay attention to the information packet for info on waste management – some towns and councils have particular rules for where you can put your garbage and when. Usually, you can only put your rubbish out on collection day.

DON'T NICK (STEAL) ANYTHING!

DON'T take anything with you 'by accident' that belongs to the cottage!

DON'T LEAVE ANYTHING UNLESS IT'S A GIFT

DO take your own belongings when you leave. It's not good to leave a lot – as the housekeeper will have to remove it before the next guests arrive. However, it's perfectly all right to leave a memento for other guests to enjoy – such as a map or local book. When we stay in Updown Cottage, we often leave a local topic book for future guests.

BE PREPARED TO PAY TO REPLACE SOMETHING YOU BROKE

If you break anything, be prepared to pay to replace it. Most cottages will require a deposit that this can come out of. So, if you break something, be prepared not to get your deposit back.

WRITE IN THE GUEST BOOK

Be sure to write in the guest book about your stay.

LEAVE A GOOD REVIEW ON TRIPADVISOR

If you enjoyed your stay – it's a good idea to leave a review on Trip Advisor. Keep in mind when writing a review there that it's not a hotel, so do not hold them to the same standard. Good reviews can make or break a self-catering cottage business. One bad review for something absurd (like you didn't like the soaps provided, so gave your whole stay 1 star) can ruin a cottage's reputation.

62. PLACES TO VISIT FOR JANE AUSTEN FANS

Jane Austen certainly ranks amongst the best Regency Period authors, if not the best authors in English Literature. While most of her works were published anonymously at a time when women could not sign contracts (much less achieve notoriety from their works), Austen achieved much of her fame after her death in 1817. Her novels from Sense and Sensibility to Persuasion offer a window in Regency society, law, and politics. Her characters are amongst the most well-remembered such as Elizabeth Bennett, Mr. Darcy, Emma Woodhouse, George Wickham, Elinor Dashwood, William Collins, Colonel Brandon, and more. Just as memorable are the locations of her novels, and she has helped to make many places throughout England famous and added to the fame of already well-known locales.

STEVENTON

Steventon is a village best known for being Jane Austen's birthplace. Her father, George, was the rector for the churches at Steventon and nearby Deane. You can still visit the Church where George Austen preached and tour the village where young Jane spent formative years that would shape her as an author.

WILTON HOUSE

While not directly connected to Jane Austen herself, Wilton House has served as an important filming location for several adaptations of her works such as 1995's Sense and Sensibility, 2005's Pride and Prejudice, and 2020's Emma. The house has belonged to a different set of characters but always maintains the grace and extravagance of the Regency era no matter which of her characters inhabited it.

BATH

Bath played a large part in Jane Austen's life, so much that its influence is felt in both Northanger Abbey and Persuasion. It's while living here that George passed away, and the family's social status and fortunes changed, resulting in many of her themes regarding the place of women in Regency society. It's worth your time to visit the Jane Austen Centre for its exhibits and fabulous walking tour that takes you to many places that were important to the Austen family.

BOX HILL

If you enjoyed the 2009 BBC adaptation of Emma, you'd want to see Box Hill, where the picnic scene of the final episode was filmed. Additionally, even if you haven't watched that series, Box Hill is an Area of Outstanding Natural Beauty and worth the trip for that alone.

CHAWTON

After the loss of the family patron, Jane, her sister, and her mother moved into a home in Chawton on her brother Edward's estate. It's likely that her time at Chawton helped to inspire the situation of Elinor Dashwood and her family in Sense and Sensibility. Today the house is a publicly registered charity and museum dedicated to Jane Austen.

LYME PARK AND CHATSWORTH HOUSE

If you want to visit Mr. Darcy's Pemberly, your best bets are to head to Lyme Park in Cheshire and Chatsworth House in Derbyshire. Each has played the part of Darcy's family estate in the 1995 miniseries and the 2005 film, respectively. Lyme House even has a statue in the pond commemorating the now-famous image of Colin Firth emerging from the same pond in a wet shirt.

JANE AUSTEN TRAIL, SOUTHAMPTON

A major attraction in Southampton, the Jane Austen Trail, is similar to the walking tour in Bath, taking you to places in the City that were important to Austen's life when she lived there. It's marked by eight plaques that take you through young Jane's life from the school she attended at age 7 in Bargate to the site of the Dolphin Hotel where she celebrated her 18th birthday with her brother Frank.

ST. MARY'S CHURCH

This elegant Church in Berry Pomeroy, Devon, has an important role in the 1995 adaptation of Sense and Sensibility as the location of Marianne Dashwood and Colonel Brandon's wedding at the end of the film. It's also a Grade I listed structure, making it worth a side trip if you're in the area.

LYME REGIS

The coastal town of Lyme Regis has certainly been a popular holiday spot in its time. Austen was one of its many visitors, and she traveled here twice in 1803 and 1804. While not having spent a significant amount of time here, it still made an impression in letters she wrote to her sister Cassandra and even got a reference in Jane's novel Persuasion.

WINCHESTER

And sadly, our list comes to an end with the place where Jane Austen died at age 41. She had a simple grave at Winchester Cathedral after her passing, though her brother Edward had a plaque installed in the Church to note her literary accomplishments below a memorial window that was installed in the 19th century.

63. PLACES TO VISIT FOR SHERLOCK HOLMES FANS

Certainly the greatest fictional detective of all time, Sherlock Holmes first appeared in the story "A Study in Scarlet" in The Strand Magazine in 1887. The creation of Sir Arthur Conan Doyle appeared over fifty-six short stories and four novels (not counting works by other authors). Of course, while Holmes himself was fictional, many of the places he visited were quite real. You can still see them today if you're visiting Britain, whether you're headed straight to London or going further afield. Below we have outlined a number of locations from Doyle's life, the stories, and their film/TV adaptations that we think you should check out.

PICARDY PLACE, EDINBURGH – ARTHUR CONAN DOYLE'S BIRTHPLACE

Anyone who's a fan of Holmes and Doyle's other works may wish to see the author's birthplace in Edinburgh. Doyle was born at No. 11 Picardy Place in Edinburgh and lived there until he was five. The original building is no longer there, but its place in literary history is marked by a statue of Sherlock Holmes.

PORTSMOUTH – HOLMES'S REAL BIRTHPLACE

While Holmes's fictional origin may begin in London, his real one is in Portsmouth. It is in this city that Arthur Conan Doyle arrived to set up his medical practice at 1 Bush Villas, which has since been demolished. The present building, Bush House, has a plaque on it marking the site of this practice where Doyle wrote his first stories while waiting for patients. The Portsmouth Museum also has a considerable exhibit dedicated to Doyle and his creations.

221B BAKER STREET – THE SHERLOCK HOLMES MUSEUM

The most famous location of all is 221B Baker Street. While entirely fictional during Doyle's time, in the present day, one can find the Sherlock Holmes Museum. In addition to a large amount of Holmes memorabilia and a shop, the rooms in the townhouse are recreated to look as they were described in Doyle's stories.

HOUND TOR, DARTMOOR – GRIMPEN MIRE (THE HOUND OF THE BASKERVILLES)

Legend has it the rocks of Hound Tor were once hunting dogs turned to stone by a vengeful witch. It was this legend that may have helped inspire Doyle's The Hound of the Baskervilles, which sees the Grimpen Mire as a stand-in for the real moors of Devon. With this literary tie in mind, Sherlock filmed its own adaptation of the story at this location.

BASKERVILLE HALL HOTEL – HOLIDAY LIKE A BASKERVILLE (WITHOUT THE HOUND)

Another inspiration for the story is the real-life Baskerville Hall near Hay-on-Wye, Wales. The hall was built by the family in 1839, and Doyle spent plenty of time here as a family friend. The hall has acted as a hotel since 1984, giving visitors the opportunity to stay in the same place that inspired one of literature's greatest detective stories.

ST. BARTHOLOMEW'S HOSPITAL, LONDON – THE FIRST MEETING OF HOLMES AND WATSON

In both the books and the BBC show, Sherlock Holmes, and Watson first meet at St. Bartholomew's Hospital at West Smithfield. It's in the morgue here where Watson first saw Holmes whipping cadavers to see how long bruises formed after death. You won't be able to see that part of the hospital, but you can imagine the odd first meeting between the two men about a spare room.

SIMPSON'S-IN-THE-STRAND – DINE LIKE HOLMES

One of the oldest restaurants in London, Simpson's-in-the-Strand has been feeding patrons since 1828. Naturally, such a famous place attracted quite the clientele, including Charles Dickens, George Bernard Shaw, and Arthur Conan Doyle. Doyle was such a fan of the place he even made Holmes a diner there as well.

SPEEDY'S SANDWICH BAR – 221B BAKER STREET IN SHERLOCK

Sherlock's 221B Baker Street can actually be found at 187 Gower Street, just above the real Speedy's Sandwich Bar. This local London eatery can be seen in the shot of many episodes, but if you want to see Holmes and Watson's abode, you're better off visiting the Sherlock Holmes Museum mentioned above.

BRISTOL – SHERLOCK FILMING LOCATIONS

While London was certainly Sherlock's home for the filming of the BBC series, many locations in Bristol substituted for England's capital during filming. Bristol South Swimming Pool marks the place where Cumberbatch's Sherlock first encounters Jim Moriarty (Andrew Scott). The Ashton Court Estate, King Street, Cathedral Square, Portland Square, and more appear throughout the program. The City even has information on them all so you can visit at your leisure.

EASTBOURNE, SUSSEX – SEE HOLMES'S RETIREMENT

In many ways, "His Last Bow" is the final Sherlock Holmes story, and in it, Doyle mentions that Holmes retired to a cottage in Eastbourne, Sussex. Today, a house in the middle of the small village of East Dean in Sussex bears a blue plaque calling itself the retirement spot for the world-famous detective. There's even an apiary behind the house that you can even imagine once belonged to Holmes.

64. BRITISH TREES

We really can't get enough of trees. From enjoying their majestic green splendor to the enriching oxygen they provide, trees offer us much and should be a part of any garden. Of course, for the Anglophile, if you want to recreate the majestic splendor of English gardens at your own home, you'll want to consider an English tree or two. There are plenty of these trees that grow quite well in the United States and would make perfect additions to your garden. We've included a selection of them below.

HAWTHORN

Hawthorn trees really come alive in the spring, with white flowers blooming all over. These white flowers give way to red berries in the summer that are a delight of birds and small animals. Hawthorn trees can get up to about 50 feet if they're not pruned. Haws are also thought to be good for the heart and lowering blood pressure, quite possibly due to the antioxidants in them.

SILVER BIRCH

Silver Birch are those gorgeously white trees with the bark peeling off of them. It can grow up to 65 feet in height and grows quite fast. It's a great tree for autumn when its leaves will go from green to gold and then a perfect white to match the snows of winter. Birds are also quite attracted to it, so don't be surprised if one of them turns it into their home.

HAZEL

In ancient times, Hazel trees were thought to offer some sort of magical protection, but today we mostly know them for their nuts. Besides, the nuts, the catkins that grow on the trees have a strange visual appeal. They can grow up to 32 feet high but can be controlled through pruning.

HOLLY

Holly trees are an evergreen that are perfect the entire year around. The pikey leaves are quite distinctive, and a combination of them and the red berries make for perfect natural decorations at Christmas. Birds enjoy it not only for the berries but the shelter it provides.

ROWAN

Like Hazel, Rowan trees were thought to have some magical properties and would be planted outside of homes to keep away witches. Like holly trees, rowans have bright red berries that attract birds and animals. Additionally, once fall comes around, the green leaves turn beautiful shades of gold, orange, and red that make for a colorful time of year.

CRAB APPLE

Crab Apple trees are ancient plants that held a great deal of symbolism for the Celts as a symbol of fertility since the trees stay fruited throughout the year. In spring, you'll be treated to lovely blossoms, and in fall, the leaves will continue to provide color for your garden. Of course, the fruit are attractive to animals and birds, making sure that your garden will welcome winged and furry friends. They only grow to a maximum of 30 feet in height, which makes them perfect for small gardens.

ENGLISH OAK

Perhaps one of the most traditionally British trees on this list, the English Oak, can be found not only all over the United Kingdom but even into Continental Europe. It's a gorgeous green tree, but there are a couple of things you'll want to keep in mind. For one, they can grow up to 115 feet high, and second, they can live for hundreds of years, so you'll want to make sure you have space for them.

ALDER

Alders are part of the birch tree family and have been part of Britain so long their name derives from the Old English "alor." The trees can grow quite tall, up to 82 feet, and grow very fast in most conditions. They're very popular with all manner of birds and insects, especially bees, if you're looking for some pollinators. It also fits nitrogen into the soil, which can also help encourage growth of your other plants.

WILD CHERRY

Wild Cherry blossoms are one of those gorgeous sights that ring in the spring. They can grow up to 82 feet, just like the alder. Don't expect to be able to eat the cherries since they're pretty bitter on this species, but the birds of your neighborhood will love them while the bees and butterflies will enjoy the blossoms' nectar.

DOGWOOD

The white flowers are one of the most memorable things about dogwood trees, and those flowers have often been used as Christian symbolism for centuries. The flowers turn red as fall approaches, and even in winter, the crimson and orange stems provide a dash of color against the drabness of the cold. They typically grow up to 32 feet in height, so they can be perfect for smaller gardens.

65. BRITISH FLOWERS

England's gardens are some of the best-known in the world. From naturally growing green spaces to the crafted landscape gardens of Capability Brown, you'll find many different types of beautiful flora throughout the country. Of course, just because it's over there doesn't mean you can't bring some of it here. Plenty of flowers in England's gardens do quite well in the United States, and you can plant them in your own garden. We've identified several below that you might want to consider to turn your home garden into a little slice of England and a nice place to enjoy your afternoon tea.

LAVENDER

A quintessential English flower, lavender not only offers a pleasant purple aesthetic but also a pleasant, relaxing scent. Since lavender is an incredibly versatile plant for potpourri, hand sanitizer, soap, shampoo, and more, you can take clippings from your plants and make your own hygiene products at home.

RAMBLING ROSES

Everyone is familiar with roses and their iconic status in the United Kingdom, but Rambling Roses are a variety that can be just as lovely. Rambling roses are shrubs that do well as a screening plant if you want to plant something along a fence or wall but also can add to arches and pillars. They need plenty of space since they can grow up to 20' feet high and 15' feet wide and come in almost as many colors as their better-known cousins.

DELPHINIUMS

Delphiniums are almost like flowering little trees. Rather than growing outwards, these flowers grow straight up – sometimes as high as six feet. They come in shades of purple, pink, and blue to add some lovely colors to your garden. Delphiniums love the sun but don't care for hot summers, so be mindful of where you live before planting them.

PEONIES

Peonies have a short season for blooming, but the plants can last for years in the right conditions. Their pink petals offer some unique blooms, and like the delphiniums, they grow to be similarly tall at five feet. The flowers come in several varieties of pink and white and are quite attractive to bees and butterflies.

HOLLYHOCK

Yet another option with height, hollyhocks can get to be up to eight feet high, though smaller plants grow up to four feet, and they look like stalks with flowers sprouting off them. They come in shades of yellow, pink, purple, and red. They tend to prefer moist soil and their height also makes them great for screening, while the colors will also attract pollinators.

PHLOX

Phloxes can be a great flower for warmer climates such as the American South since they thrive in the summer heat. They're fragrant and colorful, which guarantees they're pleasant to be around and will be sure to attract honeybees and butterflies to add even more life to your garden. They come in blue, white, and pink and will bloom for up to five weeks for some late-season color.

FOXGLOVE

If you want something to break up a monochrome group of green hedges or smaller plants in your garden, foxglove can do the job. It grows up to six feet, and the bell-like flowers will look like colorful white, yellow, purple, and pink mini-trees rising up amongst the ferns. What's more, foxglove reseeds itself, so you won't have to worry about replanting them.

PRIMROSE

Primroses are an English flower that can be amongst the first plants to welcome spring in your garden. They're normally woodland plants, so they go great alongside any trees that you may have and grow lower than some of the other plants on this list, so you can pair them together. The English variety of primrose also produces multiple flowers per stalk and comes in a variety of colors.

HARDY GERANIUMS

Hardy geraniums are the perfect flower if you don't believe you have a green thumb. They're relatively easy to grown and will stay flowering from Summer through early Winter, thanks to not needing much moisture. Hardy geraniums come in a variety of pink, purple, blue, and white, so you can add plenty of color for a good chunk of the year.

COTTAGE PINKS

As the name would suggest, this is a flower that mostly comes in pinks and reds, and it also has a spicy, clove-like scent. They bloom mostly in the summer months and so don't need a lot of moisture, too much of which can be harmful to their growth. Their scent is a little much for most animals, though, buts love them, so you may want to make sure you check for pests and only get the insects you want, like butterflies.

SNOWDROPS

Snowdrops are a lovely flower that grows in January and February throughout Britain in the Galanthus family. They're a harbinger of spring, that grows in deepest winter. These delicate little white flowers are actually rather hardy, and you will find entire woods carpeted with them in winter.

BLUEBELLS

Bluebells are a harbinger of summer and start to bloom in April. These beautiful purple flowers are frequently found in gardens, but you will also find them wild all over Britain. Like snowdrops, they will carpet the woodlands, and coming across a Bluebell wood is a bit of sublime beauty.

66. BRITISH CULTURAL INSTITUTIONS TO KNOW

Britain has a raft of important cultural institutions that are a major part of Britain's cultural life. Some have been around for hundreds of years; some are rather newer. But major events take place every year that are run by these organizations. Some, like the National Trust, have a remit to protect and preserve the nation's heritage. Some, like the Royal Opera, provide entertainment. Here's a breakdown of the most important ones.

BBC

This is probably the most important British cultural institution of them all. Every TV gets the BBC, every owner of a TV is required to pay a tax to fund it. It has several channels, several radio stations, and it sets the tone and topics of the 'national conversation.' It's trusted, it's entertaining, and it's knitted together Britain's regions, countries, and cultures into a unified national culture.

THE ROYAL OPERA

The Royal Opera is based in central London, resident at the Royal Opera House in Covent Garden. Founded in 1946 as the Covent Garden Opera Company. It brought a long annual season and consistent management to Opera in London. Since its inception, it has shared the

Royal Opera House with the dance company now known as The Royal Ballet.

BRITISH MUSEUM

Britain's 'national' museum, which is filled with artifacts from all over the world (and many with a controversial provenance). Many consider it the spoils of 'empire,' but the collection is crucially important to human history and culture. Visiting the museum is free, and it's impossible to see it all in one go – the collection is massive.

BBC PROMS

Founded over 100 years ago, the BBC Proms are a yearly celebration of classical music, held with live performances all over Britain. It culminates in the 'Last Night of the Proms,' which is a celebration of Britishness.

NATIONAL TRUST

The first pillar in Britain's efforts to protect its built and landscape heritage. The National Trust is a private charity, but given the force of law (its property holdings can never be sold), that protects important British buildings and landscape areas. It's a sprawling organization with thousands of properties and hundreds of thousands of acres under protection. They have thousands of employees protecting and curating British heritage and an army of volunteers who help keep it all ticking over.

ENGLISH HERITAGE

The second pillar of Britain's efforts to protect its built heritage. English Heritage (officially the English Heritage Trust) is a government-sponsored charity that manages over 400 historic monuments, buildings, and places around England. These include prehistoric sites, medieval castles, Roman forts, and country houses.

BRITISH LIBRARY

Britain's 'national' library of record is located in central London. It has a vast archive of books, historical documents, and important media related to British history. Every book published in Britain is placed in the library. The library building itself has reading rooms, and you can conduct your own research; they also have special exhibitions and a permanent exhibition showing off Britain's most historical documents.

OXFORD/CAMBRIDGE UNIVERSITIES

Considered two of the finest universities in the world, both Oxford and Cambridge have set the standard for university education all around the world (there's a reason that most universities in the 'new world' look like Oxford and Cambridge and operate similarly). The elite of Britain and the rest of the world tend to get educated here, and they're synonyms with the cities that host them. Oxford came first; Cambridge was founded by 'rebels' who didn't like how Oxford was run. They've had a friendly rivalry for almost a thousand years which has a visual representation every year during the Oxford and Cambridge Boat Races.

NATIONAL GALLERY

The National Gallery is an art museum in Trafalgar Square in Central London. Founded in 1824, it houses a collection of over 2,300 paintings dating from the mid-century to 1900. The Gallery is an exempt charity and a non-departmental public body of the Department for Digital, Culture, Media, and Sport. Its collection belongs to the government on behalf of the British public, and entry to the main collection is free of charge.

TATE BRITAIN

Britain's other 'national' art gallery, except this one is privately owned by a charity instead of the government. It has a massive art collection (started by the Tate sugar fortune) that spans the gamut of British and world history, and it houses the bulk of the 'Turner bequest' (JMW Turner left his private collection to the British people, but somehow it ended up split between the Tate and the National Gallery). There's also the Tate Modern Gallery on the Southbank, Tate Liverpool, and Tate St Ives.

THE TIMES

Britain's newspaper of record, if it isn't reported in the Times, it didn't happen. While it's privately owned now by Rupert Murdoch's News International, it has a special position in British media owing to its age and prestige.

THE WOMEN'S INSTITUTE

The Women's Institutes are a national network of local charities with membership limited to women who do good works in their local communities, fundraise, and have fellowship. For a good representation, see the film Calendar Girls, when a Women's Institute group did a nude calendar to raise funds for a cancer charity. Jam & Jerusalem!

ROYAL HORTICULTURAL SOCIETY

Middle England loves a good garden. The Royal Horticultural Society is more than 200 years old and has been a prestigious organization since its founding in 1804 by a group of famous gardeners and botanists. From its early beginnings, it has grown into an internationally recognized center for horticultural research and knowledge, bridging the gap between the science of botany and professional horticulture and the needs and interests of home gardeners. With royal patronage since 1860, the society has grown to control four and soon to be five gardens across England. Each year it runs the famous Chelsea Flower Show, as well as periodic smaller, seasonal shows at its London headquarters. It owns the world's largest horticultural library and gives its own 'stamp of approval' to plants considered especially suitable for discerning gardeners.

THE RNLI

Royal National Lifeboat Institution is the British equivalent to the Coast Guard, except that it's a private charity, and most of the lifeboatmen and women are unpaid volunteers. They're highly trained for sea rescue and are ready at a moment's notice to go to sea and aid those in need. It has 238 lifeboat stations and operates 444 lifeboats with 40,000 volunteers.

NATIONAL THEATRE

The Royal National Theatre in London, commonly known as the National Theatre (NNT, is one of the UK's three most prominent publicly funded performing arts venues, alongside the Royal Shakespeare Company and the Royal Opera House). Internationally, it is known as the National Theatre of Great Britain. Founded by Laurence Olivier in 1963, many well-known actors have performed at the National Theatre. It is the 'home' to Britain's theatre industry, and many famous plays will get their start here before moving to the West End.

ROYAL SHAKESPEARE COMPANY

The Royal Shakespeare Company (RSC) is a major British theatre company based in Stratford-upon-Avon, Warwickshire, England. The company employs over 1,000 staff and produces around 20 productions a year. The RSC regularly plays in London, Stratford-upon-Avon, and on tour across the UK and internationally. It is considered the 'official home of Shakespeare in Britain, and to perform with them is considered a career highlight in the acting profession.

GLYNDEBOURNE

An opera festival held every year in Sussex. It's held outside, which was a first for Opera. It started in someone's actual backyard and grew from there. It all began with a love story in 1934 when founder John Christie met soprano Audrey Mildmay (it was turned into a fascinating hit play). Glyndebourne is now one of the finest and most celebrated opera houses in the world, delivering performances to some 150,000 people across a summer Festival and an autumn tour.

BRITISH FOOD

67. FAMOUS FOODS AND DISHES

British food has been accused of being boring and bland, but dedicated Anglophiles know better. Whether it's their interesting story, their plain deliciousness, their significance in England and Great Britain, or just their funny name, you should absolutely know about these dishes – and give them a try on your next trip to Blighty.

THE CORNISH PASTY

While there are many varieties of pasties, the Cornish pasty is one of the all-time favorites. With the first references dating back to around 1300, I think I can safely say that the Cornish pasty is a classic, traditional English pasty which has been enjoyed by the English for centuries.

A Cornish pasty consists of suet pastry filled with beef, sliced or diced potato, swede, and onion, all lightly seasoned with salt and pepper. A genuine Cornish pasty has a 'D' shape and is crimped on one side, never on top. The filling should have a chunky texture, and all ingredients must go in raw.

It has been around for centuries, but the industrial revolution really made it take off. It was a favorite of the tin miners in Cornwall, who often had to eat on the move. Being portable and nourishing, the Cornish pasty was ideal for helping them through their long working days. The crimping on the side provided the workers with a nice handle to hold the pasty while eating, and the handle would have been thrown away afterward. It was a clever design because the miner's hands were contaminated with dangerous chemicals from the mines.

STARGAZY PIE

The stargazy pie hails from Mousehole (pronounced: mow-zul), Cornwall, in the South-West of England. The pie is made with whole pilchards, eggs, and potatoes, which are all covered by a pastry crust. The name comes from the dish's unique feature, which is the heads of the fish, and sometimes even the tails, sticking out of the crust gazing skyward.

The pie is traditionally eaten on Tom Bawcock's Eve, which is held in Mousehole every year on the 23rd of December. The people of Mousehole celebrate the memory of the legendary resident Tom Bawcock, who saved the village from famine. Long ago, on the 23rd of December (the year was never specified), the village was near starvation because terrible winter storms had trapped all the fishing boats in the harbor. Tom Bawcock, a brave widower, dared to go out to sea in the harsh weather. He went fishing and brought back enough fish for all those living in Mousehole, saving the village from imminent starvation. It is still served in the Ship Inn pub, Mousehole's only pub, on Bawcock's Eve every year as a tradition based on this legend.

FISH AND CHIPS

Fish and chips are an immensely popular dish and are viewed as typically British. It became particularly popular among the working classes in the U.K. around the second half of the 19th century when the invention of the train and the railway developments made it possible for the fish to be delivered quickly all over the country. This enabled many working-class people to taste fresh fish for the first time.

In 1860 the first fish and chips shop was opened in London by Joseph Malin in London's East End. He was probably the first to ever sell the fish alongside chipped and fried potatoes which, up until then, had only been found in Irish potato shops. The number of 'chippies' kept growing, and around the 1920s, there was a peak in the number of shops, with around 35,000(!) throughout Britain. Although that number has dropped, there are still over 10,000 fish and chips shops in Britain nowadays.

In chips shops in the United Kingdom and Ireland, the fish and chips are traditionally sprinkled with salt and vinegar when it is served, but it's optional. The preferred sauces for accompanying fish and chips are brown sauce and tomato ketchup, and more recently, Brits have taken to adding mayonnaise as well. In Britain and Ireland, cod and haddock are the most common fish for fish and chips, but vendors also sell others.

British chips are thicker than the American-style French fries sold by many multinational fast-food chains. Often referred to as chunky chips – in the United States, the closest equivalent are steak fries.

FULL ENGLISH BREAKFAST

The English breakfast is likely to be the first thing people come up with when asked about British food. Other names for it include 'full English breakfast,' a 'Full Monty,' or a 'fry up.' It started out in England and became so popular that the Scottish, Irish, and Welsh came up with their own varieties. An English breakfast is usually made up of but may not always include eggs, bacon, sausages, black or white pudding, potato, bread, baked beans in tomato sauce, fried mushrooms, and tomatoes.

Let's talk about the regional varieties. In Scotland, additions might include haggis, porridge, potato scones, and oatcakes. In Wales, you will get laver, lavercakes, or Laverbread (patties made of seaweed) with your breakfast. Within England, there are varieties as well, with the coastal areas often adding (smoked) pilchards or herring.

The history of the traditional English breakfast may stretch back as far as the 13th century, where the gentry of the time adored it. The breakfast table was used as an opportunity to display wealth by serving an array of elaborate dishes.

However, it was not just a meal for the wealthy. The combination of food items that we call a full English breakfast nowadays probably emerged during the industrial revolution. The working classes began to eat a full English breakfast on a regular basis because it provided them with enough energy to get through their day of harsh manual labor.

Nowadays, it is not eaten as often because in the hectic modern lifestyle there's not much time in the morning. It is also that with today's health-conscious mindset that this calorific breakfast is not a big favorite. Today, it is mostly reserved for weekends and holidays, and it is still available in many pubs and hotels.

SCONES

Scones are single-serving cakes or quick bread. They are a much-loved part of high teas, cream teas, and afternoon teas. Traditional English scones may include raisins or currants but are often plain. They are traditionally eaten sliced in half, with each half-covered with clotted cream and strawberry jam, but they can also be topped with honey, lemon curd, or any other jam or preserve.

The name might have come from the Gaelic "sgonn" (rhymes with gone), which means a shapeless mass or large mouthful," the Dutch "schoonbrood" or even the German "sconbrot." Both the Dutch and the

German term can be translated as nice or beautiful bread. However, no one is really sure where the name came from.

The word is pronounced "skahn" in Scotland and Northern England (rhymes with gone) and "skoan" in the south of England (rhymes with own), the pronunciation adopted by the U.S. and Canada.

Whether you should put the jam before or after the clotted cream is a religious argument we will not get into here!

BAKEWELL TART

A Bakewell tart is made up of a shortcrust pastry base that is covered with fruit paste, filled with almond-flavored cake mixture, and topped with sliced almonds. The fruit paste can range from strawberry jam, lemon curd, and coconut fondant to apple puree and everything in between. Other varieties can include honey, nutmeg, lemon zest in the almond mixture, cinnamon, or even preserved fruit on top.

The most popular variety is probably the cherry Bakewell, which consists of the same shortcrust pastry base topped with a red jam, filled with almond-flavored cake mixture, and topped with plain white icing and a candied cherry in the middle.

The term Bakewell tart has only been a common name since the 1960s. However, it is generally accepted that the Bakewell tart has developed from the Bakewell pudding, which is suspected to have existed since Tudor times.

BACON BUTTY

According to the Top 100 Food Index commissioned by Food Network U.K., bacon is Britain's number 1 favorite food. Though it might sound unappetizing, a bacon butty is actually just a bacon sandwich – but the preparation of an authentic specimen must be executed very carefully. Everyone has their own opinion about the "perfect bacon butty," but it's generally accepted that the bread must be white and on the dry side, the bacon crispy and full of flavor, and the condiments added for moisture and flavor without becoming the star. Check out The Gentle Art of the Bacon Butty to see a detailed butty-making chart.

HAGGIS

This could be the British food with the all-time worst reputation. The national dish of Scotland, haggis, is as classic as bagpipes and the Loch Ness monster. It's a kind of sausage made out of sheep's stomach, heart, and liver, fresh suet, oatmeal, onions, and various seasonings. On the surface, it looks rather disgusting. But it's actually quite delicious and is one of the many things the Scots take great pride in.

BANGERS AND MASH

Along with pie and mash, this dish is a British icon that's been described as the "working-class hero's meal." As any good Anglophile knows, "bangers" are pork sausages (purportedly because of the noise they used to make when cooked because of the water content), and "mash" is short for mashed potatoes. If a hearty sausage with buttery warm taters doesn't get you salivating, then top it off with fried onions and gravy. Mmmmm. The best part is you don't have to go to a pub to eat this dish; it's easily made at home as long as you can source proper English sausages (American sausages are completely different).

LANCASHIRE HOTPOT

Simple but comforting, Lancashire Hotpot is a lamb and potato casserole layered with browned onion, fresh thyme, stock, and seasoning. It's the kind of dish that cooks slowly all afternoon, then gets drawn out of the oven, bubbling and smelling like heaven. Perfect for a party with lots of friends!

ROAST BEEF AND YORKSHIRE PUDDING

These two dishes simply can't be separated; together, they create what might be Britain's most famous meal. Nothing says Sunday dinner like a juicy slice of roast beef and a crispy Yorkshire pudding, all drenched in gravy. Though it's called a pudding, this is actually nothing like the Christmas plum pudding or chocolate pudding. It's a batter pudding, and the "secret ingredient" that makes it so tasty is the drippings from the roast. Getting the Yorkshire puddings right is quite a challenge even for the ablest cook – but worth it!

STEAK AND KIDNEY PIE

The British love their internal organs, or at least those of oxen, sheep, and pigs. Once eaten as a cheap and filling meal, steak and kidney pie is now a comfort food for many Brits and Anglophiles. Usually consisting of beef, kidneys, onion, and gravy, some recipes liven it up with wine, mushrooms, and puff pastry. Cockney rhyming slang has had fun with this dish, coming up with Kate and Sidney pie, snake and kiddy pie, and snake and pygmy pie.

TOAD-IN-THE-HOLE

Last but not least, toad-in-the-hole is one of those curiously named foods that earns strange looks from outsiders. It's pretty simple, actually, like a gigantic Yorkshire pudding poured over bangers (you can also make individual toads in a muffin tin). Pick your favorite sausages, whip up the batter, and you're a little over half an hour away from classic British bliss.

SHEPHERD'S PIE

Shepherd's pie, cottage pie, is a ground meat pie with a crust or topping of mashed potato. The dish has many variants, but the defining ingredients are ground red meat cooked in a gravy or sauce with onions and a topping of mashed potato. Sometimes other vegetables are added to the filling, such as peas, sweetcorn, celery, or carrots. It is sometimes also gratinated with grated cheese. It's a good, hearty traditional meal so named because it was popular with shepherds. In early cookery books, the dish is given as a way of using leftover roasted meat of any kind, and the pie dish was lined on the sides and bottom with mashed potato, as well as having a mashed potato crust on top. You can make one with any kind of meat, but lamb is preferred.

68. BRITISH CONDIMENTS

In America and Britain, we love food. However, at some point, we felt that just the food itself wasn't enough; we had to add something to it. We had to get that extra bit of flavor. Thus, man created sauces. Some people put sauces on top, others take their food and dip it in, and still others will use the sauce as a marinade to cook the flavor right in. So some Americans may wonder what unique British condiments are out there and what they should eat them with.

MINT SAUCE

Now, admittedly, this is one I balked at initially. To me, mint is something for after-dinner when you need your breath to stop smelling like stew. However, in Britain, mint sauce is readily put on meat, specifically on lamb. The sauce is made from finely chopped spearmint leaves, vinegar, and just a bit of sugar. Aside from lamb, mint sauce is also used with mushy peas in some areas. Mint sauce can also act as a substitute for fresh mint. It is a minty and sweet compliment to your lamb meal.

HP BROWN SAUCE

HP stands for "House of Parliament," and it's the best brown sauce in Britain. It's so beloved that it has approximately 73.8% of the market.

Brown sauce is traditionally used with meat and has a spiced, tangy flavor to it. The best way I can describe it is that it could be the love child of A1 and Heinz 57. While it is acceptable to use with steak as an ingredient in stews or soups and shepherd's pie, the best use of H.P. Sauce is with a bacon sandwich, also known as a bacon butty. It's also one of the easiest British condiments to find in America.

MARMITE

The saying about Marmite is that you either love it or hate it. I'm in the latter camp, but I don't tend to like most spreadable things that aren't jellies, jams, or butter. Marmite is essentially beer waste and represents the yeast leftover from the brewing process. German scientist Justus von Liebig discovered that brewer's yeast could be concentrated into something edible in the late 19th Century, and in 1902, the Marmite Food Extraction Company was born in Burton upon Trent, England. It tends to pair more with savory foods, such as being spread over toast, dipped in crisps (potato chips), and even as a flavor of Twiglets, a crispy wheat-based snack.

HEINZ SALAD CREAM

As a condiment producer, Heinz is all over the place in the United Kingdom, and you can find their products in most restaurants and pubs. Salad cream is a yellowish condiment made with water, egg yolk, and spirit vinegar. As a condiment, it can be used not just as a salad dressing but also as a sandwich spread. While largely unknown in the States until the 21st Century, many ex-pats have created a demand for Salad Cream, and now it's carried by major grocery stores such as Wegmans, Publix, and Fresh & Easy (owned by British company Tesco).

MALT VINEGAR

Another staple of British condiments, malt vinegar, is created from malting barley, causing the starch in the grain to turn into maltose, or malt sugar. Its condiment use is mostly reserved for a single dish – battered and fried cod, the primary dish in classic fish and chips. Now, I used to date a girl who loved putting the vinegar on her chips as well as her fish, which you're welcome to do if you want to add a tangy flavor to your chips instead of dipping them in tomato ketchup. I, however, will judge you harshly for this. Malt vinegar is the perfect condiment for fish, and I always put some on before dipping my cod in tartar sauce.

69. BRITISH CHRISTMAS FOOD 101

In Great Britain, families celebrate Christmas together around the Christmas tree and watch each other open gifts, much like in the U.S.! We share many of the same traditions with Britain: trimming the tree, decorating the house with holly and mistletoe, and hanging outdoor lights.

Brits usually eat the main Christmas meal at lunchtime or early afternoon on Christmas Day. It's normally roast turkey, roast vegetables, and 'all the trimmings,' which usually means carrots & peas, stuffing, and sometimes bacon and sausages. Desserts typically include Christmas Pudding, Mince pies, and chocolates.

A mince pie is a small, British fruit-based mincemeat sweet pie, mainly served during the Christmas season. Its ingredients are traceable to the 13th century when returning crusaders brought with them Middle Eastern recipes containing meats, fruits, and spices.

The early mince pie was known by several names, including mutton pie, shred pie, and Christmas pie. Typically its ingredients were a mixture of minced meat, suet, a range of fruits, and spices such as cinnamon, cloves, and nutmeg.

Gervase Markham's 1615 recipe recommends taking "a leg of mutton" and cutting "the beef of the flesh from the bone" before adding mutton suet, pepper, salt cloves, mace, currants, raisins, prunes, dates, and orange peel. Although the modern recipe is no longer the same list of 11 ingredients once used, it still remains a popular Christmas treat enjoyed by many across the U.K.

On Christmas Eve, children in the U.K. often leave out mince pies with brandy or milk for Father Christmas and a carrot for the reindeer.

Christmas pudding is a type of pudding traditionally served as part of the Christmas dinner. It has its origins in medieval England and is sometimes referred to as either plum pudding or just "pud," though this can also refer to other kinds of boiled pudding involving dried fruits.

Despite the name "plum pudding," the pudding contains no actual plums due to the pre-Victorian use of the word "plums" as a term for raisins. The pudding is composed of many dried fruits held together by egg or suet, sometimes moistened by treacle or molasses, and flavored with cinnamon, nutmeg, cloves, ginger, and other spices. The pudding is aged for a month or longer. The high alcohol content of the pudding prevents it from spoiling during this time.

Although it took its final form in Victorian England, the pudding's origins can be traced back to the 1420s to two separate sources. It emerged not as a confection or a dessert at all but as a way of preserving meat at the end of the season. The meat was then kept in a pastry case along with dried fruits, acting as a preservative. The resultant large "mince pies" could then be used to feed hosts of people, particularly during the festive season.

Once prepared, it is doused in brandy (or occasionally rum) and flamed; the pudding is traditionally brought to the table alight.

70. TOP BRITISH SWEETS

Candy is undoubtedly a popular treat around Halloween, and as children go door to door in their fancy dress costumes in the States, they can expect anything from M&M's to those strange orange peanuts no one wants. While this practice originated in the United Kingdom, not as many families go trick or treating today, though you can still find communities where it continues or other events in which the children collect candy for the holiday. There are some popular American candies to be found in the U.K., but Britain has many of its own unique sweets, and we have ten of them below that you might enjoy for your own Halloween festivities.

MALTESERS

A surprisingly simple confection, Maltesers are honey malt balls covered in chocolate, and they are incredibly addictive. Made by Mars, they come in a variety of packages, from small boxes at your local cinema to large, shareable bags. The sweet's slogan is "The lighter way to enjoy chocolate" due to the airy nature of the malt balls, and you'll be hard-pressed to have only one.

JELLY BABIES

Most Americans might know this candy as a particular favorite of the Fourth and Twelfth Doctors. Bassett's launched the gummy candies at the end of the First World War and dubbed them "peace babies." In most cases, especially Bassett's, the gelatin candies are dusted in a light coating of sugar. They were also a favorite of Beatle George Harrison, and the band would sometimes get pelted with them by adoring fans.

AERO

Aero is a chocolate bar where the chocolate is filled with air bubbles, leading it to be described as "carbonated chocolate." Aero bars come in different flavors, such as mint, and you can even get them as a biscuit.

LICORICE ALLSORTS

Allsorts came about in 1899 when a Bassett's salesman, Charlie Thomson, accidentally dropped some samples onto a tray. The various shapes in the assortment are made of licorice, sugar, coconut, aniseed jelly, fruit flavorings, and gelatin. The various pieces actually make up the body of company mascot Bertie Bassett, though plenty of companies in the U.K. made similar varieties of allsorts.

CADBURY DAIRY MILK

Most Americans know Cadbury for their chocolate eggs around Easter, but their best-known product in Britain is the Dairy Milk chocolate. Dairy Milk can come as a whole chocolate bar, a segmented bar, or individual chocolate pieces. It's also one of the oldest chocolate sweets in Britain, dating back to 1905.

TURKISH DELIGHT

Referenced in The Lion, the Witch, and the Wardrobe, Turkish Delight is made by Fry's and has long been a popular sweet in Britain. Opinion is split on the candy. Some people love the chocolate-covered, rose-flavored confection, but others loathe it, describing it as tasting like soap. One of the ingredients is beetroot, which gives the interior its pink color and some of its flavor.

WINE GUMS

Despite the name, wine gums don't use wine in their creation at all. They're more like a standard American gummy candy. Charles Gordon Maynard alleged to have created them to appeal to adults and gave them names like port, sherry, champagne, burgundy, and claret, and they have similar flavors to match. Maynard had to work hard to convince the company founder, who was also his Methodist teetotaler father, that the sweets didn't have any wine in them.

FLAKE

Also made by Cadbury, Flake is regarded as a "gateway" chocolate bar for Americans, and it certainly has its own seductive qualities. The bar was so seductive it was the subject of plenty of suggestive ads in the 1970s and 1980s. As the name might imply, the cookie base for Flake is rather crusty and dry.

MARS BARS

Once made in the United States the same as other varieties of Mars candy bars, now they're imported and sold with other British foodstuffs in your local grocery store. Their closest American equivalent is a Milky Way, but are simply nougat and caramel covered in chocolate. Northern England and Scotland enjoy this candy in a deep-fried format, and one can typically get it at chip shops.

SMARTIES

Very different from their American cousins, British Smarties are more like M&Ms than the sugary discs we know in the States. Unlike M&Ms, Smarties actually have a different flavor for each color. Smarties can come in tube packages or bags.

TEA

71. 10 FACTS ABOUT TEA

Tea is practically a British institution. It is more popular in the UK than coffee and even has an entire ritual based around it. It first came from China through the continent and then to Britain, thanks to Queen Catherine of Braganza. Originally for the upper classes, the popularity of tea inspired many to smuggle it into the country before taxes were lowered and it became readily available to the population. Whether you are a tea connoisseur or just have a passing interest, here are some facts you might not know about Britain's favorite drink.

LITERARY CONNECTIONS

Among the entries in Samuel Pepys' famous diary, he writes of having tea for the first time on the 25th of September, 1660. He had been having a discussion about foreign affairs with friends "And afterwards did send for a Cupp of Tee (a China drink) of which I never drank before." Considering Pepys was a very wealthy individual, this entry shows how new the drink was to England and how it was still an unusual commodity in the UK.

CLIMBING THE LADDER WITH TEA

A widely reported fact says that 80% of office workers state they learn more about what's going on in the office by sharing a cup of tea with their coworkers.

CUTTING THE TEA

Aside from the obvious inclusion of caffeine as an ingredient in tea, the drink was like a drug in its early years in the UK. As mentioned previously, smuggling tea was a very lucrative business, but sometimes if the supply ran low, twigs, sawdust, and even irons that were poisonous to tea drinkers would be used as fillers. The result of this would make people ill and was one of the reasons the taxes were lowered in 1785 to permit more tea to enter the country.

THAT'S A LOT OF TEA

People in the UK drink roughly 165 million cups of tea a day, which translates to 62 billion cups per year.

WHAT'S IT WORTH TO YOU?

The UK tea market is projected to be worth £700 million each year.

NO GIRLS ALLOWED

When tea first started becoming available to the public, it was served out of coffee houses. Full of pipe smoke and noise, only men were permitted to enter, meaning that women had to enjoy tea at home or not at all. However, the Twining family opened the first teashop available to women in 1717, called The Golden Lyon. Now known as Twining's Tea Shop, it is still open to the public and is located at 216 Strand in London.

AFTERNOON TEA

Anna Maria Russell, Duchess of Bedford, is widely credited for making afternoon tea a late-afternoon meal in the 1840s. There are various kinds of afternoon tea, including high tea, old-fashioned tea, at-home tea, and more, as described in Isabella Beeton's book "Mrs. Beeton's Book of Household Management and Other Works," with meal items ranging from a hot dish, sandwiches, or baked goods such as biscuits or scones. The most expensive afternoon tea can be found at the Ritz Carlton Hong Kong, which costs patrons $8,888 per couple.

ONE LUMP OR TWO

45% of people in Britain take sugar in their tea. The remainder prefer artificial sweeteners or milk.

BAG OR LOOSE?

According to the UK Tea & Infusions Association, 96% of tea drinkers in Britain brew their tea using tea bags. For the purists, however, this isn't good enough, and they prefer to keep to the old-fashioned way of brewing it – loose by infusing the loose tea leaves – which they feel retains more flavor than when the leaves are kept in a teabag.

AT HOME OR ON THE GO

Approximately 86% of tea in the UK is consumed at home, 14% is consumed at work, in shops, and elsewhere.

72. DIFFERENT TYPES OF TEA TIMES

Tea is a culture entirely of its own in Britain. It's not a stereotype; most Brits really do love their tea and cherish a good cuppa. It's a form of relaxation and socialization that is key to 'getting' Britain (like talking about the weather). But there is a lot of confusion out there – many people don't realize the difference between High Tea or Afternoon Tea, or Cream Tea. So, here's a short list to help translate the differences.

Cuppa – Your simple cup of tea at any time of the day.
Elevenses – Late morning snack and cup of tea (second breakfast).
Afternoon Tea – A formal meal where one sits down with cucumber sandwiches, pastries, and fine tea. Usually in a hotel or restaurant around 4 PM.
High Tea – Less formal than afternoon Tea – usually a late afternoon meal after work but before proper dinner.
Cream Tea – A simpler tea service consisting of tea, scones, clotted cream, marmalade, or lemon curd.
Royale Tea – Tea service with champagne or sherry at the end.
Celebration Tea – An afternoon tea service where a cake is served for a special occasion.
Tea – Tea can also be used to denote the dinner meal, which is, of course, confusing to outsiders. I once had a pub owner in the Lake District tell me to 'enjoy my tea.' I was having a steak dinner.

Kettle – Where you boil water to make tea. Many Brits will use an electric kettle (which boils water very fast).
Put the Kettle On – To turn on the kettle to brew a cuppa. When company is coming, start the kettle as soon as they say they're on their way!
Scone – Rich pastry usually filled with currants or raisins, often served with strawberry jam and clotted cream. It's heaven. There is a debate as to whether it's 'scun' or 'scone.' Either is fine!
Tea Towel – Thin towel used for drying dishes after they've been washed. Usually, have some kind of lovely decoration on them, and many people collect them.
Tea Break – Coffee break. Most Brits will stop several times during the day to have a cuppa.
Tea Lady – A woman whose sole job in the office was to brew and serve the tea to staff. This job has mostly died out, and office workers either use a machine or make their own tea.
Tea Service – A tea service is a set of cups, saucers, and plates, with a milk pitcher, sugar bowl, and teapot.
Tea Tray – Tray used in the service of tea, usually includes the kettle, mugs, teabags, sugar, etc. Everything you need for a cuppa.
Black Tea – The most commonly consumed tea.
Builder's Tea – Tea traditionally drunk by tradesmen in the course of their workday.
Tea Taster – An expert judge of the beverage, like a wine taster.
Mother – The person who pours and serves the tea. "Shall I be mother?"
Steep – Letting the teabag or tea sit in the tea, so it brews. Generally, the longer you leave it in, the strong the tea will be.

73. HOW TO MAKE A CUP OF TEA

Tea is an integral component of British culture. There's also a lot of different ways to make tea, and lots of people will tell you there's only 'one' proper way to make tea. Some are quite fanatical about it. So, we're going break this section down.

How the British actually make a cup of Tea

The average tea-drinking Brit will drink tea several times a day, especially if they're at work (where they'll have a dedicated mug). Tea-making is a skill that almost every British person will have. The most important appliance in the home is the tea kettle. Tea kettles will boil water in less than a minute. And to make proper tea, the water must be boiling. Most Brits will also just use teabags to make their tea. Most do not fuss with loose leaf.

1. Boil water.
2. Put teabag in a mug.
3. Add sugar cubes.
4. Once water is boiled, pour water into mug.
5. Add milk if you want it.
6. Steep for a few minutes.
7. Stir.

8. Some remove the teabag after this; I prefer to keep it in as it makes the tea stronger and adds more flavor. Some people would be horrified by this as they argue the tannins in the tea give a slightly bitter taste. Do what you like.

9. Repeat for the next cuppa.

How people outside of Britain think British people make a cup of tea

There's the daily cuppa, then there's afternoon tea, which is almost a meal. This is a treat and rarely how people serve tea, even when they have guests. 99% of cups of tea in Britain are made like above. But there's this romanticism that foreigners have of British tea time, and they think that this is how they have tea all the time.

1. Prepare a teapot.
2. Prepare loose leaf tea using a tea strainer,
3. Boil water with a fancy kettle on the stove.
4. Pour boiled water into the pot over the tea strainer.
5. Let steep for a few minutes.
6. Set out teacups and saucers.
7. Add sugar to cup.
8. Add milk to cup.
9. Pour from teapot into cup and stir.
10. Serve with cucumber sandwiches.

A scaled-down version of this would be to put a bunch of teabags into a teapot and serve with regular tea mugs and a few biscuits.

How to NOT make a cup of tea

Here are a few ways to not make a cup of tea.

1. Don't try to microwave tea, ever.
2. Don't put the teabag in last.
3. Don't cut open a teabag and think that it is 'loose leaf'.
4. Don't use a teabag twice.
5. Don't over-boil the water.
6. Don't serve Lipton, ever.

I expect this to be the most controversial chapter in this book. You can address your letters to:

Anglotopia LLC
8 The Green
Suite 5331
Dover, DE 19901

74. TEA BLEND HISTORIES

Tea is a staple of the British diet. Whether you have it in the morning for breakfast, in the afternoon for high tea, or just to calm down after a long day, tea is a major beverage in your day. The real question is, however, what kind of tea will you choose? There are plenty of varieties in the United Kingdom to choose from, and each has an interesting history. We've identified ten different types of tea blends available in Britain, and perhaps their backgrounds will interest you in trying them in the future.

EARL GREY

Earl Grey is a tea blend that is flavored with oil of bergamot, which is a type of orange from France and Italy. The legend goes that a Chinese mandarin's son was saved by one of Lord Grey's men and the mandarin presented the blend to Earl gray as a thank you, though Lord Grey never actually went to China. The Grey family insists the blend was made for Lord Grey by a Chinese-mandarin-speaking person for the Earl.

LADY GRAY

Not actually invented by Lord Grey's wife, this tea blend is actually more of a modern invention. Twinings had been the original distributor of the Earl Grey blend and found that the Nordic market thought the blend was too strong. Twinings then eased off on the flavor a bit and added orange and lemon peel.

ASSAM

Scottish adventurer Robert Bruce first discovered it in 1823 when he noticed Singhpos in Myanmar brewing the tea from a local plant. Britain originally got its black tea from China, but when the Opium Wars erupted, the country had to get its tea from another location. The British East India Company then started exploring the possibility of producing the tea in Assam. A stronger tea than most, it's used heavily in our next entry.

BREAKFAST (ENGLISH, IRISH, AND SCOTTISH)

There are three different varieties of breakfast tea, all of which typically have a higher caffeine content than other blends. English Breakfast tea is actually a mixture of Assam, Ceylon, and Kenya black teas that actually comes from America rather than the UK. Irish Breakfast is also a blend of Assam teas and is typically very strong, which is why some people put milk in it to dilute its content. Scottish Breakfast tends to be the strongest of them all, typically attributed to the soft water of Scotland producing a less diluted blend.

GUNFIRE

More of a cocktail than a tea, this drink was invited by none other than the British Army, as the name might suggest. It's believed that soldiers (probably while bored) came up with this concoction in the 1890s. The cocktail has since become something of a tradition in the Armed Forces, served to the lower ranks by officers and NCOs before a morning attack or on Christmas Day when deployed. The mixture is typically one cup of black tea with one shot of rum.

DARJEELING

Archibald Campbell was a civil surgeon in the Indian Medical Service when he began planting tea in Darjeeling in 1841. He'd previously been stationed in Nepal and brought the plant Camellia sinensis with him when he came to Darjeeling. Much like champagne and France, the Tea Board of India has stated that for a blend to be called Darjeeling, it must be cultivated, grown, produced, manufactured, and processed in the tea gardens of the Sadar subdivision. It's typically thin-bodied and light-colored with a spice flavoring.

CHAMOMILE

Chamomile is actually a daisy-like plant and has a component called chrysin, which acts as a sleep aid. Chamomile tea has been prescribed since the days of Ancient Egypt when it was given as a cold remedy. The plant was also used to help mummify pharaohs and today has several medicinal benefits, from treating colds to curing stomach aches and even managing diabetes.

CHAI

Also known as Masala Chai, this tea blend also comes from Assam and is produced with a mixture of Indian spices and herbs. Chai blend also came about in part because of the East India Trading Company trying to find more tea options that didn't originate in China. Chai is normally prepared by simmering a blend of milk, water, and tea leaves as well as spices and some kind of sweetener.

CHRISTMAS

Christmas is a very magical time of year, and special editions of our favorite foods and drinks become available during the holiday season. Christmas teas are as varied as the number of ornaments on a Christmas tree, but the most popular tend to include cinnamon and cloves. Other companies might offer gingerbread chai, peppermint, and even chocolate and marshmallows. The history, of course, is fairly recent as a way to take advantage of Christmastime.

PRINCE OF WALES

This blend of black teas was named for the future King Edward VIII and was a mixture of high-grade Keemun tea from China along with other Chinese black teas. Edward gave Twinings his permission to sell a version of the tea when he was still the Prince of Wales, which is how it got the name. Many different tea companies now produce a blend of Prince of Wales, and the blends used tend to vary with no set formulas, so depending on who you buy from, you could get a slightly different taste each time.

75. FOODS TO HAVE WITH TEA

Tea, originally was just a drink from the New World, then Anna Maria Russell, Duchess of Bedford, turned it into an event. The Duchess envisioned Afternoon Tea as a meal to bridge the gap between lunch and dinner, usually taken between 4 pm and 6 pm. For the lower classes, High Tea was later developed as a meal between 5 pm and 7 pm. Of course, being a meal means that there must be food. Over the years, plenty of different snacks and food items have been offered up for an afternoon or high tea. Certain regions of Britain have developed their own preference for certain foods. Have a look at some traditional and local preferences to have with tea.

SCONES

Scones are a classic British food, a single-serving cake or quick bread, similar to the American ideal of a biscuit. There are as many varieties of scones as you can think of, with recipes that range from sweet to savory or include black currants, raisins, nuts, cheese, or dates. In Scotland, a griddle (or "girdle") scone is fried instead of baked. There are also a number of spreads available as well, whether one chooses butter, jam, or jelly.

SANDWICHES

Perhaps not as big as a sandwich you'd have for lunch or as piled high with different toppings, sandwiches for tea tend to be much simpler. These sandwiches are a bit more like finger foods since tea is only meant to be a light meal. The type of bread doesn't vary much, but the ingredients or the sandwich can typically include cucumbers, salmon, ham, fish paste, or egg and cress, which is a herb. Of course, these aren't the only ones you can have. A casual Google search will reveal multiple recipes for you to craft the perfect sandwich to have with your tea.

TEACAKES

In Britain, a teacake is a yeast-based bun that often contains fruit. Standard fruits apply, including currants, but also may include fruit peel or grapes. In Kent, people are known to put hops into their teacakes in September when the hop harvest happens. They refer to these teacakes as "huffkin." Teacakes can also take different forms, with some resembling what Americans would think of as pound cake, others looking more like scones, and still, others resembling biscuits or cookies. Some places in the North leave out the fruit for a more traditional cake flavor.

SAUSAGE ROLLS

Sausage rolls are a type of puff pastry that includes everyone's favorite pork product. What's even better is that they can be served hot or cold and still be amazing. Bakery chain Greggs reports selling about 2.5 million of them per week at their chains all over the United Kingdom. This much-loved British snack has about a million recipes that all come to the same end result, so it's more or less a matter of finding the recipe that suits your taste buds best. Depending on what you find, some recipes change the ingredients a bit, including various herbs, fruit, and other items to put a new spin on an old favorite.

BISCUITS

Typically referred to in America as cookies, they can either be homemade or store-bought and come in many different varieties. Amongst these include: digestives, chocolate, jammie dodgers, shortbread, gingerbread, jaffa cakes, hobnobs, and more. Again, it's one of those snacks where the choice of what is served really depends on the preference of the person (or what's available in the cupboard). Plenty of British companies make biscuits specifically to go with tea, such as McVitie's Rich Tea. Whatever your preference, you can be certain to find some to your liking.

76. THE ALL IMPORTANT KETTLE

The tea kettle is the most important basic element of British life. A kettle is the most versatile of British appliances. Primarily used to boil water for tea, it's useful for boiling water for any other use – like filling a hot water bottle. We don't really use kettles in the USA – simply because British electricity voltage is 230 volts, and so kettles work much faster – boiling water in under a minute. It's a critical element to making a quick cup of tea.

A tradition when moving is that the first thing you do when you move house is to buy a new kettle. Depending on where you live in the UK, a kettle will need to be regularly descaled to clear out mineral build-up. But the best kettles have 'patina' with them and will end up making your tea taste like YOUR tea. When you have company, it's important to 'put the kettle on' and always offer a cup of tea to your guests.

The tea kettle becomes a very personal thing, and like picking your preferred brand/flavor of tea, a Brit will have a preferred brand of kettle and often stick with it for life. When a kettle dies for good, it's like the death of a close friend, and much care must be taken in picking a replacement because it's a long-term commitment. It's also a code red emergency when a kettle dies, and a replacement must be found immediately.

You will also find kettles in the strangest places; I once came across a portable car tea kettle powered by a cigarette lighter in a car. It's rather amusing to think of a dutiful English spouse boiling a cup of tea at 70 mph down the motorway "cream and two sugars, dear?"

Tea kettles are serious business, sold in their millions every year.

77. BEST BRITISH BISCUITS FOR TEA

It's hard to imagine having tea without biscuits (unless you prefer scones or cucumber sandwiches, you heathen). In America, we might call these cookies, but in Britain, a cookie is often a softer baked product or what most of us think of as "drop cookies." In modern Britain, biscuits come in all shapes and sizes, with icing or jam as well as sweet or savory flavors. Enjoyed with tea, milk, or even soda, many of these are readily available in America at British food shops or the international aisle at your local grocery store.

WALKERS SHORTBREAD

Since 1898, Walkers has made shortbread, crackers, and other biscuits and presently is Scotland's leading food exporter. The recipe for your typical shortbread biscuit is one part sugar, two parts butter, and three parts flour. Walkers advertises that their shortbread contains no artificial flavors, colors, or additives. The butter gives it a high-fat content and a crumbling texture (as well as pure deliciousness). They can come in three forms, whether as individual round biscuits, pie-shaped wedges, and slab-like fingers. To this day, Walkers has won three awards from the Queen for their exports, and the company remains in the control of the Walker family.

JAFFA CAKES

Named after Jaffa oranges, McVitie and Price have been making Jaffa Cakes since 1927. The biscuits tend to be small and circular-shaped with a sponge cake base, orange jelly, and chocolate coating on top. McVitie's offers Jaffa Cakes in several varieties of cartons, tubes, and snack packs, as well as mini-cakes in pods and re-sealable pouches. Over the years, the company has offered the biscuits in lemon, strawberry, and blackcurrant flavors. Additionally, Jaffa Cakes are available as mini-rolls, candy bars, and even as muffins. Surprisingly, each one only contains 1 gram of fat.

DIGESTIVES

The term "digestive" for biscuits comes from the heavy amount of baking soda used in their recipes thought to aid in digestion. Made both by Cadbury and McVitie's (amongst others), digestives are typically made from coarse wheat flour, sugar, malt, and other ingredients. Sometimes they may include whey, oatmeal, and milk. Digestives come in a variety of flavors, whether plain, with caramel, or covered in chocolate. In a bit of a cross-over, sometimes people will treat digestives like crackers by adding cheese, and they will even appear in cracker selection packages. Digestive biscuits often form the base for cheesecakes.

WAGON WHEELS

The history of wagon wheels spans the British Empire. Canadian Garry Weston created them at the age of 22 when he worked for his father's business in Australia and introduced them at the 1948 Olympia World Foods Fair. As you might guess, the name comes from the Western wagon wheels, with Wild West films rising in popularity after World War II. In the United Kingdom, Wagon Wheels are made by Burton's, who claim on their website that people consume over 125 million worldwide. As for their makeup, they can best be described as s'mores in biscuit form, with the biscuit itself covered in a marshmallow layer and topped with chocolate.

JAMMIE DODGERS

Also made by Burton's Foods, Jammie Dodgers are a shortbread biscuit sandwich with a raspberry jam filling. Burton's advertising claims that Jammie Dodgers are the most popular kid's biscuits in the United Kingdom, and 40% of the year's sales in 2009 were consumed by adults. Presently, Burton's offers Jam & Custard as well as Banana & Toffee versions. Jammy Dodgers are also part of popular culture, with them being the favorite biscuit of Jonny Keogh on "Two Pints of Lager and a Packet of Crisps," the name of Rita's ship in "Flushed Away," and as a fake self-destruct button for the TARDIS on "Doctor Who." (They also happen to be this writer's personal favorite.)

PUBS

78. DON'T BE A PILLOCK IN A PUB – PUB ETIQUETTE

It should be straightforward – I mean, we've got bars here in the USA – but British pubs are completely different. Quite understandably, no one wants to make a public fool of themselves in that inner sanctum of British culture, the public house. Here are a few tips to make the best of your trip to the local pub.

DO'S

- Go to the actual bar to order drinks. Only very smart establishments (i.e., gastropubs) will have table service (but they'll still have a bar).
- Order beer by the pint (men) or half-pint (women); never by the bottle.
- Pay for your drinks when you're served, and expect to pay in cash. However, post-COVID most pubs are equipped for credit cards.
- Offer to buy drinks for all your party rather than just slipping off to bar on the quiet. The British tend to drink in rounds – the etiquette of rounds can get complicated,) so if your offer is taken up, don't be alarmed – you're off the hook until everyone's had a turn. Though if you want a glass of water or a packet of crisps, or some such, as well as a drink, go get that yourself. But if everyone does a round of drinks, expect to do the same.

DON'TS

- Tipping will cause confusion as it's just not done in pubs. If you must, offer to buy the bartender drink, which they may chalk up for later, but most Brits would only go to this extreme if the publican had just single-handedly rescued him and his family from a burning car.
- Don't be afraid to bring a child to the pub during the day, especially in the country. Unlike America, this won't have social services coming to take your child away!
- The pub is not the place to order frou-frou drinks. No self-respecting publican will serve Long Island Ice Tea, Buttery Nipple shots, or Espresso Martinis. This isn't to say there aren't pubs that will serve these; it's just that they're not the sort of pubs any self-respecting tippler should frequent.
- Don't ask for or expect the bar staff to pour you a particularly large measure of liquor. Though prices vary between pubs, measures do not and are strictly regulated by law. For spirits, the standard serving is 25ml; the EU has done away with the wonderful old measures: 1/6th of a gill in England and 1/4th of a gill in Scotland.
- Be a little more reticent about drumming up a conversation than you would be at home. It's not that people don't want to talk to you; it's just that they're a little taken aback when someone they'd never laid eyes five minutes before suddenly sticks out their hand and introduces themselves as Tim from Topeka. To the Brits, this sort of bumptiousness is annoying and plays to all their stereotypes of the loud American. Break the stereotype, be yourself, be patient, don't try too hard, go with the flow, and you'll find yourself welcomed and appreciated by the natives!

79. DIFFERENT TYPES OF PUBS

There are many different types of pubs throughout the British Isles, and it can be very confusing to figure out basic things like – does the pub have food? Or not? Here's a handy list of the different types of pubs we've encountered.

- **The Local** – A pub that primarily serves local patrons – the kind of place where you'll feel slightly out of place but the place to meet locals.
- **The Gastropub** – A pub that serves food. Your mileage will vary. Some will serve great food, made fresh by a chef or cook. Others will serve something right out of the microwave.
- **Public Houses** – Official name for Pubs – in history, they were houses that were open to the public for alcoholic drinks – usually tied to a specific brewery company.
- **Free Houses** – A type of pub that's not associated with a specific brewery so can serve any kind of alcohol.
- **Coaching Inns/Roadhouse** – A type of pub along major roads or towns that used to be a stopover for coaches but now is popular with passing drivers. Usually, a bit more substantial than a regular pub as it will have hotel rooms, a proper sit-down restaurant, a traditional pub bar. etc.
- **Pub hotels** – A pub with hotel rooms. Sometimes only a few.

It will often serve food but not necessarily to the quality of a gastropub (though sometimes a gastropub will have rooms).

- **Pub Chains** – Pubs owned by a major parent company – usually tied to a specific brewery or pubco. Usually, they're all the same inside, share the same menus and drinks on tap. They're popular but a bit soulless sometimes.
- **Temperance Inns** – A pub that does not serve alcoholic drinks at all – these are rare these days!
- **Country Pubs** – Pubs in the middle of nowhere popular with those who enjoy Britain's outdoors. A good place to stop when on a walk in the countryside. They'll often serve food and do Sunday roasts. A good country pub should be kept secret, lest it becomes too popular.

80. 15 INTERESTING BRITISH PUBS TO VISIT FOR A PINT

Everyone loves a good pub, whether they're out on holiday or headed to their local. It's a place with good beer, (hopefully) good food, and plenty of chances to socialize with others. Of course, many pubs have some pretty interesting names. Each name has its own special history, perhaps forgotten by the locals and not understood by the tourists. Have a read below and find out some interesting histories of these pub names.

THE NOBODY INN – DEVON

My sources indicate that there are two potential origins for this pub's name. The first posits that the name originated with a landlord who never answered the door. Another suggests that, after a landlord had died, his casket was brought back to the pub for a wake, and the place was completely empty. The fact that the pub's sign depicts a man knocking may give some credence to the former origin.

THE BUCKET OF BLOOD – CORNWALL

Now a family-friendly establishment, back in the day, it was a pub that made the Mos Eisley Cantina look friendly. This pub was once a home for smugglers and thieves, and as such, had a pretty violent history. One morning, the landlord went out to draw water from the well and pulled forth a bucket of blood instead. At the bottom of the well, investigators found the mutilated body of a Revenue Officer, seemingly dispatched by the pub's patrons.

THE GOAT AND COMPASSES – HULL

One origin supposes that the pub's name originates from a corruption of the Puritan phrase "And God encompasses us all." It's unknown who corrupted the original phrase, though it's unlikely the pub would have been named such by a teetotaling Puritan and was probably a very clever joke on them.

THE DRUNKEN DUCK – AMBLESIDE, CUMBRIA

The story for this one is pretty funny. Supposedly, the landlady came out of the pub one morning to find a bunch of dead ducks in the road (wait for it). While she was plucking them to prepare them for cooking, the ducks started to rouse and revealed they weren't quite dead. A search of the yard discovered a leaking beer barrel from which the ducks had apparently been drinking. Rather than go through with her original plan to cook the ducks, she knitted them sweaters instead until their feathers grew back.

THE LEGEND OF OILY JOHNNIES – WINSCALES, CUMBRIA

Not at all related to a story about condoms, this pub (also in Cumbria) was once called The Oak Tree. The landlord opted to change it after the passing of one of his favorite patrons, a man named Johnnie, who sold paraffin oil.

THE CASE IS ALTERED – BENTLEY

Another pub with a couple of origins, The Daily Mail, postulates that the origin comes from a legal dispute between the landlord and the licensing authorities. A website dedicated to the pub, however, states that the name comes from a landlady who was quite permissive with patrons not paying off their tabs, but once she got married, it was a very different case. The last pub in the village, a decline in business led the owners to offer up shares in the pub to keep it running and make necessary repairs and renovations.

SPREAD EAGLE PUB – LONDON

Not to be confused with a sexual position, "spreadeagle" is a term that also refers to the heraldic eagle that would appear on a coat of arms. To this day, the pub's sign even bears a stylized eagle with its wings spread. Very close to Regent's Park in Camden, it has a lovely dark blue exterior and serves mainly Young's Ales. The Young's Double Chocolate is a particular favorite of mine and a lot like drinking an alcoholic Toblerone. You can probably also find Wells Banana Bread, which tastes exactly like it says on the bottle.

DEACON BRODIE'S TAVERN – EDINBURGH

This pub on the Royal Mile in Edinburgh is named for one of its most infamous citizens. William Brodie was a deacon of the Guild of Wrights and a member of the town council. By day, he was a cabinet-maker, but by night, he was a thief. He used his day job to case houses and then a break-in at night to rob people of their valuables. He was caught and hung for his crimes, an image depicted on the pub's t-shirts. This double-life shocked many of the city's citizens and was partly the inspiration for Robert Louis Stevenson's The Strange Case of Dr. Jekyll and Mr. Hyde.

THE SALTWATER BRIG – NEWTOWNARDS, NORTHERN IRELAND

Situated in Northern Ireland because we needed one for Northern Ireland, the Saltwater Brig doesn't have much on its website about its name, but it's not too hard to ferret out its origins. It can be found in Newtownards, southwest of Belfast, and sits right next to Strangford Lough, a saltwater inlet connected to the Irish Sea. A "brig" is the naval term for a prison aboard a ship, so logically its sea connection inspired this unique name. Complete with a dining room, a game room, and a traditional pub, it's the kind of place that has everything you could want, no matter what mood you're in.

BULL & SPECTACLES – BLITHBURY, STAFFORDSHIRE

Once known as the Bull's Head, the story goes that, some years ago, a drunken man climbed up the pub and put his eyeglasses on the bull. Rather than be annoyed, the owners decided to change the name. The building itself is a rural inn dating back to 1650 and is said to be haunted by three ghosts.

MARSDEN GROTTO – SOUTH SHIELDS

Also known as "The Grotto," this pub is actually located within a sea cave dug into the cliff face. To get to the pub, you take a lift from the top of the cliffs near the car park down to the Grotto. The place was formed by Jack Bates, also known as "Jack the Blaster," because he used explosives to make the original cave larger so that he could live in it. That was back in 1782. It's rumored to be haunted due to it being a notorious hideout for smugglers at different times before it became a pub. When Peter Allan purchased it in the 19th Century and conducted excavations, they discovered 18 skeletons in the cave.

THE CROOKED HOUSE – DUDLEY

It is exactly what it says on the tin, a building that makes the Leaning Tower of Pisa appear level. It was built in 1765 as a farmhouse, but mining in the area ate away at the foundation and caused the building to start leaning. It was scheduled for demolition in the 1940s but was saved by Wolverhampton and Dudley Breweries, who kept the leaning nature of the structure while reinforcing it to make it structurally safe. The level floors and lopsided walls can create some interesting optical illusions as your glass slides across a level table, or you can get a marble to roll uphill.

EAGLE & CHILD – OXFORD

Not exactly unique for being weird or having some quirky theme, this pub is notable for being the place where the Inklings would gather. This literary discussion group from Oxford university included two very notable names in literature – C.S. Lewis and J.R.R. Tolkien. The group would often distribute their manuscripts to each other for critiques, and at one of the last meetings in 1950, Lewis distributed his proofs for what would become The Lion, the Witch, and the Wardrobe. Great traditional pub and worth a look to say you drank in the same place as these literary legends.

FRANKENSTEIN – EDINBURGH

A bit more of a touristy spot, anyone who visits can't deny the monstrous nature of the decorations. Just like the name might suggest, the interior looks like something out of a mad scientist's laboratory tucked into a castle. It's a great place to recount your favorite scenes from the original Karloff classic, Peter Cushing's The Curse of Frankenstein, or even Mel Brooks' Young Frankenstein. In addition to an array of alcoholic beverages, it serves some traditional Scottish meals, including haggis, neeps, and tatties, for those in your tour group with an adventurous appetite (I, for one, love them).

THE SIGNAL BOX INN – CLEETHORPES

The pub bills itself as the smallest in the world, with interior space that measures 8' by 8' for a total of 64 square feet. Besides the bar that stretches most of the width, there's a small bench. Most of the seating is actually outside the pub to accommodate visitors; you simply go in to order your pint and go back out to the pub garden to drink it. No food in this place except for packaged snacks like crisps, but with five pint pulls, you have a chance to sample some real, local ale.

LONDON

81. LONDON BLACK TAXI ETIQUETTE TIPS

As a native Chicagoan, I have taken plenty of cab rides. I know how to hail a cab and the etiquette to use when interacting with the driver, which, to be perfectly honest, is very little. However, when taking a taxi ride in London, the procedure is sharply different.

Here is a list of the steps to properly hail a cab in London.

- Like in most cities, the taxi's light on top of the cab must be on. The light signals that the taxicab can be hired.
- When hailing a cab in London, generally I wave – I don't yell out Taxi.
- If you are at a busy train station or airport, there is a chance that there is a queue (line) for a taxi. This system is very orderly, and you must wait in the line unless you would like your life to end at the moment of jumping the queue.
- When the taxi has pulled over after you've hailed it, or it's your turn in the taxi rank, politely go to the front window and ask the driver if he or she will take you to your destination. Unlike in the U.S., the destination is discussed before entering the cab.
- To talk to the cab driver, there is an intercom system, usually located near the seats. Be polite, and it is polite to say hello. Generally, conversation should be on lighter matters. Most London cab drivers are friendly and are happy to chat.

- When you have reached your destination, you may leave a tip. Usually, round-up to the nearest pound or 10% of the fare is acceptable. If you feel your cabbie has gone over and above service, you are welcome to tip more. If your cabbie did the bare minimum, don't feel guilty for not tipping.
- Generally, avoid Mini-cabs – they aren't licensed like Black Cab drivers, and you may not be able to trust them.
- Avoid Uber as the drivers are also not trained like Black Cab drivers are.
- Download an app that lets you book Black Taxis in advance (which one taxi drivers prefer is always changing, so we can't recommend a specific one in this book).
- All taxi drivers are legally required to take credit cards, do not buy the line 'machine is broken.'
- Don't expect a cabbie to help with your bags. If they do, be sure to tip them.
- A black cab driver may balk at going 'south of the river' because it's far from everything.

By using these tips to hail a taxi in London, you are assured not to make a cultural snafu. It is also important to know that London taxi cab drivers must study and take a test in order to drive a cab in London. I would argue that they are the most reliable cab service in the world. They will not drive you around the same block three times to run up the meter. Trust your London cabbie; he or she is extremely qualified.

82. TUBE HISTORY 101

The London Underground is one of the most important aspects of London life that informed how railways took over Britain and created London suburbs. Everyone likes to think that America invented the idea of the suburb, but London did as the Underground expanded into the countryside around London. Millions of people use it every day, and it's as critical a part of London's daily life as the water or the electricity. And you may not have known that an American played a key role in its early development!

The world's first underground railway, the London Underground, was constructed as a response to the City's rapid growth during the 19th Century. Today, it is the 11th-busiest subway system on the planet, with 1.379 billion passengers using it from 2016-2017. Its tunnels stretch for 249 miles throughout London, often overlapping and giving passengers plenty of options for getting from one place to another. The history of the Underground, its tunnels, and the people connected to it are truly fascinating. We hope that as you partake of this chapter, you'll submerge yourself in the history and lore and discover more than you knew about the Tube.

The Industrial Revolution of the late 18th and early 19th saw a shift in Britain's population from the farms of the countryside to the factories of the cities. Being the capital, London saw one of the largest influxes of new citizens, with the population of Greater London tripling from 1,011,157 to 3,094,391 between 1801 and 1861. The increase in population also led to an increase in the amount of road traffic as residents of Outer London traveled to Inner London for work and back home each day. At the same time, the nation's seven major railways met in London bringing in, even more people and upwards of 200,000 people were crossing into the City of London each day.

The solution proposed was railways that would run steam trains underground to help move the City's new residents. By the 1850s, the groundwork had been set to create the system that the City would require. The first steam-powered railway trains were running across the country by the 1830s, linking Britain in an unprecedented manner. From 1825 to 1843, Isambard Kingdom Brunel and Thomas Cochrane had developed the tunneling technology that built the Thames Tunnel, enabling transportation of goods and people under the river and further linking the two sides of the City. Around this time, City Solicitor Charles Pearson had begun to argue for an underground transportation system and supported several schemes to have one built, including one in 1846 that included a central railway station that would be used by multiple railways. However, in that same year, a Royal Commission denied his plan.

Pearson pushed for his underground railway again in 1852 and this time found limited success with the creation of the City Terminus Company, which ran a rail line between Farrington and King's Cross. Unfortunately, while the scheme had the support of the City, the railway companies weren't interested, and it wouldn't be until the creation of the North Metropolitan Railway. The Bayswater, Paddington, and Holborn Bridge Railway Company was the impetus behind the Met's creation, which connected the Great Western Railway at King's Cross to the City Terminus Company's rail line, which the railway company had acquired. The company's attempts to get a bill through Parliament were often met with resistance until Royal Assent was given finally in 1854, by which point the company changed its name to the Metropolitan Railway, and its plans extended to include the London and North Western Railway as well as the Great Northern Railway.

Despite the difficulty in getting the funds raised due to the ongoing Crimean War, the Metropolitan Railway first opened in 1863, transporting 38,000 people on its first day and borrowing trains from other railways to assist. The first year saw a total of 9.5 million passengers, a number that increased to 12 million in the following year. This success meant that many new companies petitioned Parliament for new underground railways, and the District Railway soon followed. The two networks together would eventually form the basis of the Circle Line as well as parts of the Piccadilly Line and the District Line. The rivalry between the two railways' owners, James Forbes and Edward Watkin, meant that the process of linking the two took twenty years and the lines continued to experience problems until the railways were amalgamated in 1933.

Over the next few decades, other lines would form from the various railway companies, including the Hammersmith & City Line (formed out of the Metropolitan Railway), the Northern Railway (formed by the City and South London Railway as well as Charing Cross, Euston, and Hampstead Railway), and the Waterloo & City Line (established by the London and South Western Railway). At the same time, steam engines started to give way to electric railways, though some steam engines would continue to see use even into the 1960s. The Underground Electric Railways Company of London, founded by American transport magnate Charles Tyson Yerkes, was established in 1902 and provided power to many of the electric railways. Digging technology also advanced to permit even deeper tunnels than the sub-surface lines that were first built.

The Metropolitan and District Railway lines were essentially created by digging trenches and putting a roof over them, so the first legitimately underground was the Northern Railway, which opened in 1890. This line ran from Stockwell to King William Street and later expanded to Moorgate, Euston, and Clapham Common. Meanwhile, CCE & HR established the Hampstead Tube, and by the late 1920s, the two integrated into what we know as the Northern Line. Meanwhile, the Waterloo & City Railway opened in 1898 and was named after its two stations. Two years later, the Central London Railway opened, running a line from Shepherd's Bush to Bank. The Baker Street and Waterloo Railway opened in 1906 as one of the subsidiaries of the UERL and became known by its more popular name of "Bakerloo." In the same year, the UERL formed the Great Northern, Piccadilly, & Brompton Line that ran from Finsbury Park to Hammersmith.

A couple of major changes took place shortly afterward. The first, led by UERL publicity officer Frank Pick, was a clear brand for the company's lines. Borrowing from the London General Omnibus Company, Pick developed the roundel symbol for the UERL that would become synonymous with the Underground. He also introduced common signage and advertising throughout the lines that would become the basis for all other underground railways in the City. It wouldn't be twenty-five years between the creation of Pick's branding scheme that order would come to the chaos of London's fractured subterranean transport system when the London Passenger Transport Board was established in 1933. The Board effectively merged the City's transportation networks, including the underground railways, into a single entity that became London Transport.

Another major change for the Underground occurred two years prior, in 1931, when former UERL employee Harry Beck would produce his first design of the Underground map that would become the standard layout. Before Beck's map, diagrams of the underground railways tended to be geographical in nature and looked like a plate of brightly colored spaghetti rather than an easily understood interface. By "straightening the lines, experimenting with diagonals and evening out the distance between stations," Beck created a map that was simple and elegant, better understood by consumers than previous models. Beck attempted to sell it to the UERL in 1932, but the company wasn't interested. When he tried again in 1933, the UERL bought it off of him for £10 (or roughly £600) today. When the firm became part of London Transport, the map went with it and was altered several times over the decades, but Beck's initial design remained the basis for every subsequent version.

Beyond transport, the Underground found another use during the early 1940s when it became a key part of the City's war efforts. While people had taken shelter in the Underground's tunnels during the first bombing raids of World War I, there was an increased use of the disused tunnels as air-raid shelters from 1940 to 1945. Additionally, the government made use of the Underground tunnels to store national treasures and as administrative offices for themselves and for the military. Some Tube stations even became small factories churning out munitions and airplane parts for the war. In many ways, the Underground network became its own small city during World War II.

Following the war, Clement Atlee's Labour government came to power, and a wave of nationalizing industries caught London Transport in its wake, incorporating the body into the British Transport Commission in 1948. The BTC ignored some of the maintenance needs of the aging Underground system but began construction on two new lines: the Victoria Line and the Jubilee Line. As the City had stopped growing due to the Green Belt that engulfed it, the two new lines would be focused more on alleviating current congestion rather than extending the network to new destinations. The Victoria Line opened in 1968, and the Jubilee followed in 1979, the latter named after Queen Elizabeth's Silver Jubilee in 1977. Beginning in 1969, the iconic phrase "Mind the Gap" could be heard over the stations' PA systems. The automated message was devised after it became too difficult for station staff and train drivers to verbally remind the passengers themselves, choosing a short phrase to save on costs. Sound engineer Peter Lodge recorded the phrase himself (as well as "Stand clear of the doors") after the original actor hired wanted royalties for his work. Other actors were later recorded saying the phrase, including Emilia Clarke, Phil Sayer, and Oswald Laurence, whose voice had been used since 1969 and was restored to Embankment Station on request of his widow so that she could continue to hear his voice.

Eventually, the administration of London Transport was turned over to the Greater London Council, which instituted a system of fair zones in 1981 to help lower the rates on its buses and underground trains. In the ensuing years, London Transport introduced the Travelcard and the Capitalcard. 1984 saw the Underground become part of London Regional Transport under the Secretary of Transport, which would be a prelude to Prime Minister Margaret Thatcher's government dismantling the Greater London Council in 1986 and moving many of its responsibilities to the government or borough councils. The 80s also saw one of the worst disasters in the Underground's history when a fire started on one of King's Cross station's wooden escalators as the result of a still-lit match. The fire led to the deaths of thirty-one people, and the subsequent report led to new safety regulations.

Moving onto the 1990s, many of the trains received a fresh coat of paint after it proved difficult and costly to remove graffiti. In 1990, the Hammersmith & City line was crafted out of the Metropolitan Line, which it had been part of since the railway was created over a hundred years prior to this. Extensions continued in anticipation of the new millennium, and, at the same time, the return of a centralized London Government meant another change in administration for the Underground. Prime Minister Tony Blair's Labour government meant to create a new governmental organization for the City's boroughs and crafted the Greater London Authority, which took effect in 2000. At the same time, it created a new transportation body in Transport for London. TfL helped to create a public-private partnership in which TfL ran the trains while private companies helped to upgrade the lines.

Despite this, the government retained control of the Underground until 2003, when it returned to local control. The Oyster card was introduced that same year, along with busking in designated areas. As the decade went on, the Overground was introduced to relieve congestion along with new lines and stations, and the Overground has been credited as one of the causes of East London's revitalization. Crossrail then became the City's next great innovation, meant to further relieve congestion of the lines running between the home counties and through the City. In honor of the Queen's long reign, it was renamed as the Elizabeth Line. Last year, the London Underground moved to being open twenty-four hours per day on the weekends, mirroring the practices of other major world cities.

The first and one of the largest metro subway systems in the world, the London Underground, continues to have a major role in the City. It is part of London's history, and its changes continue to reflect the change in the metropolis itself. The next time you find yourself on one of the Underground's trains, reflect on everything the system has been through over 150+ years and how you travel the same path as millions.

83. STRANGE LONDON EVENTS

London certainly sees its share of annual parades, festivals, and events from its Carnival to the Lord Mayor's Show. Many of them highlight the history and cultural heritage of the City, though some are a little on the weird side. Certain events in London might seem odd to observers at first, but they can be just as fun. From annual traditions with a long history to races with a holiday link, we have outlined five of what we believe are the strangest yearly events in London below.

PETER PAN CUP

The Peter Pan Cup takes place on Christmas Day but isn't necessarily related to the holiday itself. Members of the Serpentine Swimming Club line up on the shore in Hyde Park to go for the chilliest of races as they plunge into the Serpentine's cold waters. The races have been going on since 1864, and the club also holds races on Saturdays, with the distance depending on the water's temperature. On December 25, the Serpentine's temperature sits at about 40 degrees Fahrenheit, but that doesn't stop the club members from finishing their hundred-yard competition. Keep in mind that you have to be a member of the Serpentine Swimming Club to participate, but anyone is welcome to watch.

CHAP OLYMPIAD

Being a chap means hearkening back to bygone days of fun and frivolity, all the while looking rather impeccably dressed. Each summer, The Chap magazine gets together the best-dressed gentlemen (and finely-dressed ladies) from around to engage in a variety of games such as the Tea Pursuit bicycle relay, French Connection (contestants attempt to knock French cheese off a pole with a baguette), Butler Baiting (a chap take on a three-legged race) and Riding Crop Rumpus (best to let you look that up for yourselves).

SANTACON

Another Christmas event, it's not strange to see groups on a hen or stag night out drinking in fancy dress, but this takes it up to eleven. Decked out in the finest red and white fake furs and hats, dozens of Santas descend on London's bars and pubs, oftentimes joined by fellow drinkers dressed as reindeer, elves, and Mrs. Claus. Of course, on this long drinking night, there are plenty of carols sung, and good cheer spread, and organizers endeavor to make sure that no one has too jolly a time if you know what we mean.

SPITALFIELDS PANCAKE RACE

One more excuse to get dressed up in costume, the Spitalfields Pancake Race sees a number of teams of four in fancy dress show up every year. The goal of the race is to sprint from one end of the course to the other while flipping a pancake in a pan – and not spilling the pancake. While this may seem like the silliest event on this list, it's all for a good cause as the proceeds go to support London Air Ambulance. No matter whether you win or lose, you'll be rewarded with pancakes.

LONDON BRIDGE SHEEP DRIVE

You might guess that the London Bridge Sheep Drive has a long tradition, and you'd be right. The sheep drive goes all the way back to 1180 AD, when the Worshipful Company of Woolmen, one of the oldest livery companies in the City, would serve as overseers for wool packers and wool merchants. Freemen of the City would often drive their sheep over London Bridge to market, where their goods would be overseen by the livery company. Today, the drive serves as a way to promote wool as an environmentally-friendly textile and to continue to promote the industry.

84. FUNNY LONDON PLACE NAMES

Street names can be funny things. Most often, the name originates from long ago, and the original meaning behind the name was lost. People forget the person it was named for, or the trade that was located there has since moved on. Still, the names remain, and their meaning often becomes something new and hilarious. Enjoy these twenty-five London streets with funny names.

UPPER BUTTS

Upper Butts is a street located in Hounslow, and the origin of Butts is thought to be related to archery targets, which once upon a time were also referred to as butts. The Butts surname is thought to come from people who lived near these targets.

MAN IN MOON PASSAGE

Thought to come from an inn or pub that used to be in this location. Pubs with this name often depict the moon with a face and has a bundle of sticks, a lantern, or a dog.

LOVE LANE

The origin of this street name is not as romantic as it may seem. In the Middle Ages, "Love Lane" was a place you could go if you were willing to pay for a "good time" with a lady.

HANGING SWORD ALLEY

Possibly named after a sword fighting or fencing school that used to be here, but more than likely for the Tudor home known by its sign of the hanging sword. Its colorful nickname was "Blood Bowl Alley," as it existed in an area exempt from city laws after the Reformation, which meant it was quite the criminal hangout.

ROTTEN ROW

This place was anything but rotten, as its original name was "Route de Roi," which is "The King's Road" in French. King William III built it to travel to and from Kensington Palace, and it became quite a fashionable route later on.

BACK LANE

A "back lane" is a smaller street that ran behind the main street, much like an alleyway that runs behind homes in some neighborhoods.

BIRDCAGE WALK

This street name comes from King James I's love of exotic birds and how he used to keep them nearby.

COCKPIT STEPS

This street used to be the site of royal cockfights. The Royal Cockpit was there during the 1700s, but all that remains today are the steps.

SHERBORNE LANE

This street really used to smell back in the day when it was known as "Shiteburne Lane" and was known as home to public toilets.

SWALLOW STREET

The first section of the street was built in 1671 and named after Thomas Swallow, a 16th century tenant of the area.

WARDROBE PLACE

The street was once home to a building that the monarchy used to store clothes for state visits.

FRIDAY STREET

This was more likely named for a fish market that operated on Fridays. Other nearby streets are also related to products such as Milk Street and Wood Street.

MINCING LANE

The street used to be home to nuns from the Church of St. Helens Bishopgate, and the medieval name for nuns was "mynchen."

TRUMP STREET

Not named for the former American President, like its neighbors Milk Street and Bread Street, it was related to a particular item that was sold there. In this case, that business was making Trumpets.

MOUNT PLEASANT

The street is actually the opposite of how it sounds, as it was actually a medieval dumping ground. It's cleaned up a lot since then.

CRIPPLESGATE STREET

It's said that when Edmund the Martyr's body was brought through the city gate here in 1010, several cripples were miraculously cured, though it's also likely that it was named after a "crepul" or a covered tunnel that was built for sentries.

FLASK WALK

This street is somewhat related to what you imagine, as it was home to quite a lot of pubs in the 17th and 18th centuries, but its origins actually come from the fact that those taverns used to sell flasks of water from a nearby medicinal spring.

PUDDING LANE

Not as sweet as you might think, "pudding" was an ancient term for animal guts, which would be pushed down the street into the Thames waste removal system from all the butchers' shops. Interestingly enough, this is where the Great Fire of London began in 1666.

OLD JEWRY

After William I became king, he invited Jews to come live in London, and many of them settled in this area in what became the City's Jewish quarter.

HA-HA ROAD

A "ha-ha" is actually a sunken ditch that serves as a boundary marker for a property, which was preferred by some landowners instead of a wall that might block their view.

CRUTCHED FRIARS

A "crutch" or "crouch" is another name for a Latin crucifix, and this street was the site of the Convent of the Courched Friars, which formed in 1298.

VINE STREET

Not home to a lot of plants, it was actually named for a pub known as The Vine, which operated here in the 18th century.

COCK LANE

You might think this was named for a rooster, but it actually has some dirty connotations, as the street was home to many a brothel in olden days. It was the only place where brothels could operate legally, and the Cock Lane Ghost later became a sensation for the street in the 18th century.

FRENCH ORDINARY COURT

A French restaurant used to operate here in the 17th century that served fixed-price meals, which were referred to as "ordinaries."

KNIGHTRIDER STREET

Not related to David Hasselhoff, this was once a much longer street that knights would take on their way to Smithfield for jousting tournaments during the 14th and 15th centuries.

85. LONDON'S OLDEST BUSINESSES

People have been exchanging money for goods for centuries, and London has seen some kind of commerce since the Romans first built the City as we know it. Most companies that we know of today, however, are fairly recent inventions in the grand scheme of things. It wouldn't be until the 17th or 18th centuries that most shops and restaurants would even come into being. Some businesses, such as pubs, are even older, though, for the purpose of this list, we'll be limiting how many pubs are included since several of the City's pubs are even older than other industries in London. What follows is an interesting mix of businesses that have operated since the 16th century and are still open today.

YE OLDE MITRE – 1546

It's almost fitting that London's oldest business should be a drinking establishment. Besides being one of London's most hidden pubs, Ye Old Mitre is also one of the oldest, with its history dating back to 1546. The pub was built for the servants of the Bishops of Ely who worked at nearby Ely Palace, which was featured in the works of Shakespeare. One of its oldest features is a cherry tree that Queen Elizabeth I is said to have danced around with her once-favorite Sir Christopher Hatton. Enter the tavern, and you′ll encounter a pub with lots of wooden panels and no music or screaming TVs at all. The pub doesn't open on Saturday and Sunday, except during the Great British Beer Festival every year.

LONDON GAZETTE – 1665

The London Gazette began its history in 1665 as another paper – The Oxford Gazette. At the time, most "newspapers" looked more like gossip magazines (and some would argue that they still are), so the Gazette established itself to be an authoritative information source. The reason for the name difference was that the paper started during another outbreak of the Black Death. King Charles II had moved the court to Oxford, and his courtiers wouldn't touch a London newspaper for fear of catching the disease. The Gazette was the first official journal of record and newspaper of the Crown. When the fear of the disease dissipated and the Court of St. James returned to London, the Gazette came with it and changed its name to the London Gazette. The Gazette often relied on dispatches from overseas for its news reports, and anyone "mentioned in dispatches" was said to have been "gazetted."

YE OLDE CHESHIRE CHEESE – 1667

Another candidate in our list of oldest businesses in London is the pub known as Ye Olde Cheshire Cheese. It was built only a year after the Great Fire, but on its site used to be a pub called the Horn, which was built in 1538. A unique feature of Ye Olde Cheshire Cheese is its cellar which dates to a 13th-century monastery. Of course, there are a few older pubs that managed not to get burned down by the ire, but this is one of the oldest to open afterward that is still in operation today. The pub's patrons over the years are full of literature's greatest names, including Dr. Samuel Johnson, Voltaire, Charles Dickens, and Mark Twain. Its lack of natural lighting gives it that dingy feel that appeals to tourists and locals alike.

C. HOARE & CO. – 1672

Founded in 1672, C. Hoare & Co. is the oldest bank in the United Kingdom and the fourth oldest in the world. Founder Richard Hoare had begun his career as an apprenticed goldsmith. It was the year he was granted Freedom of the Goldsmiths' Company that he founded his business and is treated as the founding of the bank. Moving from "The Sign of the Golden Bottle" in Cheapside to Fleet Street in 1690, the banking side of Hoare's business slowly overtook the goldsmithing until it was Hoare's main occupation in 1702, the same year he made his son "Good Henry," and he was knighted by Queen Anne. The bank has enjoyed its independent status since its founding and is now led by the 10th and 11th generations of the Hoare family.

LOCK & CO. HATTERS – 1676

Founded in 1676, James Lock & Co. is the world's oldest hat shop. Despite the name, it was actually founded by Robert Davis, whose son Charles took on James Lock as his apprentice in 1747. James also married Robert's daughter, further cementing his legacy with the business. The businesses passed down from fathers to sons for generations, in the meantime outfitting many famous names from Admiral Horatio Nelson to Oscar Wilde. Even to this day, Lock & Co. uses its famous conformateur to measure a person's head to create a bespoke hat, and the shop displays many of the famous persons for which it has done work.

TOYE & CO. – 1685

Known formally as Toye, Kenning, & Spencer, Toye & Co. is one of the most important jewelry firms in the United Kingdom, holding a Royal Warrant to Queen Elizabeth II. For the Crown, Toye & Co. makes gold and silver laces, insignias, and embroidery, as well as supplying Honours badges and ribbons. It is also the sole supplier of the buttonhole Honours emblem. The Toye family were Huguenot refugees when they arrived in London in 1685 and once again took up their trade of weaving, lace-making, embroidery, and gold and silver wire making. Toye & Co. has served the Crown through fifteen monarchs since its founding and has branched out to everything, including electioneering buttons, trophies, and even the robes and banners for Queen Elizabeth II's coronation. One of the company's proudest achievements is that many of its craftspeople are families who have been passing their skills on to their children and grandchildren.

LLOYDS OF LONDON – 1688

Edward Lloyd owned a coffee house on Tower Street that he started in 1686 that catered mainly to sailors, merchants, and ship-owners. Soon after, Lloyd began to offer maritime insurance. By the 1730s, Lloyds had opened an office at 16 Lombard Street and established quite a name for itself in the maritime insurance industry. Wars in the late-18th century and early 19th century helped Lloyds prosper even more, and the firm quickly became Britain's leading insurer of ships and sailors (which regrettably included insuring ships and slaves in the slave trade). Lloyds also shaped much of the insurance industry, publishing the first Lloyds List and instituting a policy of having a "Lead" underwriter who would set the rates for the others. Today the Lloyds Building is one of the most recognizable and intriguing pieces of architecture in the City.

EDE & RAVENSCROFT – 1689

In the legal profession, one needs to look professional when appearing in court, and Ede & Ravenscroft has been assisting the nation's judges and barristers since 1689. It was founded in that year by William and Marsha Shudall but didn't adopt its current name until 1903, when Joseph Ede inherited the business and merged with wig-maker Ravenscroft. The shop makes more than just legal attire, though, and possesses a royal warrant for robes for Queen Elizabeth II, the Duke of Edinburgh, and the Prince of Wales. They also supply robes for graduation ceremonies and make any number of suits and formalwear, including bespoke items. Today the company has three locations across London and is very close to the famous fashion district Savile Row.

BERRY BROS. & RUDD – 1698

The oldest seller of alcohol in the City, Berry Brothers & Rudd was founded by the Widow Bourne at No. 3 St. James's Street in 1698. Mrs. Bourne had the fortune of establishing her grocer's shop across the street from St. James's Palace, which ended up becoming the principal residence of the monarch, King William III. Despite the popular location, Berry Bros. did not receive a royal warrant until 1903, and Queen Elizabeth II gave her own warrant to the shop in 1995. In that same year, Berry Bros. & Rudd moved itself into the future by being the first wine merchants to open an online wine shop. The shop remains the premier wine and spirits merchant for the City, celebrating over 300 years of business.

TWININGS & CO. – 1706

Thomas Twining's ambitions must have seemed impossible when he purchased a small coffee shop to sell a new beverage that was taking the country by storm. He opened the country's first tea room in the Strand in 1706, transforming it into an empire as Britain's demand for tea grew. The location was perfect as it straddled the line between Westminster and the City of London, putting him in the perfect place to cater to the gentry. It also helped his business that, while women were discouraged from coffee houses, there was nothing keeping them from entering Twinings' tea rooms. In a feat of trademarking, Twining's logo was created in 1787 and remains the oldest logo in continuous use. Queen Victoria made the company an official warrant holder in 1837. Today, it remains the top name in tea all over the globe.

86. WHAT IS A LONDONER?

We've covered Brits, now what exactly is a Londoner? Given the size of Greater London, do the residents identify by the metropolis as a whole or by their particular area, such as Westminster or East London? The answers to these questions are quite complex and reflect the shifting demographics of modern London. London exists more in people's minds than in practice.

First off, it's worth noting how diverse the City can be. The Center for London think tank has observed that over forty years, migration to London has meant that a significant portion of the population is non-native to the City. In the 2011 census, approximately 36.7% of Londoners were from outside the United Kingdom, and that doesn't cover non-native Londoners who come from other parts of the UK. Ultimately, the Center for London conducted a poll that found roughly 25-32% of London residents are also natives to the City. Even amongst the population of native Londoners, there is a great amount of ethnic variety, ensuring that the City's population is a diverse one.

And while the City may have a majority that comes from outside of London, polling data shows a strong sense of local identity. As Center for London evidences, a 1977 poll stated that 73% of the population considered themselves Londoners compared to a 2017 poll where this number grew to 89%. No matter one's age, sex, gender identity, sexual orientation, ethnicity, or political affiliation, living in London has given its residents a strong sense of identity as Londoners. Some even identify themselves as Londoners before identifying as British, which is arguably due to both the foreign-born birthplaces of most Londoners and differing political views from the rest of the country, which was evident from the results of the Brexit vote in 2016.

Even within London, local identities remain prevalent. These identities are largely cultural, based on the banding together of local communities, whether it be an ethnic minority that formed its own community in places such as Tower Hamlets or Brixton, or a community that formed in low-income neighborhoods such as Cockneys in East London. Britain Thinks conducted a poll in 2014 that found a third of Londoners preferred a more local identity such as North, South, East, or West London. Ethnic communities, the study found, were also places of strong local identity. The Eastern European Resource Center discovered through anecdotal evidence that many new Londoners often associated with their local neighborhood or borough prior to identifying themselves with the wider City.

This goes to show that, in any situation, location identity is something that is not inherent but acquired. London identity can exist whether one grew up there or moved there. For the former, London identity grows with age and awareness. For the latter, moving to the City is a choice and identifying oneself with London is a part of that choice. Both ultimately foster a sense of home and of community that grows with time. It may start with a local area, whether Shoreditch or Peckham but eventually recognizes London as a whole. This could mean that Londoners have dual or multiple identities, overlapping senses of belonging, recognizing their birthplace, ethnicity, neighborhood, City, and country. Londoners ultimately come in all types, from all walks of life and places on the globe. Their sense of identity is a strong one that acknowledges that they are part of one of the world's greatest cities.

It's important to understand the differences between the City of London (the square mile original settlement) and Greater London. All of them are London. Generally, if you live within the M25 orbital motorway, you can consider yourself a Londoner. But there are a few exceptions to places outside of this. Anyone within commutable distance to London might consider themselves a Londoner, which encompasses most of Southwest England. Really though, when you ask someone where they're from – they'll just say London, but when you talk to them more, you'll get a better idea of what part of London and where they're actually from. Shoreditch is a much different place than Westminster. It's like someone from Northern Illinois saying they're from Chicago, but they actually live in Naperville. London is an idea for most people.

87. NAMES OF LONDON

LONDON – the very name strikes such a chord with people who love that fair City. It conjures up an image of beautiful buildings, long history, the Thames, black taxis, red buses, red phone boxes, charming locals, and so much more.

London has been known by several names throughout its history, and it also has different names all over the world based on the language spoken.

Here's a fun list of a few.

Londinium – This was the original Roman name for the City they founded on the banks of the Thames and the root of all the future iterations. It varied based on language and translation – here are some examples: c. 115; Londinion c. 150; Londinio, Lundinio 4th century; Lundinium late 4th century; and Londini early 2nd century and c. 105.

Lundenwic – The port on the Thames founded by the Anglo-Saxons in the 7th or 8th century, about a mile away from the original Londinium settlement. It means literally 'London settlement or trading town.'

Londontown – A colloquial and affectionate nickname for London. Not quite accurate as London has never been a town – it's always been a city from its founding. The phrase was made famous by the song A Nightingale Sang in Berkley Square and later in an album called London Town by Sir Paul McCartney.

Londres – This is the French, Catalan, Portuguese, Spanish, and Filipino language name for London. The 'r' is silent and is pronounced as you would in Italian (see below).

Londra – Italian name for London.

The Big Smoke – London was given this label in the 19th century due to its choking smog and pollution caused by coal-burning fires. It's a name that stuck as another name for London. It's also been known as The Old Smoke. London's legendary fog became a relic of history thanks to air pollution laws in the 1950s and 1960s.

City of London – The Square Mile – This is the original settlement that forms the core of London. It's about 1 square mile in size on the banks of the Thames, and it has its own government structure separate from the rest of London. The outline of the City is still made up of the outlines of the original Roman Wall (and you can still see bits of it in random places around the City).

Greater London Authority – The current overall government for all the various boroughs that make up London. It has a mayor (currently Sadiq Khan) and an elected assembly with 25 members. It's only been around since the year 2000 when it was created by the Labour government. It is made up of the 32 boroughs in the historical London area along with the City of London (which has its own government).

London County Council – The former authority that governed London, but it was abolished by Margaret Thatcher in 1986 (it was political, she hated its leader Ken Livingstone – later London's first elected mayor). Its grand building is now home to some of London's most popular tourist attractions, such as the London Aquarium and the London Dungeon.

Metroland – An informal name for a suburban area northwest of London, England, served by the Metropolitan Line on the London Underground. It now has come to represent the golden age idea of London suburban life in the pre-World War II era as London spread out into suburbia via the Tube and other rail lines.

LHR – The airport abbreviation for London Heathrow airport.

LGW – The airport abbreviation for London Gatwick airport.

London City – The small airport located in the Docklands that has short-haul flights to the rest of Europe.

LDN – The new shortened version of London is often used in marketing but also used by people sending text messages.

BRITISH ENTERTAINMENT

88. DOCTOR WHO 101

Doctor Who is one of the most important British TV shows that has ever been made – and is so important; it deserves its own section in this book. Even if you're not a fan of the show or never intend to watch it, it's baked into modern British culture and exists in the vernacular (TARDIS-like, 'bigger on the inside' etc.). This sci-fi show is one that many children grew up watching, and it's had a huge impact on how the British consume TV, and also how British sci-fi developed as distinct from American sci-fi. This chapter will explain why!

One of the world's most popular television series, Doctor Who, has been on the air since 1963 (with a gap from 1989 to 2005). The show was conceived as a way to teach children about history but quickly came to lean more and more on its science-fiction adventure premise. While practically an institution in the United Kingdom, Doctor Who was essentially a cult-hit in the United States and other nations until it exploded in popularity following a 2005 revival. As you read on, we will explain a bit of the show's history, its essential characters, and the ways you can enjoy the Doctor Who universe across multiple media.

HISTORY

Doctor Who began in 1963 as the brainchild of BBC Head of Drama Sydney Newman. The network wanted a new science-fiction show, and

Newman was the person who conceived the idea that it would be a program that would educate about history and introduced concepts such as the time-traveling TARDIS. Together with producer Verity Lambert, director Waris Hussein, and star William Hartnell, the show launched on November 23rd. It would run continuously with a series of different actors in the title role and numerous producers, directors, and other actors until it was canceled by then-Head of Series Peter Creegan.

An attempt was made to revive the program in 1996 for the Fox Network in the United States, but low ratings (it was pitted against the season finale of Roseanne) meant the TV movie starring Paul McGann was not picked up for a series. The show would continue on in novels, comics, and audio formats only until revived in 2005 by producer Russell T. Davies. It has run continually since with the most recent Doctor portrayed by actress Jodie Whittaker.

WHO IS THE DOCTOR?

Simply put, the Doctor is an alien. No real name is ever given for the character, with "The Doctor" being a name originally given to the character by their first companions in the series, Ian Chesterton and Barbara Wright. The Doctor's species hails from the planet Gallifrey, which long ago mastered travel in time and space, and so dubbed themselves the "Time Lords." Considered a renegade among their people, the Doctor stole one of their time-traveling ships (called a TARDIS) and left the planet with their granddaughter.

As an alien, the Doctor has a number of distinct biological differences from humans. Apart from having two hearts, the most notable difference is that the Doctor is able to completely regenerate his (or her) body when close to death. This was originally how the series got around the change in actors from William Hartnell to Patrick Troughton. Not only does the Doctor's physical appearance change, but their entire personality changes as well, and regenerations are not limited by sex or race. To date, thirteen different actors have portrayed the Doctor as the primary protagonist of the series, with John Hurt and Jo Martin playing previously unknown regenerations. As such, you'll normally hear fans refer to a particular Doctor by their order of appearance or nickname (such as the 13th Doctor for Jodie Whittaker or The War Doctor for John Hurt).

No matter what time they find themselves or in what form, the Doctor always fights for and helps others, attempting to win their battles not through force but with the use of their intellect.

THE TARDIS

As mentioned, the TARDIS is a time-traveling device used by the

Time Lords to visit other worlds and eras. Its name is an acronym that stands for "Time and Relative Dimensions in Space." It is "transcendentally transdimensional," which means its inner dimensions are much larger than its exterior (or, as some characters are want to say, "it's bigger on the inside").

When first encountered by Ian and Barbara in 1963, it appears as an old police telephone box. The original idea for the show was to have the TARDIS change its appearance to blend into any time via a "chameleon circuit," but budgetary constraints forced the show to keep using the police box (explained in-universe by the circuit being broken), which has since become an icon of the program. The TARDIS itself is also sentient and has a tendency to take the Doctor and his companions where IT wants to go or where it feels the Doctor is needed.

THE SONIC SCREWDRIVER

The primary tool of the Doctor, the Sonic Screwdriver, is capable of much more than manipulating screws. From unlocking doors to scanning aliens, the Sonic Screwdriver has taken on whatever abilities were dictated by the plot while having very few weaknesses (including an inability to work on wood). First appearing in the Second Doctor story "The War Games," it has taken on numerous appearances and is a top piece of memorabilia for any Doctor Who fan.

THE COMPANIONS

The Doctor's Companions throughout the series have acted as an audience surrogate, and more often than not, are ordinary humans. In addition to the Doctor's granddaughter, Susan, the first companions were schoolteachers Ian and Barbara. Numerous actors have appeared as companions during the show's run, including such well-known individuals as Karen Gillan, Arthur Darvill, Billie Piper, Freema Agyeman, and Bradley Walsh.

VILLAINS

They say you can judge someone by the quality of their enemies, and the Doctor has acquired many notable villains over fifty-eight years. Amongst the most notable are the Daleks and the Cybermen. The Daleks were created by a mad scientist named Davros in the aftermath of an alien nuclear war, mutants that are squid-like in appearance with a single eye but utilize armored personal vehicles that have been compared to salt-and-pepper shakers. The Daleks hate every living creature that is not exactly like them and will even turn on other Daleks that are deemed to be "impure."

The Cybermen, on the other hand, are humans who willingly or unwillingly had their brains placed in cybernetic bodies, becoming emotionless, nigh-invulnerable galactic conquerors. Originally from an Earth-like twin world called Mondas, more recent Cybermen have also come from a parallel dimension. Additionally, one of the more popular recent monsters since the show's revival in 2005 are the Weeping Angels, beings that appear to be stone statues until you turn your back on them and live by sending a person back in time and stealing their potential future.

Seriously, an entire article could be spent on the Doctor's enemies alone, so don't worry too much if you don't immediately know who the Doctor is facing in a given episode. The show does a good job of explaining them to new viewers.

OTHER MEDIA

In addition to television, Doctor Who has appeared in practically every type of media in existence. Novels and comics have been some of the earliest examples. Different publishers from Arrow to the BBC itself have published stories over the years and can be enjoyed regardless of whether they fit within the show's present continuity. Different publishers have also produced Doctor Who comics, the most notable of which have appeared in Doctor Who Magazine since 1979 and today are also published by Boom! Studios, the latter of which featuring different stories than DWM.

Only two attempts have been made to bring Doctor Who to movie screens. 1965's Dr. Who and the Daleks and 1966's Daleks' Invasion Earth 2150 AD feature Peter Cushing as "Dr. Who" and bear little resemblance to the television show. In the movies, Cushing plays an ordinary human using the name Dr. Who who travels in his invention, the TARDIS, with his two granddaughters (Barbara and Susan) as well as Barbara's boyfriend Ian and police officer Tom Campbell (played by Bernard Cribbins). Both films are lifted directly from the series' serials "The Daleks" and "The Dalek Invasion of Earth."

Perhaps the most notable external media aside from the novels and comics are a series of audio adventures from Big Finish Productions. The company has produced a number of series over the years featuring past Doctors and their companions, as well as new characters introduced to the franchise. The BBC also produces its own audio stories with currently contracted actors from the show. While the canon of these stories is hotly debated amongst fans, the show has acknowledged certain events and characters from time to time, as when the Eighth Doctor mentioned several of his audio companions before regenerating into the War Doctor.

In many cases, these additional stories are some of the only places where you can follow certain Doctors' adventures, such as the Eighth Doctor, the War Doctor, and Jo Martin's Doctor, who had little screen time but enjoy a high level of popularity with fans.

WHERE TO WATCH

If you want to see more Doctor Who, "Classic" Doctor Who stories (from 1965 to 1989) can be found through the Britbox streaming service, while newer Doctor Who episodes are available through BBC America and HBO Max.

89. BRITISH SPORTS

The British sporting world is diverse – the Brits, after all, invented many sports the world loves to play. The joke is that they're much better at inventing good sports than they are at winning them. Here is a guide to some common words and phrases you'll encounter.

Association Football – The official name for football or soccer as it is called in the USA.

FA – The official governing body of football, they set the rules and run the leagues.

English Premier League – The Premier League is an English professional league for men's association football clubs. At the top of the English football league system, it is the country's primary football competition. Contested by 20 clubs with a system of relegation for underperforming clubs.

ECB – England Cricket Board – The governing body of Cricket in England and Wales.

The Ashes – The Ashes is a Test cricket series played between England and Australia that is very widely watched. The Ashes are regarded as being held by the team that most recently won the Test series. It is held every four years.

Test Cricket – Test cricket is the longest form of the sport of cricket and is considered its highest standard. Test matches are played between national teams with "Test status," as determined by the International Cricket Council (ICC). The 2 teams of 11 players play a 4-innings match, which may last up to 5 days. The name Test stems from the long, grueling match being a "test" of the relative strengths of the two sides.

Six Nations – The Six Nations Championship is an annual international rugby union competition involving six European sides: England, France, Ireland, Italy, Scotland, and Wales.

Rugby Union – Rugby union, is a contact team sport that originated in England in the first half of the 19th century. One of the two codes of rugby football, it is based on running with the ball in hand. In its most common form, a game is between two teams of 15 players using an oval-shaped ball on a rectangular field with H-shaped goalposts on each try line.

Rugby League – Rugby league football is a full-contact sport played by two teams of thirteen players on a rectangular field. One of the two codes of rugby football, it originated in England in 1895 as a split from the Rugby Football Union over the issue of payments to players. Its rules gradually changed with the aim of producing a faster, more entertaining game for spectators. In rugby league, points are scored by carrying the ball and touching it to the ground beyond the opposing team's goal line; this is called a try and is the primary method of scoring.

FIFA – The official international body that manages the rules and regulations of Football. They also set up the framework for each country's national team.

UEFA – The Union of European Football Associations is the administrative body for association football in Europe, although several member states are primarily or entirely located in Asia. It is one of six continental confederations of the world football's governing body FIFA. UEFA consists of 55 national association members.

World Cup – International Competition held every four years where the top national teams compete for the world championship. Run by FIFA. Next will be in 2018.

UEFA European Championship (Euro Cup) – Championship competition featuring national teams from European countries only, held every four years and managed by UEFA. Usually held two years after/before the next World Cup.

Rugby World Cup – The Rugby World Cup is a men's rugby union tournament contested every four years between the top international teams. The tournament was first held in 1987 when the tournament was co-hosted by New Zealand and Australia. New Zealand is the current champion, having defeated Australia in the final of the 2015 tournament.

Wimbledon – General term for The Championships, Wimbledon, the oldest tennis tournament held in the world every June.

All England Club – The All England Lawn Tennis and Croquet Club, also known as the All-England Club, based at Church Road, Wimbledon,

London, England, is a private members' club. It is best known as the venue for the Wimbledon Championships, the only Grand Slam tennis event still held on grass.

Snooker – Snooker is a cue sport that originated in India in the 19th century. It is played on a table covered with a green cloth, or baize, with pockets at each of the four corners and in the middle of each side cushion. Using a cue and 22 colored balls, players must strike the white ball to pot the remaining balls in the correct sequence, accumulating points for each pot.

The Boat Race – The Boat Race is an annual rowing race between the Oxford University Boat Club and the Cambridge University Boat Club, rowed between men's open-weight eights on the River Thames in London, England. It is also known as the University Boat Race and the Oxford and Cambridge Boat Race.

90. BRITISH TV CHANNELS

The British have come a long way from having only one station on their televisions to triple-digit channels. Where the BBC was once the only game in town, stations are popping up all over the place. With that in mind, here's your guide to the stations of the British Isles, from the BBC to ITV and everything in-between. Many of these stations are available on Freeview, a free-to-air digital television service available to anyone who has the right receiving equipment. Freesat is its satellite television counterpart.

This list is primarily limited to Terrestrial (over-the-air) channels that anyone can receive with an antenna and a receiver. Like the US, the UK has a few hundred different cable and satellite channels – many of which are just British counterparts of American channels – these channels are not on this list.

There are two types of television in the UK; there's the BBC which is supported by a yearly license fee that all owners of televisions have to pay. There are no commercials on the BBC. Then there's commercial TV, which is everything else. Commercial TV has advertisements.

UK Television is now all digital – much like the USA. They completed the switch to digital TV in 2012 (it was done in time for the Olympics), the process began in 2007. Freeview is the primary digital television system, and most TV's come with it built-in now. While the UK is digital, they have different formats. Some channels are available in HD – HD defined by the BBC, a TV that broadcasts in 1080i resolution – meaning 1080 interlaced lines of resolution. However, not all the channels are available in HD. The HD channels are simply the same channel as the standard channels, just broadcast in HD.

Non-HD Digital TV is broadcast in SDTV – Standard Definition Television, also popularly known as PAL Format TV. It has 576 lines of resolution and is pretty crisp. The shape is widescreen, so it matches with most HD broadcasts, just has fewer lines of data.

BBC One – The flagship of the British Broadcasting Corporation, it was launched in 1936, and like other BBC stations, funded through the television license. BBC One represents a mixed-genre station with news, sports, comedy, drama, etc. Landing a program on this channel almost guarantees that someone will be watching.

BBC Two – While BBC One is considered the station with more "mainstream" or "popular" programs, BBC Two is its more-educated cousin. In recent years, the station has moved away somewhat from its original mission and features more mainstream fare. Its most popular program currently is Top Gear, and can often be a testing ground for newer programs that can eventually 'graduate' to BBC One.

BBC Three – This channel serves as the younger, hipper member of the family, dedicated to programs for viewers in the 16 to 34 years old category. Shows such as The Mighty Boosh got their start on the channel. However, a few years ago, the BBC announced that BBC Three would move to an online-only format, launching protests from many viewers and celebrities such as Greg James, Matt Lucas, and Jack Whitehall. The channel stopped broadcasting in 2015 and went digital-only. As of 2021, there was talk of bringing it back to the airwaves.

BBC Four – Adopting many of the types of programs that used to air on BBC Two, BBC Four is dedicated to broadcast at least 100 hours of new arts programs, 110 hours of new factual programs, and show at least 20 international films per year. Everything from The Proms to American programs such as Parks and Recreation can be seen here. It only broadcasts for part of the day.

BBC News – A twenty-four hour news channel in the vein of CNN and the first British competitor to Sky News.

BBC Parliament – Akin to C-SPAN in the States, BBC Parliament broadcasts Parliamentary sessions as well as sessions and news from Wales, Scotland, and Northern Ireland. It also shows its own original programming related to government affairs.

CBBC – A channel with a target audience of 6 to 12 year olds, it airs everything from classic children's programming such as Blue Peter to The Sarah Jane Adventures, a more kid-friendly spin-off of Doctor Who.

CBeebies – The original name for fans of CBBC programming, the network dedicates itself to fun and educational programming for children under the age of 6.

ITV – One of the first independent stations to go on the air in the United Kingdom, ITV stands for "Independent Television." As a competitor to the BBC, it airs programs from multiple genres as well as broadcasting news and sports. Popular programs such as Downton Abbey, Ant & Dec, and the original Avengers are or have been in its programming. Unlike the BBC, all ITV channels are supported by commercials. In Scotland, ITV is called STV.

ITV2 – Airs many American programs and also rebroadcasts of programs from ITV.

ITV 3 – A channel dedicated mainly to drama programs.

ITV 4 – This ITV channel is primarily dedicated to men's programming, including sports, comedies, and action programs and films.

C-ITV – ITV's children's programming channel, a rival to CBBC and CBeebies.

Channel 4 – A third commercial competitor was launched in 1982. While Channel 4 is a commercial station much like ITV, it is also a public company like the BBC. While airing multi-genre popular programming, it also has public service commitments to broadcast culturally diverse and innovative programs.

Channel 4+1 – Channel 4, but one hour later, so if you're late for your favorite program, you can watch it there instead.

More4 – More4 is a digital television channel, run by British broadcaster Channel 4. The channel was launched on 10 October 2005. The channel is carried on Freeview and has a focus on lifestyle content.

Channel 5 – It is the fifth and final national terrestrial network after BBC One, Two, ITV, and Channel Four. It comprises both general entertainment programs from the UK and abroad as well as internally commissioned programs. Channel 5 is considered the most down-market of the British TV stations and has a tendency to fill their schedule with American shows. Though in recent years, this has been changing since they hired BBC producers and controllers. Some of the best documentaries and the new 'All Creatures Great and Small' have been on Channel 5.

Dave – Dave is a UKTV owned Channel that focuses on male-centered programming and airs a lot of Top Gear Repeats. UKTV said the name of the channel was chosen because "everyone knows a bloke called Dave."

Yesterday – Yesterday is a television channel broadcasting in the United Kingdom as part of the UKTV network of channels. The channel originally launched on 30 October 2002 and relaunched in its current format on 2 March 2009. Yesterday focuses on history programming and shows a lot of great BBC documentaries that originally aired on the main networks.

UKTV Gold – This UKTV channel airs primarily classic British comedies.

Alibi – Airs British crime dramas.

Quest – Quest provides factual, lifestyle, entertainment programs, and other imported material, as well as coverage of football. The channel is operated by Discovery, Inc.

Sky – The flagship channel of British Sky Broadcasting, the child of Rupert Murdoch, it is the oldest non-terrestrial station in the UK, having launched in 1982. The majority of its content is multi-genre, with plenty of programs imported from the United States. They air a mix of news, drama, comedy, and more. Also, when most people say they have Sky, they mean the satellite service, which offers up tons of satellite channels.

Sky Arts – This is a British free-to-air television channel offering programs 24 hours a day dedicated to highbrow arts, including theatrical performances, movies, documentaries, and music (such as opera performances and classical and jazz sessions).

The +1 Networks – Many of the main networks now offer a +1 service where it's simply the same channel except everything airs one hour later. It's a great way to catch a show if you missed its original airtime.

91. THE BRITISH INVASION 101

The rise of the 1960s American counter-culture owes much to the British. Throughout this turbulent and eventful decade, British music groups and cultural icons migrated in waves to the United States, bringing with them new ideas and influences that would help create the defining culture of the age. Music in the 1960s is inextricably associated with the cultural and political developments of the era, including the emergence of psychedelic drug use, the political anti-war and anti-capitalist movements, and the way in which particular bands defined revolutionary anthems for the civil rights movement.

KEY DATES

- January 1964 – The Beatles release their first single in the United States
- August 1964 – A Hard Day's Night is released in the United States
- May 1965 – 9/10 singles in US charts came from British & Commonwealth artists
- May 1965 – The Rolling Stones head US charts with (I Can't Get No) Satisfaction

The music of the 1960s represented the identity and ideologies associated with the baby boomer generation, including the emergence of new aesthetics in art, fashion, and popular culture, left-wing ideology, and sexual liberation. At the heart of this cultural revolution was the amalgamation of influences and styles from the United Kingdom with the musical genres and styles of the United States.

The British Invasion was not simply the migration of a fully formed British 'style' across the Atlantic: rather, it was a cultural phenomenon, born of both British and American influence and formed in the crucible of 1960s American politics.

THE 1960S: THE RISE OF THE BABY BOOMERS

The defining feature of the 1960s and the factor that shaped the rise of the counter-culture that surrounded the British invasion was the generation gap between the inter-war generation and the so-called baby boomers. The term 'generation gap' originated in the 1950s and was used to describe the radically different aspirations and socio-economic characteristics that separated the baby boomers from their parents. For the inter-war generation, the 1950s represented a period of material comfort that they had never previously experienced. This generation grew up in the wake of the Depression and spent their early adulthood in the Second World War. As a result, their aspirations were conditioned by the lack of material comfort and political uncertainty that governed their lives, and they sought to actively profit from the newfound comfort and stability of the post-war period. The post-war boom resulted in a cultural focus on the family and the domestic sphere, particularly for women, who had taken on diverse working roles during the war, and were now encouraged to return to the domestic sphere and dedicate themselves to the family. The rise of the suburbs in this period was a product of this cultural trend.

However, the experiences of the subsequent generation termed the 'baby-boomers,' were radically different from those of their parents. The baby-boomers were raised in this suburban domestic idyll, which had been created from the aspirations of their parents, but proved to be politically and socially stifling. The counter-culture of the baby-boomer generation was, in part, a reaction to the materialism and consumerism that dominated 1950s society and a yearning to be liberated from the social constraints imposed by their parents. The baby boomers viewed their parents as politically complacent and stuck in a narrow-minded domesticated environment that prevented them from challenging social injustice. In addition to this, the baby-boomers had grown up without the shadow of conscription, in relative material comfort, and therefore had the opportunity to engage in a variety of leisure activities in their youth, creating the notion of 'teenage' years as a new space in which youth identities could be forged. This meant that they fostered a new culture, and were materially comfortable enough to challenge their parents' worldview. This was the generation that needed an anthem: music that would operate as a rallying cry and enable them to express ideas and frustrations that had been constrained by the domesticated, suburban idyll of the post-war period.

THE BRITISH ARE COMING! THE MUSIC OF THE 1960S

American society at the beginning of the 1960s was, therefore, primed and ready for a new musical movement. At the same time, a radically new sound, based on a British interpretation of American rock and roll and blues, was developed, mainly in the north of England. At the head of this new 'Merseybeat' trend were the Beatles, who, after gaining considerable success at home, smashed on to the American stage in 1964. In January 1964, the Beatles released their single I Wanna Hold Your Hand in the US and followed it up with a tour in February 1964. Beatlemania soon took root across the United States, and the unique, fresh style of their music resonated with baby boomers in all parts of the country.

The music of the 1960s represented a cultural revolution due to the radical change in the types of rhythm, melody, instrumentation, and lyrical content of popular music, in contrast to the dominant sounds of the 1950s. In the 1960s, rock began to emerge on the international music scene, making a significant impact and transforming conventional musical styles. Rock music produced a new musical aesthetic and gave the baby boomer generation a distinctive musical identity, as these new forms of music were marketed directly at younger generations and were not typically consumed by older members of British and American society. In particular, in this period, the influence of British rock bands was extremely significant, particularly in the emerging rock scene in the United States. British bands such as The Rolling Stones, the Beatles, and the Hollies adapted traditional American styles such as blues and soul, and incorporated them into their music, creating a distinctive and original sound.

The rise to international fame of the Beatles gave added publicity and musical expression to the psychedelic movement, particularly with the release of Sgt. Pepper's Lonely Hearts Club Band and Magical Mystery Tour. Music was extremely important in fueling the counter-culture movement by creating anthems that were used to unify various movements and create an iconic call to arms. The extent of the Beatles' fame meant that they were by far the most dominant popular expression of the counter-culture movement, and to a certain extent, they ensured its transition into the mainstream and the absorption of some aspects of counter-culture and anti-establishment discourse within dominant forms of popular culture.

Significantly, the Beatles also opened the way for more British artists to break out onto the American music scene. The Rolling Stones, the Animals, and the Kinks all found considerable success in the United States and set the tone for the decade. Female artists such as Dusty Springfield, Petula Clark, and Lulu also managed to break into the American market. In particular, the impact of psychedelic rock bands such as Pink Floyd had a huge influence on the development of American sounds of the 1960s. Artists such as The Who also provided rock anthems for a generation that were used to galvanize the movement further.

MUSIC AND POLITICS: 1960S COUNTER CULTURE

The importance of these musical trends was that they produced a new musical identity for the young baby boomer generation that formed an accompaniment to the broader subversive cultural movement that was breaking out throughout the United States and Europe. In the 1960s, the revolt of the baby boomers against their parents and the domestic ideal associated with suburban life was the dominant driver of cultural production, as young people sought to produce radically new cultural identities, articulated in opposition to those represented by their parents. As the decade wore on, the impact of progressive rock bands such as Pink Floyd added innovative layers to this new identity, reflecting the cultural associations of the hippie movement, consumption of psychedelic drugs, sexual liberation, and the breakdown of traditional societal norms. Bands such as The Who, Pink Floyd, and The Beatles all produced music with psychedelic elements, often incorporating musical influences from diverse cultures such as India or Latin America, which was a product of new encounters with esoteric spirituality and philosophy. The broader cultural trends of the 1960s found expression in popular music, which was heavily influenced by broader cultural developments, and also served as an important carrier for the popularisation of these new ideas.

Music in the 1960s also took on an important political role. The folk revival was particularly significant in the anti-war movement and became a dominant form of expression for student activists and protesters. The hippie culture and aesthetic, together with the increased emphasis on lyrical content, made folk music a particularly good vehicle for political expression. This may be observed in the work of singer-songwriters such as Leonard Cohen, Bob Dylan, Joni Mitchell, and Pete Seeger, all of whom were profoundly influenced by British folk singers and songwriters such as Ewan McColl, who used music as a way to comment on the political developments and upheavals of the period. Although the iconic folk anthems of the political movements of the latter part of the decade were dominated by American and Canadian artists, the musicians of the British Invasion had established the foundations for their creative innovations.

LEGACY

The British Invasion had a lasting and profound effect on the music of the 1960s, both within the United States and internationally. The impact of British bands and musicians on American culture lent credibility to Britain as a cultural powerhouse, where the music industry had been traditionally dominated by the United States. This provided an avenue for subsequent British acts to establish a base in the United States, albeit with mixed degrees of success in the decades that followed.

Much of the debate surrounding the British Invasion focuses on the extent to which the rock music stars of the 1960s were actually that different from their American counterparts. Indeed, it is clear that many of the acts arising from the Merseybeat scene and other movements of 1960s Britain took inspiration from American genres and movements, including rock and roll, Motown, and American folk. This approach, however, oversimplifies the nature and significance of the British Invasion as a cultural phenomenon: rather than seeing it as a wholesale 'invasion,' it should perhaps be regarded as a synthesis of British and American influences and styles, formed in a process of cross-Atlantic dialogue, and popularised in the United States.

The British Invasion represented a defining moment in 1960s counter culture and gave voice to a generation of Americans seeking new forms of expression. The iconic images, styles, and sounds of the 1960s were defined by this cultural profusion that found its niche in the collision of British and American styles.

92. 10 BRITISH SHOWS FOR POLITICS JUNKIES

General Elections are always interesting times in the British political calendar. There is no shortage of British TV shows centered on politics. Here's a list of our favorites if you want a keen understanding of all things British politics.

HOUSE OF CARDS

Many fans of the Netflix House of Cards may not know that the show was actually based on a British TV show of the same name. The premise is the same – the antihero of House of Cards is Francis Urquhart, a fictional Chief Whip of the Conservative Party, played by Ian Richardson. The plot follows his amoral and manipulative scheme to become the leader of the governing party and, thus, Prime Minister of the United Kingdom. If you love the Kevin Spacey version, you'll love this just as much.

A VERY BRITISH COUP

This classic drama is very much a product of its time – the late 1980's Thatcher years. Harry Perkins, an unassuming, working-class, very left-wing Leader of the Labour Party and Member of Parliament for Sheffield Central, becomes Prime Minister in March 1991. The priorities of the Perkins Government include dissolving all newspaper monopolies, withdrawal from the North Atlantic Alliance, removing all American military bases on UK soil, unilateral nuclear disarmament, and true open government. Newspaper magnate Sir George Fison, with allies within British political and civil service circles, moves immediately to discredit him, with the United States the key, but covert, conspirator. The most effective of the Prime Minister's domestic enemies is the aristocratic Sir Percy Browne, Head of MI5, whose ancestors "unto the Middle Ages" have exercised subtle power behind the scenes. However, Harry finds support in Joan Cook, a loyal Member of Parliament (MP) and Home Secretary; and Thompson, Perkins' Press Secretary; Inspector Page, his Head of Security and Sir Montague Kowalski, the Government Chief Scientific Adviser. It provides an intimate view of the machinations of a particularly British political conspiracy. Well worth a watch.

YES (PRIME) MINISTER

This is my most favorite British TV show of all time. Jim Hacker is a newly minted government minister who faces opposition and manipulation from Humphrey Appleby, a civil servant who does the real governing. The show is very funny and also a product of its time (Thatcher was said to be a fan). The show traces Hacker all the way to the top (where the show becomes Yes, Prime Minister).

THE POLITICIAN'S HUSBAND

This short drama series follows David Tennant as he plays the scheming husband of a politician on the rise. After his role in Doctor Who, it's amazing to watch Tennant take such a deliciously evil turn.

THE RISE AND FALL OF MARGARET THATCHER

If you were disappointed by Meryl Streep as Margaret Thatcher a few years ago, you'll defiantly enjoy this set of three dramas set at different stages during Thatcher's career. This box set features three BBC telemovies that Thatcher factors into as a central character. First up is the 2008 Margaret Thatcher – The Long Walk to Finchley, starring Andrea Riseborough as a young Thatcher, a chemist working her way up the parliamentary ladder. Next on the program is 2002's The Falklands Play, starring Patricia Hodge as Thatcher in a dramatization of the backstage intrigues that belied the Falklands War of 1982. Finally, 2009's Margaret stars Lindsay Duncan as the Iron Lady, in an intimate saga dramatizing the political machinations and maneuvering that led to Thatcher's downfall. Not currently streaming, but you can pick up the US DVD on Amazon.

WINSTON CHURCHILL: WILDERNESS YEARS

The story of Winston Churchill's life between 1929, when he lost his cabinet position, and 1939, when he joined Great Britain's War Cabinet – a period he described as the most difficult in his life. It's an 8 part series and was well regarded when it aired in 1981. This series is harder to find, but it's on DVD in the UK. I've seen it, and it's quite good. If you can't find it – give The Gathering Storm a try – it's about the same period but is in 1 film package. They also appear to be on YouTube.

THE THICK OF IT

Before he was The Doctor, Peter Capaldi was Malcolm Tucker, the foul-mouthed spin doctor in the modern equivalent to Yes Minister. We follow the bumbling machinations of a government minister as he is pulled in different directions by his lackeys and Malcolm Tucker. Also, check out In The Loop, a feature film set in the same universe but with actors playing different characters (except Malcolm Tucker).

NO JOB FOR A LADY

Jean Price is the idealistic, newly-elected Labour Party Member of Parliament for a deprived inner-city constituency. She must try to balance her work with her family life, learn the ways of the House and try to keep her principles.

THE AMAZING MRS PRITCHARD

This delightful show was created in 2006 and doesn't take itself too seriously, but it's still a lot of fun. The story follows Mrs. Ros Pritchard, a successful manager of a supermarket. When a couple of politicians make a spectacle of themselves outside her shop, Ros decides to stand for election herself, just to prove that she could do better. Her story grips the nation, and eight weeks later, no one is more surprised than Ros herself when she wins the General Election and becomes the next Prime Minister. How will power change her and her family? Also, a young Carey Mulligan stars in one of her first roles.

STATE OF PLAY

This was recently remade into a movie starring Ben Affleck, but the original British drama is a fantastic political thriller. A thriller set in London, in which a politician's life becomes increasingly complex as his research assistant is found dead on the London Underground and, in a seemingly unrelated incident, a teenage pickpocket is shot dead. Lots of British acting greats star in this short series, including John Simm, Philip Glenister, Billy Nighy, and David Morrissey.

93. WHAT IS THE BOAT RACE?

Every spring on the Thames, a rivalry going back almost 800 years is played out. It can be high drama as the teams battle the weather, each other and sometimes public interlopers. I'm talking about, of course, the Oxford Cambridge Boat Races. This major event pits the men's and women's rowing teams against each other on a grueling 4.2 mile long trip up the Thames. The race is a scene of high drama every year and is exhilarating to watch. We've gathered together ten interesting facts about the race you might not know.

WAR DEFERMENT

The men's race was first held in 1829 and has been held annually since 1856, except during the first and second World Wars. Due to the Coronavirus pandemic, it was canceled in 2020 as well.

LADIES, TOO

The first women's race was in 1927 and has been held annually since 1964. A big change came in 2015 when the women's race was now held on the same day as the men's on the same course (the ladies go first).

THE COURSE

The course covers a 4.2-mile (6.8 km) stretch of the Thames in West London, from Putney to Mortlake. It's possible to go down to the riverside and watch the race go by. The boats are usually followed by a flotilla of boats with judges and film crews. It's quite a sight to see! In 2021, the race was held in the Cambridgeshire fens on the River Ouse. The 2022 race may have to relocate to somewhere else as well due to emergency structural work on Hammersmith Bridge on the Thames.

THE BLUES

This one is confusing. The official color of Oxford is blue. The official color of Cambridge is blue. They only differ in the shade. Oxford Blue is a dark blue, and Cambridge Blue is might lighter – more a pastel teal.

WINS AND LOSSES

As of 2021, Cambridge has won the race 85 times, and Oxford has won it 80 times in the men's race. There was one dead heat in 1877. In the women's race, Cambridge has won 45 times and Oxford 30 times.

MILLIONS AND MILLIONS

Fifteen million people regularly watch the race on television, making this one of the biggest sporting events in Britain every year. It also marks the beginning of 'The Season,' the calendar of upper-class social events that coincide, such as Ascot, Wimbledon, etc.

THE OFFICIAL NAME?

Initially, it was always called 'The Boat Race.' Then it became 'The Boat Races' when the women's race was included. Due to sponsorship, the name changes almost everywhere. In 2021, it was the Gemini Boat Races.

SINKINGS

The Thames can be a temperamental beast, and the race usually goes on no matter how choppy the water is or how rainy it is. This leads to sinking. In the 1912 race, run in extremely poor weather and high winds, both crews sank. Cambridge also sank in 1859 and in 1978, while Oxford did so in 1925 and again in 1951; the 1951 race was re-rowed on the following Monday. In 1984 the Cambridge boat sank after colliding with a barge before the start of the race, which was then rescheduled for the next day. In 2016, at Barnes Bridge, the Cambridge women began to sink and received advice from the umpire to pull to the side. The Cambridge cox indicated that she wanted to continue to complete the course and was allowed to do so (total jerk move).

TRAINING

The crews spend most of the year training for this race. They have dedicated team management and workout spaces. They're often the top athletes in the rowing field (often they're Olympians), and many come to Oxford or Cambridge just to do the race (while doing their advanced studies). It's not uncommon for the teams to be made up of multiple nationalities – there is almost always at least one American in each boat, sometimes more.

DISRUPTION

In 2012's race, an Australian chap swam into the course and disrupted the race (almost getting his head chopped off in the process). Trenton Oldfield was protesting against spending cuts and what he saw as the erosion of civil liberties and a growing culture of elitism within British society. The race was stopped for 30 minutes while he was fished out of the water. After the race restarted, the boats clashed, and an oar was broken. Its safe to say, the whole race was a disaster, and it was high drama on the Thames. Cambridge eventually won. Oldfield was later tried and convicted of causing a public nuisance, fined £750, and sentenced to 6 months in prison. He was almost deported from Britain in 2013 because of the conviction but won the right to stay (with his English wife and child) on appeal.

WORLDWIDE AUDIENCE

The BBC is the official broadcaster of the race, and they broadcast it worldwide. It's usually broadcast live on the BBC World News Channel, which is available in the USA and available in many other countries and territories. It's also usually streamed online for free in some fashion. It's worth watching! If you're ever in London in early April, definitely make an effort to see the race in person. It's a lot of fun!

And whom does Anglotopia root for every year? The Oxford Blues, of course. GO OXFORD!

94. 10 BRITISH COMEDIES

I've seen dozens of British comedies over the years. More than I can count! But I have ten personal favorites that I think would be instructive for all Anglophiles to watch. These shows are streaming regularly, but we're not going to note whereas it will change rather quickly. We recommend using the app JustWatch to keep up with where your favorite shows are streaming. Or get them on DVD, our preferred way to own great British media!

REV.

Rev. is a delightful comedy starring Tom Hollander and Olivia Colman. It's about a Church of England priest who comes to an inner-city flock in London. It has a fascinating rotating cast of characters and deals with some heavy, philosophical ideas. Tom Hollander excels as the morose priest, Olivia Colman, is magnificent as his long-suffering wife. It's funny, dark, and magnificent – one of the finest British comedies to come out of Britain in the last few years.

MIRANDA

You may recognize Miranda Hart from her dramatic role on Call, the Midwife, but she's a seasoned comedian, and her show is a delight.

The series is based on Hart's semi-autobiographical writing, following a television pilot and the BBC Radio 2 comedy Miranda Hart's Joke Shop. The various episodes revolve around this setup and the scenarios Miranda gets herself into. Miranda (Miranda Hart) is 6 feet 1 inch (1.85 m) tall and gets called 'Sir' once too often. She has never fitted in with her old boarding school friends, Tilly (Sally Phillips) and Fanny (Katy Wix), and finds social situations awkward, especially around men. She is a constant disappointment to her mother, Penny (Patricia Hodge), who is desperate for her to get a proper job and a husband. It's a great show!

THE INBETWEENERS

Warning: This show is extremely vulgar. But also amazing. The show follows the life of suburban teenager Will McKenzie (Simon Bird) and three of his friends at the fictional Rudge Park Comprehensive. The episodes involved situations of school bullying, broken family life, indifferent school staff, male bonding, and largely failed sexual encounters. It's hilarious, and the use of foul language is simply amazing.

THE VICAR OF DIBLEY

The Vicar of Dibley is a BBC television sitcom created by Richard Curtis (Love Actually) and written for its lead actress, Dawn French, by Curtis and Paul Mayhew-Archer, with contributions from Kit Hesketh-Harvey. It aired from 1994 to 2007. The Vicar of Dibley was set in a fictional small Oxfordshire village called Dibley, which is assigned a female vicar following the 1992 changes in the Church of England that permitted the ordination of women. The main character was an invention of Richard Curtis, but he and Dawn French extensively consulted the Revd Joy Carroll, one of the first female priests, and garnered many character traits and much information.

GAVIN AND STACEY

The show follows the romance between Gavin from Billericay in Essex, and Stacey, from Barry in the Vale of Glamorgan. Initially, Gavin lives with his parents, Pam and Mick, and spends his time with his best friend, Smithy. Stacey lives with her widowed mother, Gwen, but is frequently visited by her Uncle Bryn and her best friend, Nessa. The series follows the key moments in their relationship; as they have their first meeting, meet each other's families, become engaged, get married, look for a house, briefly split up, look for new jobs, and try to conceive. This show is really about the ensemble casts of characters, and it's a true delight.

PEEP SHOW

This is one of Mrs. Anglotopia's and I's favorite shows of all time. Peep Show is a British sitcom starring David Mitchell and Robert Webb. The television program is written by Jesse Armstrong and Sam Bain, with additional material by Mitchell and Webb, amongst others. Peep Show follows the lives of two men from their twenties to thirties. Mark Corrigan (Mitchell), who has steady employment for most of the series, and Jeremy "Jez" Osbourne (Webb), an unemployed would-be musician, are the main characters of the show. The pair met at the fictional Dartmouth University and now share a flat in Croydon, South London. This show was made for binge-watching.

BLACK BOOKS

Black Books is a British sitcom created by Dylan Moran and Graham Linehan that was broadcast on Channel 4 from 2000 to 2004. Starring Moran, Bill Bailey, and Tamsin Greig, the series is set in the eponymous London bookshop Black Books and follows the lives of its owner Bernard Black (Moran), his assistant Manny Bianco (Bailey), and their friend Fran Katzenjammer (Greig). It's like Notting Hill but funnier and somewhat dark.

COUPLING

This show has often been called the British version of Friends, but that sells it rather short as the show is way funnier and way edgier. Coupling is a British television sitcom written by Steven Moffat that aired on BBC2 from 12 May 2000 to 14 June 2004. Produced by Hartswood Films for the BBC, the show centers on the dating and sexual adventures and mishaps of six friends in their thirties, often depicting the three women and the three men each talking among themselves about the same events, but in entirely different terms. The show is somewhat based on the love life of show creator Steven Moffat – who's more famous now as the showrunner of Doctor Who (and it's fun to spot all the Who references in the show).

RED DWARF

As a bit of a sci-fi geek, Red Dwarf is one of my favorites. Red Dwarf tells the adventures of the last human alive and his friends, stranded three million years into deep space on the mining ship Red Dwarf.

THE THICK OF IT

This is a great show for those interested in the mess that is politics. It's one of our favorites and stars an ensemble cast of inept British government apparatchiks who attempt to mostly save their own butts. The star of the show is by far Malcolm Tucker played brilliantly by Peter Capaldi. His ability to swear is a gift, and like The Inbetweeners above, you will hear swear words used in a way you never thought possible. It's a fantastic show and an excellent insight into modern British politics.

THE IT CROWD

This comedy is set in the IT department of a British corporation, with an interesting cast of characters in Roy and Moss, who are managed by Jen, who knows nothing about computers. Their zany adventures become more about hilarity than IT, but it's led to some very popular commons jokes about computers that have endured almost 20 years later. If I'm ever feeling down, this comedy will definitely put me in a better mood!

YES (PRIME) MINISTER

This is my all-time favorite British comedy. It's a fascinating education in government, how it works, politics, and scheming politicians. It's a window into life in Britain in the 1980s and reflects a lot of the attitudes of the British civil service that still apply even today. The show started out following Jim Hacker as the hapless new Minister of Administrative Affairs. His foil is Sir Humphrey Appleby, the perfect caricature of a civil servant trying to prevent the minister from ever doing anything. The 'straight man' is Bernard Wooley, who is always available for a pithy remark. The show evolved into 'Yes, Prime Minister' when Hacker manages to become Prime Minister.

GHOSTS

This is one of my favorite 'new' British comedies (it premiered only in 2019). It follows a young British couple who happen to inherit a beautiful and crumbling old stately home. The problem is that it's haunted by all the people who died associated with the house, who become visible only to the main character. The Ghosts at first do everything they can to stop the couple from turning the place into a hotel. Come for the stately home stuff and stay for the interesting backstories of the ghosts and how they ended up dead. It's funny, mildly scaring and fascinating.

95. BBC 101

While no longer alone amongst Britain's media powerhouses, at one time, the British Broadcasting Corporation (BBC) was the only game in town. Since its incorporation in 1922, the corporation has been responsible for informing and entertaining the British public, tasks for which it continues to excel at 95 years later. Over this time, the BBC has provided not only the United Kingdom but the world with reliable news and some of mankind's most legendary programs from "Doctor Who" to "Monty Python's Flying Circus." Its personnel have influenced radio and television, and its buildings are some of the most famous in Britain. As we delve into the near-century long broadcasting history of the BBC, we invite you, dear reader, to join us on a journey from the first radio signal to the present and discover what a fascinating chronicle this media giant possesses.

The United Kingdom's first radio broadcast took place in June 1920 at the Marconi factory, and from there, radio became so prolific a communication tool that the General Post Office had to step in as the licensing official to control the growth of the medium. By 1922, the GPO had more than 100 requests for licenses from manufacturers and other organizations, and so to ensure a measured development of radio broadcasts, the GPO recommended issuing only one license to a consortium of manufacturers (including Marconi) under the title of the British Broadcasting Company, Ltd. The company formed officially on

18 October 1922 and made its first broadcast on channel 2LO from the seventh floor of Marconi House on 14 November that year.

To head this new broadcasting conglomerate, the government-appointed John Reith as the first General Manager for the BBC in mid-December 1922. Mr. Reith had served in the army during World War I and had had no experience in broadcasting before applying for the manager post on seeing a newspaper advertisement for the position. He was admittedly out of his depth for the position, having to deal with copyrights, patents, music publishers, artists' associations, performance rights, and more, though he felt he had the credentials to "manage any company" given his military background. Despite this lack of prior experience, he proved to be an immensely capable manager who helped shape the BBC during its formative years and remained in charge until 1938. Making up the rules as he went along, Reith proved an innovative leader who had to use his army engineer's background to craft standards and practices that the corporation would follow for decades.

In September 1923, one of the BBC's most influential documents began publication with the first issue of the Radio Times. The periodical provided a schedule of the corporation's limited programs but also served as an educational resource for budding amateur enthusiasts as well as carrying the manufacturers' advertisements for the newest radio equipment. The RT was also the only place to find the radio schedule, as newspapers viewed it as a competing medium and thus refused to publish it. The magazine began as a joint effort between the BBC and publisher George Newnes, and the latter type-set printed and distributed the RT himself until the corporation bought the publication fully under its control in 1925.

The BBC's first major test came during the General Strike in 1926. At the time, the BBC was in renegotiations with the GPO over its license, an issue that was left up to the Crawford Committee. Several of the manufacturers wanted out due to the unprofitable nature of the consortium, while Reith wanted the BBC to become a public service. Reith wanted the BBC to maintain its monopoly and serve the public interest, feeling its expansion should be funded by the government for the general welfare.

Meanwhile, the General Council of the Trades Union Congress was trying to get the British government to stop wage reduction and improve the conditions for the nation's coal miners. Negotiations between the TUC and the government broke down, and the strike began on 3 May 1926. The strike had the effect of temporarily halting newspaper production, rendering the BBC the only source of regular news.

Behind closed doors, Reith was firmly on the side of the government with regards to the strike, even letting the Prime Minister broadcast from his own home. This helped to keep the government out of the BBC's business insofar as it did not attempt to use the radio service as its mouthpiece. The BBC then presented some of the most even coverage of the strike, representing the viewpoints of both the workers and the government during the work stoppage. This cemented the BBC's audience as well as establishing its reputation for fair and balanced reporting. The company came out of 1926 in a strong position, and the Government accepted the Crawford Committee's recommendation that the BBC have a new status as a non-commercial, Crown-chartered organization in 1927, then becoming the British Broadcasting Corporation. The original 1927 charter established objectives, powers, and obligations of the BBC, entrusting John Reith as its Director-General to execute the document's provisions.

1928 would see another leap for the BBC as construction began on Broadcasting House. The corporation had operated its radio broadcasts out of Marconi House and buildings in the Strand and Savoy Hill, but Broadcasting House would be its first purpose-built headquarters for radio broadcasting. G. Val Mayer designed it in an Art Deco style for the exterior, while Raymond McGrath designed the interior in a similar vein. Its Portland stone structure contained all the studios, and the building's steel shell provided acoustic "buffering." For a time, its construction was held up as nearby residents were concerned about it blocking the natural light for their homes on Langham Street. It took four years to complete, and programs slowly began moving over in 1932, with the first broadcast being that of Henry Hall and the BBC Dance Orchestra on 15 March. That same year, King George V would become the first monarch to use radio as a broadcast medium to reach his subjects.

Meanwhile, as Broadcasting House was going up, something else revolutionary was being born. Scottish engineer John Logie Baird had been experimenting with television since 1924, beaming the first images across a room and later demonstrated his experiments at Selfridge's and the Royal Institution. He also used BBC frequencies to broadcast some of his images from studios at Covent Garden in 1929. In 1930, he would broadcast the BBC's first televised drama, "The Man with the Flower in His Mouth," ushering in the television era for the broadcaster. Baird's technology could only broadcast thirty lines of resolution, as opposed to 2,160 lines of resolution by the latest 4K televisions. Limited regular broadcasts then began in 1934, and the BBC established its first television studio at Alexandra Palace in 1936, along with starting the BBC Television Service.

By 1937, technology advanced enough that televisions had 405 lines of resolution. 1937 would also see the BBC's first outside television broadcast as the corporation filmed the coronation of King George VI. Unfortunately, the outbreak of World War II in 1939 would see a suspension of the television service for the duration of the conflict. In response to the danger presented by the London Blitz, the BBC would move much of its radio broadcasting out of London to Bristol and then

Bedford. St. Paul's Church in Bedford actually became the home studio for the daily service until 1945. The BBC Television Service would resume on 7 June 1946 with Jasmine Bligh as the first presenter back on the air. October 1946 would see the beginning of television programming dedicated solely to children, with shows such as "Muffin the Mule" being broadcast from the corporation's new television studios at Lime Grove.

One of the biggest changes to the BBC to occur post-war was the introduction of the television license. As mentioned earlier, at the advent of the company back in 1922, the General Post Office was responsible for issuing licenses to amateur and professional radio operators. Besides broadcasting, those who wanted to receive radio broadcasts paid a fee of 10 shillings. With the resumption of the BBC Television Service in 1946, the Post Office merged the receiving radio broadcast license with television reception, and the cost for both was a mere £2 (roughly £76 today). With the advent of color television in the 1960s (more on that later), a surcharge was added to cover the new technology. The cost has subsequently risen nearly every year, though the license fee was frozen in 2016 at £145.50 while the BBC's Charter was renegotiated and now sits at £147 as of April 2017. While some try to get by without the license, the penalty for owning a television and not having a license is roughly £1,000 plus any incidental legal costs and compensation.

Television would only grow as a medium, with Newsreel beginning in January 1948 and the first televised Olympic Games in the summer. While only 100,000 British homes had televisions by this time, the BBC still broadcast 68.5 hours of live coverage during the games. The next year would see the return of live weather broadcasts that had been pursued tepidly before the war. Things were relatively quiet until ITV came along in 1955 to challenge the BBC's monopoly on the television airwaves. The new company was a direct result of the Television Act 1954, which created the Independent Television Authority (later the Independent Broadcast Authority) to regulate the growing medium and license franchises. More insight into the government was provided during the 1950s as the first live broadcast proceedings of the House of Commons were made in 1950, and the coronation of Queen Elizabeth II was transmitted in 1953.

One major event that took place in 1956 was the establishment of the Radiophonic Workshop. The workshop was established because the BBC wanted to develop its own music and sound effects for the radio and television programs it produced. The workshop would craft some of the most innovative sounds over the next few decades, including Doctor Who's famous TARDIS dematerialization sound effect and the program's theme tune. The Radiophonic Workshop would not close up shop until 1993 when the corporation determined the department was no longer viable. In 1958, one of the BBC's most important children's programs would be born when "Blue Peter" premiered on 16 October. Head of

Children's Television at the time, Owen Reed, wanted a program that catered to children ages 5 to 8 and represented a "voyage of adventure." Still running today, it would have a major influence with lines such as "And now for something completely different" and the famed Blue Peter Badge becoming established parts of British culture.

Blue Peter would also become one of the first television programs to move into the famed BBC Television Centre when it opened in 1960. Much like Broadcasting House before it, Television Centre was purpose-built for TV broadcasting. The building was designed by Graham Dawborn, who was initially stumped by having to design a building for the triangular property. The story goes that he went to a local pub where he drew the boundaries of the land on an envelope with a big question mark over it. This ended up becoming the basis for his design that would permit eight TV studios, offices, production galleries, recording studios, and separate entrances for guests and delivery trucks.

Construction on Television Centre actually began in 1950, but government restrictions on the building made the process a lengthy one. The sanctions on building and the licensing of materials stopped the construction until 1953, and in the meantime, the BBC opted to renovate its studios at Lime Grove, Hammersmith, and Shepard's Bush Empire. Stage One, including the TVC scenery block, was the first part of the center built, while Stage 2 and the canteen block followed in 1954. The next year would see work begin on the circular office block that composed Stage 3. By the time the building opened in 1960, studio TC3 was the first to be completed. The studio would become home to many of the BBC's most famous programs from "Monty Python's Flying Circus" to "Strictly Come Dancing."

When the Independent Television Authority determined that ITV didn't have enough quality programming, it gave the license for a new television station to the BBC, ultimately creating BBC Two in 1964. The new station caused the name of BBC Television Service to change to BBC One. BBC One would become the home to most of the mainstream and popular programs over the years, while BBC Two was populated with the more intellectual programs and films, including documentaries such as "The Ascent of Man," and eventually automotive magazine "Top Gear." BBC Two would also become a testing ground for other shows that would eventually move to BBC One, such as "Have I Got News for You" and "The Great British Bakeoff." The channel later broadcast the corporation's first dedicated block of morning children's programming, which would eventually evolve into CBBC and CBeebies.

Science-Fiction television programming would change forever in 1963. The BBC's then Head of Drama, Sydney Newman, wanted a new program that would help teach kids about history by using time travel. The program that he eventually developed with the corporation's first female producer, Verity Lambert, would become the worldwide phenomenon that is "Doctor Who." Featuring the alien known as The Doctor, his granddaughter Susan, and her teachers Ian and Barbara, the first episode hit a stumbling block as it was overshadowed by news concerning the death of US President John F. Kennedy when it premiered the same week. The first episode was rebroadcast a week later, but the program really took off with the introduction of the Doctor's most famous enemies, the Daleks. After leading actor William Hartnell was forced to leave the show in 1966 due to ill health, the writers came up with the concept of regeneration so that Doctor Who could continue with a new actor as the Doctor. This plot device kept the original version of the show going until 1987, coming back for a 1996 television pilot film and the current program that began in 2005.

1966 would also see another major innovation for the BBC with the advent of color television. The corporation announced that it would soon bring color to television screens in 1966, though it would be another year before its first colorized broadcast to the public. The BBC had actually experimented with color transmissions for the first time in 1957 with broadcasts made to both houses of Parliament, but would not bring the technology to the masses for another nine years. BBC Two was the first to experiment with color broadcasts when it televised Wimbledon with the new technology on 1 July 1967. BBC Two Controller David Attenborough said at the time that at least five hours of programming per week would be dedicated to color, but by December, 80% of the channels shows were in color. At the time, a color receiver cost about £250 along with the supplemental license fee. Color would be extended to BBC One in 1969 and was completely in effect by 1976.

Local radio stations such as Radio London also began to appear at the time, spurred on by the existence of pirate radio ships. These maverick stations, such as Radio Caroline, were headquartered on ships anchored in the North Sea and broadcast popular music that wasn't as widely available on BBC Radio. As they weren't government-sponsored, they also featured copious amounts of advertising that eventually forced the BBC to permit nationally based advertising services. The corporation was also encouraged to diversify its broadcasts across multiple stations, having Radio 1 play popular music to compete with the pirates, Radio 2 featured "easy listening," Radio 3 had classical music and cultural programming, and Radio 4 focused primarily on news and information.

The 1970s continued to push innovation as the BBC partnered with Open University to bring higher education to the masses through early morning and late-night educational programs. Even today, Open University and the BBC's partnership continues to bring new ways of learning to the public through online videos that cover everything from the color spectrum to how cars are built. 1972 saw the introduction of news programming aimed at children and young people called "Newsround." With John Craven at the helm, "Newsround" brought kids current events from all over the world and even broke news stories such as Pope John Paul II's assassination and the Challenger explosion. 1974 then saw the introduction of Ceefax. Ceefax was a Teletext service that originally begun as a captioning system for the corporation's programs but grew to provide full pages of information on news, sports, and more. It ceased to be used in 2012 when the information service switched over to being completely digital.

Many of the BBC's most endearing television programs also got their start in the 1970s. Leaving Monty Python to follow his own path, John Cleese started the show "Fawlty Towers" with his then-wife Connie Booth. Other comedies such as "Are You Being Served?", "Last of the Summer Wine" and "Porridge" also kept audiences laughing. However, comedy wasn't the only new programming that got the viewer's attention. Now known the world over for his exceptional nature documentaries, David Attenborough began broadcasting his "Life of Earth" series in 1979, which led to decades of bringing the true majesty of nature to the public.

The 1980s marked new challenges for the United Kingdom and the BBC. With the premiership of Margaret Thatcher beginning in 1979, her Conservative government brought a wave of deregulation that further loosened the BBC's grip on the radio and television industries in Britain. Under the Broadcasting Act 1980, the Independent Broadcasting Authority became further empowered to create another TV license. Competitor ITV was joined by the commercially-sponsored Channel 4 in 1982 and its Welsh counterpart, S4C. However, audiences were still tuning into the BBC in droves thanks to new programs such as "Eastenders" and "Breakfast Time," as well as major events including the Falklands War, Live Aid, and the Wedding of Prince Charles to Diana Spencer, the non-royal who became beloved as the "People's Princess."

New technology drove innovation in the 1990s. The 24-hour news stations that had become popular in the United States convinced the BBC to launch its own constant news channel in 1997. While the BBC was only second to get into the game in Britain, BBC News 24 immediately made its impact in a world where constant access to the news was becoming necessary to keep the public informed. BBC Radio also expanded itself to BBC Radio 5, which also covered news, opinion, and sports in 1994. 1997 saw the advent of the BBC's website, bbc.co.uk, and the corporation provided its first digital channel the next year with BBC Choice. Choice not only offered news and information on demand but also played host to many "behind the scenes" shows that let audiences in on how their favorite programs were made. This station became BBC Three in 2003, airing more innovative programs such as "The Mighty Boosh" and "Being Human" until it was finally closed in 2016, becoming a web-only service.

As the British government instituted a devolution of its powers at the beginning of the millennium to national assemblies in Wales, Scotland, and Northern Ireland, so the BBC split off some of its responsibilities to regional branches in Cardiff, Glasgow, and Belfast. This meant that the regional headquarters had more ability to produce their own programs not only for local audiences but for national consumption as well. This was perhaps best exemplified by the revival of "Doctor Who" in 2005, which was produced and largely filmed at BBC Broadcasting House Cardiff. Meanwhile, much of the original drama and comedy production moved to Broadcasting House Belfast, and much of the national television production, including many beloved panel shows, started to be done out of BBC Pacific Quay, which opened in 2007. BBC North also gained expansive responsibilities in the mid-2000s at New Broadcasting House in Manchester. Other regions under the corporation purview include BBC West, BBC North West, and BBC Yorkshire, amongst others.

The digital frontier was even more firmly embraced come the 2000s as iPlayer was launched so that anyone could view BBC programs on the computers and electronic devices; that way, they wouldn't miss a moment of the revived "Strictly Come Dancing." The "Red Button" was introduced the next year that permitted viewers to get more information on the program they were watching, answer quiz questions, and interact with their shows in an all-new way. All these innovations were put to use in 2012 for the Summer Olympic Games in London and part of the revamping of Broadcasting House, which underwent a major renovation from 2003 to 2013. The new wings and renovations brought everything under one roof after Television Centre had closed in 2012. One of the best programs that really shows off the revamped Broadcasting Centre is "W1A", which features Hugh Bonneville as the new Head of Values, tasked with promoting the core purpose of the BBC while constantly flummoxed by his subordinates.

In 2016, another chapter in the ongoing saga between the BBC and the Conservative Party began as the corporation's charter was due to be renewed. The BBC's Royal Charter only lasts for ten years, thus requiring it to be renewed periodically, which naturally has a tendency towards some executive meddling by Her Majesty's government. When the charter came up for renewal most recently, some ministers desired to move the corporation away from reliance on the government, while others wanted more monitoring of the BBC's programming and approval of the charter by both the Lords and the Commons. The approved charter, while championing diversity in programming and presenters that should please regional audiences, has also been criticized for allowing communications regulator Ofcom to have more say over how the news is presented. The new charter also closed the loophole that let people watch BBC programs through iPlayer without a television license and a "unitary board," replacing the BBC Trust as the governing body of the corporation. In a further attempt to privatize the BBC's production, the charter permits private companies to have the opportunity to produce BBC programs, taking some of the shows out of the house. In one good move, the new charter will last for eleven years instead of ten to make it less likely that it will become a political football for parties to use in election years.

Even as the new charter changes the workings of broadcasting, the BBC continues on its purpose, established by John Reith at the corporation's outset, to: "Inform, educate, and entertain." Since its creation in 1932, the BBC has sought to excel in all three areas amidst improving technology and increasing competition. Today, it continues to give audiences the very best in programming with "BBC News," "Doctor Who," "EastEnders," "QI," and more. Joining forces with ITV to create Britbox, the BBC ensures that its reach continues not only across the United Kingdom but the whole world. Always embracing new technology and methods to meet its core mission, one can only imagine how the BBC will evolve to meet the needs of the future amidst its new charter.

96. SHAKESPEARE 101

Did you know there is a 'Shakespeare day?' What is Shakespeare Day? Well, April 23rd marks the day that William Shakespeare was born (though this is also disputed to the point no one knows for sure), but it's also actuality the day he died as well. Since there are hundreds of books and resources where you can learn every aspect of the Bard's life, we decided to focus on a few factoids you may not know about the Bard.

1. Shakespeare was prolific – his complete works consist of 884,647 words. Wow! When you consider they were all handwritten – you can imagine the sore wrists!

2. Shakespeare not only loved creating stories, but he also created words that didn't exist yet in the English language. In fact, he coined over 500 words – a few examples: schoolboy, lackluster, never-ending, madcap, day's work, etc.

3. He wrote 39 plays, but only 38 have survived to the modern era. The lost play? Cardenio. The content of the play is not known, but it was likely to have been based on an episode in Miguel de Cervantes' Don Quixote involving the character Cardenio, a young man who has been driven mad and lives in the Sierra Morena.

4. His longest play was 4,042 lines (Hamlet), and his short play was 1,787 (The Comedy of Errors).

5. There are no surviving Shakespeare heirs. Shakespeare and his wife Anne Hathaway had three children together – a son, Hamnet, who died in 1596, and two daughters, Susanna and Judith. His only granddaughter Elizabeth – daughter of Susanna – died childless in 1670. Shakespeare, therefore, has no descendants.

6. He was an Actor's Writer. Shakespeare's profession was acting. He is listed in documents of 1592, 1598, and 1603 as an actor. We know that he acted in a Ben Jonson play and also in his own plays, but it's thought that, as a very busy man, writing, managing the theatre, and commuting between London and his home in Stratford where his family was, he didn't undertake big parts. There is evidence that he played the ghost in Hamlet and Adam in As You Like It.

7. He never went beyond grammar school, probably finishing in his early to mid-teens. In those days, grammar school was way more advanced than now: Students learned Latin, math, and religion; they read classical literature and studied using a hornbook (paper glued to a piece of wood and covered with a clear animal horn).

8. Shakespeare is the most translated author ever. His work is read in at least 80 languages, including Klingon, Chinese, Italian, Armenian, Bengali, Tagalog, Uzbek, and Krio (spoken by freed slaves in Sierra Leone).

9. There is a portion of his life we know nothing about. To the dismay of his biographers, Shakespeare disappears from the historical record between 1585, when his twins' baptism was recorded, and 1592, when the playwright Robert Greene denounced him in a pamphlet as an "upstart crow." The insult suggests he'd already made a name for himself on the London stage by then. What did the newly married father and future literary icon do during those seven "lost" years? Historians have speculated that he worked as a schoolteacher, studied law, traveled across continental Europe, or joined an acting troupe that was passing through Stratford.

10. We're probably not spelling his name correctly. When you look at his own signatures from his life and from contemporaries who wrote about him – the name spelled is differently more than 80 times.

11. The epitaph on his grave has a curse in it to deter grave robbers: 'Good friend for Iesvs sake forbeare, To dig the dust enclosed here. Beste be ye man yt spares these stones, And curst be he yt moves my bones.' He is buried at the Holy Trinity Church in Stratford-upon-Avon.

97. GOING TO THE CINEMA

One of the most fascinating things about Britain is how different something so simple can be. Such as: going to the movies. It's completely different in Britain. So, how is going to the movies different in the UK?

IT'S THE CINEMA, NOT THE MOVIES

Up first is the linguistic usages. They don't call them 'movies' in the UK – they call them films. They also don't call it a movie theater; they call it a cinema. So, you go see a film at a cinema. You don't go see a movie at a movie theater. It's a minor difference, but a big one when searching for film tickets/directions on Google UK (searching for movie tickets will get you strange results and not what you're looking for).

BOOKING YOUR SEAT

While you don't have to book in advance for your film, it's advisable to get the best seat and make sure you can get into the popular shows. That said, when you book a ticket, whether it's online or at the box office, you have to choose your seat. This is the biggest difference between going to the movies in the USA versus going to the movies in the UK. Choosing your seat just makes sense. You get to sit exactly where you want, and no one else can take your seat. What's to stop you from taking someone else's seat? A very zealous staff that makes sure everyone is in the right seat.

(Editor's Note: Since this was originally written, COVID-19 hit the world, and suddenly booking your assigned seat at a theater in the USA has become part of the new normal).

TWO TIERS OF SEATING

While most of the modern multiplexes in Britain have stadium-style seating, they also offer a 'premium' option when purchasing your tickets. The ticket costs a few pounds more, but you get a larger and comfier seat that has a better view of the screen. It's one size fits all here in the States.

SWEET OR SALTY POPCORN

This really threw me for a loop. At the concession stand, the attendant asked me if I wanted my popcorn sweet or salty. What? Sweet popcorn? What is that? No thanks, I'll take the salty version.

NO BUTTER

They do not put butter (or the petrochemical concoction US theaters call butter) on their popcorn. I asked, and the concession attendant looked at me funny. So, while I had my salty popcorn, it was very dry though my arteries thanked me.

INCONSISTENT ICE IN THE DRINK

When I saw the Hobbit in London at the BFI IMAX, the attendant didn't put ice in my bucket of soda. When we saw The Railway Man at the Vue Cinema in Bristol, they put ice in the drink. So, when in the UK at the cinema perhaps ask for ice in case you might not get it.

CANDY SELECTION IS COMPLETELY DIFFERENT

The candy on offer at the concession stands is very different. While the concepts of the candy might be the same, the brands and types are all unfamiliar. I wanted gummy bears. I got something called 'wine gums,' which were close but had interesting flavors. It was fun to try something new.

THEY SERVE BEER

This was also a huge difference. They sold beer at the concession stand. I don't think I've ever been to a multiplex in America that serves beer at the movies. I know there are some artisan theaters that serve alcohol, but it's generally unheard of here. While I don't drink at all, Mrs. Anglotopia enjoyed beer and nachos, which was a strange and very American combination to find at a UK cinema. This is starting to change, though.

LOTS AND LOTS OF COMMERCIALS

Multiplexes in the USA often show commercials nowadays, but it's often during the pre-roll that shows before a movie actually starts. In the UK, you can expect 15-20 minutes of proper commercials before it even gets to the coming attractions trailers. While this would generally be annoying, we had not seen most of the commercials before, and some of them were rather clever, so we just sat back and enjoyed the show.

THE RATING SYSTEM IS DIFFERENT

The UK does not use the MPAA movie ratings systems – why would they? They have their own system that has more tiers and honestly makes a little more sense. The Railway Man had a rating of 15, meaning it was suitable for 15 years and up. In the US, I'm sure the movie will get an R rating because of the violent scenes of torture.

THE SELECTION OF FILMS IS DIFFERENT

While big-budget movies like The Hobbit opened globally the same day, not all movies get this treatment. Some are delayed based on various factors relating to international rights and local tastes. So, the selection Of movies on offer while we were in the UK was mixed between movies that opened in the US at the same time and movies that either opened in the US months ago or movies that opened in the UK first (usually UK productions) and would open in the USA later this year. There was also a healthy dose of foreign films on offer (foreign as in not British or American).

So, when you're in the UK, I would encourage you to look at the movie listings; you may find a gem that won't be showing in the US for months, and you can see it first, or you may spot a movie you missed and have a chance to see. We had a lovely time going to the cinema while we were in Britain and if you have a few hours to spare and are looking for something to do; then you can't go wrong with taking in a film.

98. TOP 100 BRITISH FILMS

In 1999, the British Film Institute released a ranked list of the top 100 British films ever made. We're going to reproduce that list here, along with handy checkboxes so you can mark off the ones you've seen (or mark off as you make your way through the list).

Rank	Movie	Year	Director
☐ 1	The Third Man	1949	Carol Reed
☐ 2	Brief Encounter	1945	David Lean
☐ 3	Lawrence of Arabia	1962	David Lean
☐ 4	The 39 Steps	1935	Alfred Hitchcock
☐ 5	Great Expectations	1946	David Lean
☐ 6	Kind Hearts and Coronets	1949	Robert Hamer
☐ 7	Kes	1969	Ken Loach
☐ 8	Don't Look Now	1973	Nicolas Roeg
☐ 9	The Red Shoes	1948	Powell and Pressburger
☐ 10	Trainspotting	1996	Danny Boyle
☐ 11	The Bridge on the River Kwai	1957	David Lean
☐ 12	if....	1968	Lindsay Anderson

☐ 13	The Ladykillers	1955	Alexander Mackendrick
☐ 14	Saturday Night and Sunday Morning	1960	Karel Reisz
☐ 15	Brighton Rock	1947	John Boulting
☐ 16	Get Carter	1971	Mike Hodges
☐ 17	The Lavender Hill Mob	1951	Charles Crichton
☐ 18	Henry V	1944	Laurence Olivier
☐ 19	Chariots of Fire	1981	Hugh Hudson
☐ 20	A Matter of Life and Death	1946	Powell and Pressburger
☐ 21	The Long Good Friday	1980	John Mackenzie
☐ 22	The Servant	1963	Joseph Losey
☐ 23	Four Weddings and a Funeral	1994	Mike Newell
☐ 24	Whisky Galore!	1949	Alexander Mackendrick
☐ 25	The Full Monty	1997	Peter Cattaneo
☐ 26	The Crying Game	1992	Neil Jordan
☐ 27	Doctor Zhivago	1965	David Lean
☐ 28	Monty Python's Life of Brian	1979	Terry Jones
☐ 29	Withnail and I	1987	Bruce Robinson
☐ 30	Gregory's Girl	1980	Bill Forsyth
☐ 31	Zulu	1964	Cy Endfield
☐ 32	Room at the Top	1959	Jack Clayton
☐ 33	Alfie	1966	Lewis Gilbert
☐ 34	Gandhi	1982	Richard Attenborough
☐ 35	The Lady Vanishes	1938	Alfred Hitchcock
☐ 36	The Italian Job	1969	Peter Collinson
☐ 37	Local Hero	1983	Bill Forsyth
☐ 38	The Commitments	1991	Alan Parker
☐ 39	A Fish Called Wanda	1988	Charles Crichton
☐ 40	Secrets & Lies	1996	Mike Leigh
☐ 41	Dr. No	1962	Terence Young
☐ 42	The Madness of King George	1994	Nicholas Hytner
☐ 43	A Man for All Seasons	1966	Fred Zinnemann
☐ 44	Black Narcissus	1947	Powell and Pressburger

☐ 45	The Life and Death of Colonel Blimp	1943	Powell and Pressburger
☐ 46	Oliver Twist	1948	David Lean
☐ 47	I'm All Right Jack	1959	John Boulting
☐ 48	Performance	1970	Nicolas Roeg and Donald Cammell
☐ 49	Shakespeare in Love	1998	John Madden
☐ 50	My Beautiful Laundrette	1985	Stephen Frears
☐ 51	Tom Jones	1963	Tony Richardson
☐ 52	This Sporting Life	1963	Lindsay Anderson
☐ 53	My Left Foot	1989	Jim Sheridan
☐ 54	Brazil	1985	Terry Gilliam
☐ 55	The English Patient	1996	Anthony Minghella
☐ 56	A Taste of Honey	1961	Tony Richardson
☐ 57	The Go-Between	1970	Joseph Losey
☐ 58	The Man in the White Suit	1951	Alexander Mackendrick
☐ 59	The Ipcress File	1965	Sidney J. Furie
☐ 60	Blow Up	1966	Michelangelo Antonioni
☐ 61	The Loneliness of the Long Distance Runner	1962	Tony Richardson
☐ 62	Sense and Sensibility	1995	Ang Lee
☐ 63	Passport to Pimlico	1949	Henry Cornelius
☐ 64	The Remains of the Day	1993	James Ivory
☐ 65	Sunday, Bloody Sunday	1971	John Schlesinger
☐ 66	The Railway Children	1970	Lionel Jeffries
☐ 67	Mona Lisa	1986	Neil Jordan
☐ 68	The Dam Busters	1955	Michael Anderson
☐ 69	Hamlet	1948	Laurence Olivier
☐ 70	Goldfinger	1964	Guy Hamilton
☐ 71	Elizabeth	1998	Shekhar Kapur
☐ 72	Goodbye, Mr Chips	1939	Sam Wood
☐ 73	A Room with a View	1985	James Ivory
☐ 74	The Day of the Jackal	1973	Fred Zinnemann
☐ 75	The Cruel Sea	1953	Charles Frend

☐ 76	Billy Liar	1963	John Schlesinger
☐ 77	Oliver!	1968	Carol Reed
☐ 78	Peeping Tom	1960	Michael Powell
☐ 79	Far from the Madding Crowd	1967	John Schlesinger
☐ 80	The Draughtsman's Contract	1982	Peter Greenaway
☐ 81	A Clockwork Orange	1971	Stanley Kubrick
☐ 82	Distant Voices, Still Lives	1988	Terence Davies
☐ 83	Darling	1965	John Schlesinger
☐ 84	Educating Rita	1983	Lewis Gilbert
☐ 85	Brassed Off	1996	Mark Herman
☐ 86	Genevieve	1953	Henry Cornelius
☐ 87	Women in Love	1969	Ken Russell
☐ 88	A Hard Day's Night	1964	Richard Lester
☐ 89	Fires Were Started	1943	Humphrey Jennings
☐ 90	Hope and Glory	1987	John Boorman
☐ 91	My Name Is Joe	1998	Ken Loach
☐ 92	In Which We Serve	1942	Noël Coward and David Lean
☐ 93	Caravaggio	1986	Derek Jarman
☐ 94	The Belles of St Trinian's	1954	Frank Launder
☐ 95	Life Is Sweet	1990	Mike Leigh
☐ 96	The Wicker Man	1973	Robin Hardy
☐ 97	Nil by Mouth	1997	Gary Oldman
☐ 98	Small Faces	1995	Gillies Mackinnon
☐ 99	Carry On ... Up the Khyber	1968	Gerald Thomas
☐ 100	The Killing Fields	1984	Roland Joffé

99. TOP 100 BRITISH TV SHOWS

In the year 2000, the British Film Institute compiled a list of the top 100 British TV shows of all times. The list is a mixture of dramas, comedies and factual entertainment. Some have never even aired in the USA. Some have been big hits in the USA. We're reproducing the list here in a checkmark fashion so you can mark them off (though finding some of them might be a challenge). Since the list was made in 2000, we'll provide a list of our favorite British TV shows since the year 2000 below.

Rank	TV Show	Channel	Year(s)
☐ 1	Fawlty Towers	BBC2	1975–1979
☐ 2	Cathy Come Home (The Wednesday Play)[4]	BBC1	1966
☐ 3	Doctor Who	BBC1	1963–1989, 1996
☐ 4	The Naked Civil Servant	ITV (Thames Television)	1975
☐ 5	Monty Python's Flying Circus	BBC1 / BBC2	1969–1974
☐ 6	Blue Peter	BBC1	1958–
☐ 7	Boys from the Blackstuff	BBC2	1982

☐ 8	Parkinson	BBC1	1971–1982, 1987–1988, 1998–
☐ 9	Yes Minister / Yes, Prime Minister	BBC2	1980–1988
☐ 10	Brideshead Revisited	ITV (Granada)	1981
☐ 11	Abigail's Party (Play for Today) [5])	BBC1	1977
☐ 12	I, Claudius	BBC2	1976
☐ 13	Dad's Army	BBC1	1968–1977
☐ 14	The Morecambe & Wise Show	BBC2 / BBC1 / ITV (Thames)	1961–1983
☐ 15	Edge of Darkness	BBC2	1985
☐ 16	Blackadder Goes Forth	BBC1	1989
☐ 17	Absolutely Fabulous	BBC2 / BBC1	1992–1996
☐ 18	The Wrong Trousers	BBC2	1993
☐ 19	The World at War	ITV (Thames)	1973–1974
☐ 20	The Singing Detective	BBC1	1986
☐ 21	Pennies from Heaven	BBC1	1978
☐ 22	The Jewel in the Crown	ITV (Granada)	1984
☐ 23	Who Wants to Be a Millionaire?	ITV	1998–
☐ 24	Hancock's Half Hour	BBC	1956–1961
☐ 25	Our Friends in the North	BBC2	1996
☐ 26	28 Up	ITV (Granada)	1985
☐ 27	The War Game	BBC1	1965
☐ 28	The Magic Roundabout	BBC1	1965–1977
☐ 29	That Was the Week That Was	BBC	1962–1963
☐ 30	An Englishman Abroad	BBC1	1983
☐ 31	The Royle Family	BBC2/BBC1	1998–
☐ 32	Life on Earth	BBC2	1979
☐ 33	The Old Grey Whistle Test	BBC2	1971–1987
☐ 34	University Challenge	ITV (Granada) / BBC2	1961–1987, 1994–

☐ 35	Porridge	BBC1	1974–1977
☐ 36	Blue Remembered Hills (Play for Today)	BBC1	1979
☐ 37	Mastermind (original format)	BBC1 / BBC2	1972–1997
☐ 38	I'm Alan Partridge	BBC2	1997
☐ 39	Cracker	ITV (Granada)	1993–1996
☐ 40	Coronation Street	ITV (Granada)	1960–
☐ 41	Top of the Pops	BBC1 / BBC2	1964–
☐ 42	Inspector Morse	ITV (Central)	1987–2000
☐ 43	Grange Hill	BBC1	1978–
☐ 44	Steptoe and Son	BBC1	1962–1965, 1970–1974
☐ 45	Only Fools and Horses	BBC1	1981–1996
☐ 46	Auf Wiedersehen, Pet (series 1[citation needed])	ITV (Central)	1983
☐ 47	Tiswas	ITV (ATV)	1974–1982
☐ 48	Elgar	BBC	1962
☐ 49	Nuts in May (Play for Today)	BBC1	1976
☐ 50	Father Ted	Channel 4	1995–1998
☐ 51	The Avengers	ITV (ABC)	1961–1969
☐ 52	Tinker Tailor Soldier Spy	BBC2	1979
☐ 53	The Forsyte Saga	BBC2	1967
☐ 54	Hillsborough	ITV (Granada)	1996
☐ 55	Dennis Potter: The Last Interview (Without Walls Special)	Channel 4	1994
☐ 56	Bar Mitzvah Boy (Play for Today)	BBC1	1976
☐ 57	Edna, the Inebriate Woman (Play for Today)	BBC1	1971
☐ 58	Live Aid	BBC1 / BBC2	1985
☐ 59	World In Action	ITV (Granada)	1963–1998
☐ 60	Thunderbirds	ITV (ATV)	1965–1966
☐ 61	Talking Heads / Talking Heads 2	BBC1 / BBC2	1988 / 1998

☐ 62	Ready Steady Go!	ITV (Rediffusion)	1963–1966
☐ 63	Z-Cars	BBC1	1962–1978
☐ 64	Culloden	BBC1	1964
☐ 65	The Ascent of Man	BBC2	1973
☐ 66	A Very British Coup	Channel 4	1988
☐ 67	Civilisation	BBC2	1969
☐ 68	Prime Suspect	ITV (Granada)	1991–
☐ 69	The Likely Lads / Whatever Happened to the Likely Lads?	BBC2 / BBC1	1964–1966 /1973–1974
☐ 70	Have I Got News for You	BBC2 / BBC1	1990–
☐ 71	The Snowman	Channel 4	1982
☐ 72	Walking with Dinosaurs	BBC1	1999
☐ 73	Nineteen Eighty-Four	BBC	1954
☐ 74	The Fall and Rise of Reginald Perrin	BBC1	1976–1979
☐ 75	Quatermass and the Pit	BBC	1958–1959
☐ 76	Between The Lines	BBC1	1992–1994
☐ 77	Blind Date	ITV (LWT)	1985–
☐ 78	Talking to a Stranger (Theatre 625)	BBC2	1966
☐ 79	The Borrowers	BBC1	1992–1993
☐ 80	One Foot in the Grave	BBC1	1990–2000
☐ 81	Later... with Jools Holland	BBC2	1992–
☐ 82	Tutti Frutti	BBC2	1987
☐ 83	The Knowledge	ITV (Thames)	1979
☐ 84	House of Cards	BBC1	1990
☐ 85	This Is Your Life	BBC1 / ITV (Thames)	1955–1964, 1969–
☐ 86	The Tube	Channel 4	1982–1987
☐ 87	The Death of Yugoslavia	BBC2	1995
☐ 88	Till Death Us Do Part	BBC1	1966–1975
☐ 89	A Very Peculiar Practice	BBC1	1986–1992
☐ 90	TV Nation	BBC2	1995

☐ 91	This Life	BBC2	1996–1997
☐ 92	Death on the Rock (This Week)	ITV (Thames)	1988
☐ 93	The Nazis: A Warning from History	BBC2	1997
☐ 94	Drop the Dead Donkey	Channel 4	1990–1998
☐ 95	Arena	BBC2	1975–
☐ 96	The Railway Children	BBC1	1968
☐ 97	Teletubbies	BBC2	1997–
☐ 98	Spitting Image	ITV (Central)	1984–1996
☐ 99	Pride and Prejudice	BBC1	1995
☐ 100	Made in Britain	ITV (Central)	1982

100. TOP 100 BRITISH SONGS

Like British Film and TV, British music has had a huge impact on the world, with many of the world's most popular bands being of British origin. It's very difficult to make a 'best of' list when there's so much great British music out there, so we've opted to go with the most popular music based on sales. This list was originally compiled by Billboard and represented the most popular British music sold in the United States (for all of history). The list is obviously dominated by The Beatles and The Rolling Stones. Others you have probably heard of – others you have not – either way, this is a good primer on building a playlist of the best in British music.

Rank	Song	Musician/Band
☐ 1.	"Stranger on the Shore"	Acker Bilk
☐ 2.	"Telstar"	The Tornados
☐ 3.	"I Want to Hold Your Hand"	The Beatles
☐ 4.	"She Loves You"	The Beatles
☐ 5.	"Can't Buy Me Love"	The Beatles
☐ 6.	"Love Me Do"	The Beatles
☐ 7.	"A World Without Love"	Peter and Gordon

☐ 8.	"A Hard Day's Night"	The Beatles
☐ 9.	"The House of the Rising Sun"	The Animals
☐ 10.	"Do Wah Diddy Diddy"	Manfred Mann
☐ 11.	"I Feel Fine"	The Beatles
☐ 12.	"Downtown"	Petula Clark
☐ 13.	"Eight Days a Week"	The Beatles
☐ 14.	"I'm Telling You Now"	Freddie and the Dreamers
☐ 15.	"Game of Love"	Wayne Fontana and the Mindbenders
☐ 16.	"Mrs. Brown, You've Got a Lovely Daughter"	Herman's Hermits
☐ 17.	"Ticket to Ride"	The Beatles
☐ 18.	"(I Can't Get No) Satisfaction"	The Rolling Stones
☐ 19.	"I'm Henry VIII, I Am"	Herman's Hermits
☐ 20.	"Help!"	The Beatles
☐ 21.	"Yesterday"	The Beatles
☐ 22.	"Get Off of My Cloud"	The Rolling Stones
☐ 23.	"Over and Over"	The Dave Clark Five
☐ 24.	"We Can Work It Out"	The Beatles
☐ 25.	"My Love"	Petula Clark
☐ 26.	"Paint It Black"	The Rolling Stones
☐ 27.	"Paperback Writer"	The Beatles
☐ 28.	"Wild Thing"	The Troggs
☐ 29.	"Sunshine Superman"	Donovan
☐ 30.	"Winchester Cathedral"	The New Vaudeville Band
☐ 31.	"Ruby Tuesday"	The Rolling Stones
☐ 32.	"Penny Lane"	The Beatles
☐ 33.	"All You Need Is Love"	The Beatles
☐ 34.	"To Sir, with Love"	Lulu
☐ 35.	"Hello, Goodbye"	The Beatles
☐ 36.	"Hey Jude"	The Beatles
☐ 37.	"Get Back"	The Beatles with Billy Preston
☐ 38.	"Honky Tonk Women"	The Rolling Stones

☐ 39.	"Come Together" / "Something"	The Beatles
☐ 40.	"Let It Be"	The Beatles
☐ 41.	"The Long and Winding Road" / "For You Blue"	The Beatles
☐ 42.	"My Sweet Lord" / "Isn't It a Pity"	George Harrison
☐ 43.	"Brown Sugar"	The Rolling Stones
☐ 44.	"How Can You Mend a Broken Heart?"	Bee Gees
☐ 45.	"Uncle Albert/Admiral Halsey"	Paul McCartney and Linda McCartney
☐ 46.	"Maggie May" / "Reason to Believe"	Rod Stewart
☐ 47.	"A Horse with No Name"	America
☐ 48.	"Crocodile Rock"	Elton John
☐ 49.	"My Love"	Paul McCartney and Wings
☐ 50.	"Give Me Love (Give Me Peace on Earth)"	George Harrison
☐ 51.	"Angie"	The Rolling Stones
☐ 52.	"Photograph"	Ringo Starr
☐ 53.	"You're Sixteen"	Ringo Starr
☐ 54.	"Bennie and the Jets"	Elton John
☐ 55.	"Band on the Run"	Paul McCartney and Wings
☐ 56.	"The Night Chicago Died"	Paper Lace
☐ 57.	"I Shot the Sheriff"	Eric Clapton
☐ 58.	"Whatever Gets You thru the Night"	John Lennon
☐ 59.	"Lucy in the Sky with Diamonds"	Elton John
☐ 60.	"Pick Up the Pieces"	Average White Band
☐ 61.	"Philadelphia Freedom"	The Elton John Band
☐ 62.	"Sister Golden Hair"	America

☐ 63.	"Listen to What the Man Said"	Paul McCartney and Wings
☐ 64.	"Jive Talkin'"	Bee Gees
☐ 65.	"Fame"	David Bowie
☐ 66.	"Island Girl"	Elton John
☐ 67.	"Saturday Night"	Bay City Rollers
☐ 68.	"Silly Love Songs"	Wings
☐ 69.	"Don't Go Breaking My Heart"	Elton John and Kiki Dee
☐ 70.	"You Should Be Dancing"	Bee Gees
☐ 71.	"Tonight's the Night (Gonna Be Alright)"	Rod Stewart
☐ 72.	"You Make Me Feel Like Dancing"	Leo Sayer
☐ 73.	"Blinded by the Light"	Manfred Mann's Earth Band
☐ 74.	"When I Need You"	Leo Sayer
☐ 75.	"Dreams"	Fleetwood Mac
☐ 76.	"I Just Want to Be Your Everything"	Andy Gibb
☐ 77.	"How Deep Is Your Love"	Bee Gees
☐ 78.	"Stayin' Alive"	Bee Gees
☐ 79.	"(Love Is) Thicker Than Water"	Andy Gibb
☐ 80.	"Night Fever"	Bee Gees
☐ 81.	"With a Little Luck"	Wings
☐ 82.	"Shadow Dancing"	Andy Gibb
☐ 83.	"Miss You"	The Rolling Stones
☐ 84.	"Too Much Heaven"	Bee Gees
☐ 85.	"Da Ya Think I'm Sexy?"	Rod Stewart
☐ 86.	"Tragedy"	Bee Gees
☐ 87.	"Love You Inside Out"	Bee Gees
☐ 88.	"Pop Muzik"	M
☐ 89.	"Crazy Little Thing Called Love"	Queen

☐	90.	"Another Brick in the Wall (Part II)"	Pink Floyd
☐	91.	"Coming Up"	Paul McCartney
☐	92.	"Another One Bites the Dust"	Queen
☐	93.	"(Just Like) Starting Over"	John Lennon
☐	94.	"Morning Train (Nine to Five)"	Sheena Easton
☐	95.	"The One That You Love"	Air Supply
☐	96.	"Ebony and Ivory"	Paul McCartney and Stevie Wonder
☐	97.	"Don't You Want Me"	The Human League
☐	98.	"Up Where We Belong"	Joe Cocker and Jennifer Warnes
☐	99.	"Come On Eileen"	Dexys Midnight Runners
☐	100.	"Let's Dance"	David Bowie

101. FURTHER READING

It's a bit weird to recommend other books to read about Britain when you're holding one in your hand. But this book cannot contain everything, and I've read hundreds of books about Britain over the years, so I would be remiss in not recommending a few. These are the books I consider most important either because they're good and enjoyable or because they provide useful context to British history and culture that makes being an Anglophile so much fun. I include non-fiction and fiction. And to be clear, this is a very personal list. But starting with these books will lead you to many other interesting books!

NOTES FROM A SMALL ISLAND AND ROAD TO LITTLE DRIBBLING BY BILL BRYSON

Notes from a Small Island is probably the best – and my favorite – book by an outsider about Britain. After living in Britain for over a decade, Bryson decides to journey through it one last time before moving back to America. This affectionate and fascinating portrait of Britain is funny and interesting. He wrote a sequel about ten years ago that updates many of the thoughts and places he had originally traveled to. Best to read them as a pair and compare the differences over a 20 year period of time.

WATCHING THE ENGLISH BY KATE FOX

If you want a scholarly and forensic examination of English culture and why the English do what they do, then this wonderful book is for you.

KINGDOM BY THE SEA BY PAUL THEROUX

Another 'American travels around Britain' book – this book by novelist Theroux takes us on a journey through the 80s Thatcherite Britain. It's not as sunny as Bryson's books, but no less interesting.

BRIDESHEAD REVISITED BY EVELYN WAUGH

This is the definitive fiction book about the decline of Britain's aristocracy in the lead-up to World War II. It paints an achingly beautiful portrait of Britain between the wars and the relationship between a painter and an aristocratic family. Read the book, then watch the expansive and classic ITV drama starring Jeremy Irons.

THE DECLINE AND FALL OF THE BRITISH ARISTOCRACY BY DAVID CANNADINE

If you want a keen understanding of why Britain's famous aristocracy declined and then almost disappeared, this book is a forensic examination. It's dense, and it's long, but it's all fascinating as you read about families who lost their wealth, their great houses, and so much more.

THE SHEPHERD'S LIFE AND ENGLISH PASTORAL BY JAMES REBANKS

James Rebanks is a shepherd of the Lake District who has written two books that are beautiful portraits of farming life in modern Britain. James has an amazing way with words as he beautifully describes the Cumbrian landscape and how his family has farmed it for generations. Rebanks is one of Britain's greatest writing voices, and I cannot wait to see what he does next. Read both his books cover to cover – they're amazing!

THE SEA ROOM BY ADAM NICHOLSON

What happens when you inherit a small uninhabited Scottish Island in the Hebridean sea? You try to learn everything you can about it and the people who once inhabited it. Nicholson affectionately tells the story of the island, while also telling his story of becoming a steward of it.

THE LAST WOLF BY ROBERT WINDER

This is a beautiful history of the English landscape, framed around the idea that killing all the wolves allowed Britain's sheep farming industry to go on steroids and create the landscape and economic powerhouse we have today.

HOW TO BE A BRIT BY GEORGE MIKES

This humorous book was written by an immigrant to Britain (originally from Hungary) and is an outsider's perspective on what it means to be British, and crucially how to be British if you so choose. It's also very funny and considered the definitive guide to British humor and culture.

THE IRON LADY BY JOHN CAMPBELL

Love her or hate her, Margaret Thatcher had one of the biggest impacts on modern Britain than any other person. This breezy biography puts her life in context and gives you all the unbiased key information you need to understand everything she did, along with the impact those decisions had on Britain.

CHURCHILL BY ANDREW ROBERTS

There are hundreds of biographies on Sir Winston Churchill and countless other books about aspects of his life. This one is by far the best one-volume biography. It covers his whole life and is a perfect springboard for future research into his life.

LIFE IN THE ENGLISH COUNTRY HOUSE BY MARK GIROUARD

If you want to understand the world around Downton Abbey and other upper-class TV shows and films, this book is the perfect user's guide providing everything you could possibly want to know about English country houses.

ACKNOWLEDGMENTS

We must take a moment to thank the contributors to Anglotopia over the years. The DNA of many articles we've published over the years has been adapted for this book.

I must particularly thank John Rabon, who has written for Anglotopia for almost ten years. A big chunk of the explainers and list chapters in this book were originally compiled by him, and we've simply adapted them to work in the book. Thank you, John, for your tireless work writing for the site and battling the pedants with me in the trenches of the internet.

I also want to thank those who purchased this book during the Save Anglotopia Appeal in spring 2021. Many bought the book based on a one-paragraph synopsis sight unseen and a cover mockup, a massive vote of confidence that we would produce a book worth buying. Thank you for trusting us, and we hope you're pleased with the final result. This book would not exist without you!

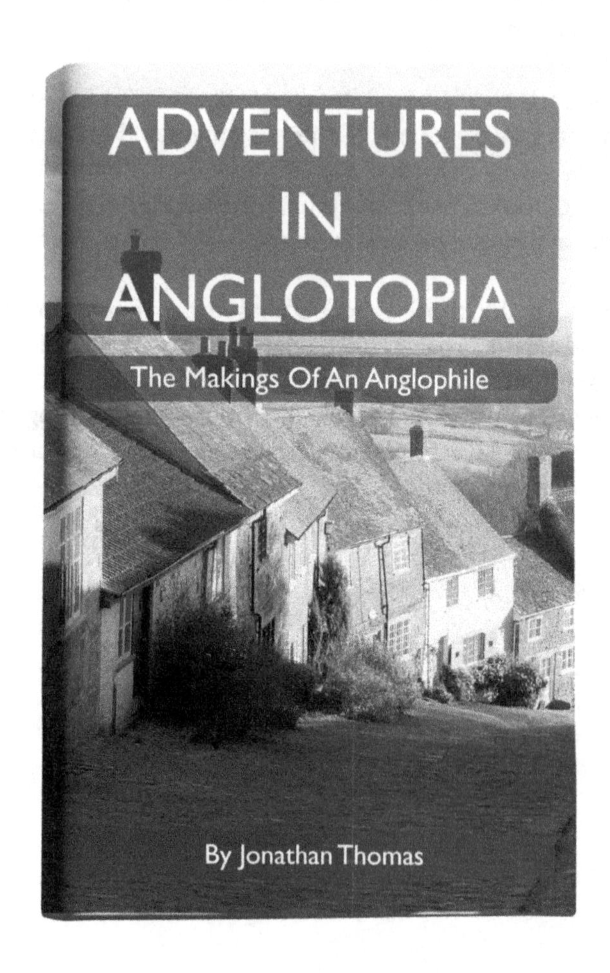
ADVENTURES
IN
ANGLOTOPIA
The Makings Of An Anglophile
By Jonathan Thomas

Now Available from Booksellers Everywhere

Adventures in Anglotopia
The Makings Of An Anglophile

By Jonathan Thomas

What makes an Anglophile? What makes someone love a country not their own? Adventures in Anglotopia is a journey to answer this question, framed through a childhood exposed to British culture and then nearly twenty years of travel in Britain. It's an exploration of why one American man loves Britain so much but also why Britain is such a wonderful place, worthy of loving unconditionally.

The narrative arc of the book answers this question by covering interesting topics related to Britain such as visiting for the first time, culture, stately home, tea, history, British TV, literature, specific places, and much more. Each chapter focuses on a specific topic, all building to the end where Jonathan reveals his 'Great British Dream.'

Come on a journey that will take you the length and breadth of Britain and its rich history.

ISBN: 978-0985477080

Available from all bookstores and direct from Anglotopia at https://adventuresinanglotopia.com

CPSIA information can be obtained
at www.ICGtesting.com
Printed in the USA
LVHW022206030921
696923LV00007B/20